Visit us at

www.syngress.com

Syngress is committed to publishing high-quality books for IT Professionals and delivering those books in media and formats that fit the demands of our customers. We are also committed to extending the utility of the book you purchase via additional materials available from our Web site.

SOLUTIONS WEB SITE

To register your book, please visit **www.syngress.com**. Once registered, you can access your e-book with print, copy, and comment features enabled.

ULTIMATE CDs

Our Ultimate CD product line offers our readers budget-conscious compilations of some of our best-selling backlist titles in Adobe PDF form. These CDs are the perfect way to extend your reference library on key topics pertaining to your area of expertise, including Cisco Engineering, Microsoft Windows System Administration, CyberCrime Investigation, Open Source Security, and Firewall Configuration, to name a few.

DOWNLOADABLE E-BOOKS

For readers who can't wait for hard copy, we offer most of our titles in downloadable e-book format. These are available at **www.syngress.com**.

SITE LICENSING

Syngress has a well-established program for site licensing our e-books onto servers in corporations, educational institutions, and large organizations. Please contact our corporate sales department at corporatesales@elsevier.com for more information.

CUSTOM PUBLISHING

Many organizations welcome the ability to combine parts of multiple Syngress books, as well as their own content, into a single volume for their own internal use. Please contact our corporate sales department at corporatesales@elsevier.com for more information.

Virtualization for Security

Including Sandboxing, Disaster Recovery, High Availability, Forensic Analysis, and Honeypotting

John Hoopes Technical Editor

Aaron Bawcom
Paul Kenealy
Wesley J. Noonan
Craig A. Schiller
Fred Shore

Andreas Turriff
Mario Vuksan
Carsten Willems
David Williams

Unique Passcode

48305726

PUBLISHED BY
Syngress Publishing, Inc.
Elsevier, Inc.
30 Corporate Drive
Burlington, MA 01803

Virtualization for Security

Including Sandboxing, Disaster Recovery, High Availability, Forensic Analysis, and Honeypotting

Printed and bound in the United Kingdom

Transferred to Digital Print 2011

ISBN 13: 978-1-59749-305-5

Publisher: Laura Colantoni
Acquisitions Editor: Brian Sawyer
Technical Editor: John Hoopes
Cover Designer: Michael Kavish
Copy Editors: Leslie Crenna, Emily Nye, Adrienne Rebello, Gail Rice, Jessica Springer, and Chris Stuart

Project Manager: Andre Cuello
Page Layout and Art: SPI
Developmental Editor: Gary Byrne
Indexer: SPI

For information on rights, translations, and bulk sales, contact Matt Pedersen, Commercial Sales Director and Rights, at Syngress Publishing; email m.pedersen@elsevier.com.

Library of Congress Cataloging-in-Publication Data

Hoopes, John.
   Virtualization for security : including sandboxing, disaster recovery, high availability / John Hoopes.
      p. cm.
   ISBN 978-1-59749-305-5
   1. Virtual computer systems. 2. Virtual storage (Computer sciences)--Security measures. 3. Database security. I. Title.
   QA76.9.V5H66 2009
   005.8--dc22

                                                                                                    2008044794

Contents

Chapter 1

An Introduction to Virtualization

Solutions in this chapter:

- What Is Virtualization?
- Why Virtualize?
- How Does Virtualization Work?
- Types of Virtualization
- Common Use Cases for Virtualization

☑ Summary

☑ Solutions Fast Track

☑ Frequently Asked Questions

Introduction

Virtualization is one of those buzz words that has been gaining immense popularity with IT professionals and executives alike. Promising to reduce the ever-growing infrastructure inside current data center implementations, virtualization technologies have cropped up from dozens of software and hardware companies. But what exactly is it? Is it right for everyone? And how can it benefit your organization?

Virtualization has actually been around more than three decades. Once only accessible by the large, rich, and prosperous enterprise, virtualization technologies are now available in every aspect of computing, including hardware, software, and communications, for a nominal cost. In many cases, the technology is freely available (thanks to open-source initiatives) or included for the price of products such as operating system software or storage hardware.

Well suited for most inline business applications, virtualization technologies have gained in popularity and are in widespread use for all but the most demanding workloads. Understanding the technology and the workloads to be run in a virtualized environment is key to every administrator and systems architect who wishes to deliver the benefits of virtualization to their organization or customers.

This chapter will introduce you to the core concepts of server, storage, and network virtualization as a foundation for learning more about Xen. This chapter will also illustrate the potential benefits of virtualization to any organization.

What Is Virtualization?

So what exactly is virtualization? Today, that question has many answers. Different manufacturers and independent software vendors coined that phrase to categorize their products as tools to help companies establish virtualized infrastructures. Those claims are not false, as long as their products accomplish some of the following key points (which are the objectives of any virtualization technology):

- Add a layer of abstraction between the applications and the hardware
- Enable a reduction in costs and complexity
- Provide the isolation of computer resources for improved reliability and security
- Improve service levels and the quality of service
- Better align IT processes with business goals
- Eliminate redundancy in, and maximize the utilization of, IT infrastructures

While the most common form of virtualization is focused on server hardware platforms, these goals and supporting technologies have also found their way into other critical—and expensive—components of modern data centers, including storage and network infrastructures.

But to answer the question "What is virtualization?" we must first discuss the history and origins of virtualization, as clearly as we understand it.

The History of Virtualization

In its conceived form, virtualization was better known in the 1960s as time sharing. Christopher Strachey, the first Professor of Computation at Oxford University and leader of the Programming Research Group, brought this term to life in his paper *Time Sharing in Large Fast Computers*. Strachey, who was a staunch advocate of maintaining a balance between practical and theoretical work in computing, was referring to what he called multi-programming. This technique would allow one programmer to develop a program on his console while another programmer was debugging his, thus avoiding the usual wait for peripherals. Multi-programming, as well as several other groundbreaking ideas, began to drive innovation, resulting in a series of computers that burst onto the scene. Two are considered part of the evolutionary lineage of virtualization as we currently know it—the Atlas and IBM's M44/44X.

The Atlas Computer

The first of the supercomputers of the early 1960s took advantage of concepts such as time sharing, multi-programming, and shared peripheral control, and was dubbed the Atlas computer. A project run by the Department of Electrical Engineering at Manchester University and funded by Ferranti Limited, the Atlas was the fastest computer of its time. The speed it enjoyed was partially due to a separation of operating system processes in a component called the supervisor and the component responsible for executing user programs. The supervisor managed key resources, such as the computer's processing time, and was passed special instructions, or extracodes, to help it provision and manage the computing environment for the user program's instructions. In essence, this was the birth of the hypervisor, or virtual machine monitor.

In addition, Atlas introduced the concept of virtual memory, called one-level store, and paging techniques for the system memory. This core store was also logically separated from the store used by user programs, although the two were integrated. In many ways, this was the first step towards creating a layer of abstraction that all virtualization technologies have in common.

The M44/44X Project

Determined to maintain its title as the supreme innovator of computers, and motivated by the competitive atmosphere that existed, IBM answered back with the M44/44X Project. Nested at the IBM Thomas J. Watson Research Center in Yorktown, New York, the project created a similar architecture to that of the Atlas computer. This architecture was first to coin the term *virtual machines* and became IBM's contribution to the emerging time-sharing system concepts. The main machine was an IBM 7044 (M44) scientific computer and several simulated 7044 virtual machines, or 44Xs, using both hardware and software, virtual memory, and multi-programming, respectively.

Unlike later implementations of time-sharing systems, M44/44X virtual machines did not implement a complete simulation of the underlying hardware. Instead, it fostered the notion that virtual machines were as efficient as more conventional approaches. To nail that notion, IBM successfully released successors of the M44/44X project that showed this idea was not only true, but could lead to a successful approach to computing.

CP/CMS

A later design, the IBM 7094, was finalized by MIT researchers and IBM engineers and introduced Compatible Time Sharing System (CTSS). The term "compatible" refers to the compatibility with the standard batch processing operating system used on the machine, the Fortran Monitor System (FMS). CTSS not only ran FMS in the main 7094 as the primary facility for the standard batch stream, but also ran an unmodified copy of FMS in each virtual machine in a background facility. The background jobs could access all peripherals, such as tapes, printers, punch card readers, and graphic displays, in the same fashion as the foreground FMS jobs as long as they did not interfere with foreground time-sharing processors or any supporting resources.

MIT continued to value the prospects of time sharing, and developed Project MAC as an effort to develop the next generation of advances in time-sharing technology, pressuring hardware manufacturers to deliver improved platforms for their work. IBM's response was a modified and customized version of its System/360 (S/360) that would include virtual memory and time-sharing concepts not previously released by IBM. This proposal to Project MAC was rejected by MIT, a crushing blow to the team at the Cambridge Scientific Center (CSC), whose only purpose was to support the MIT/IBM relationship through technical guidance and lab activities.

The fallout between the two, however, led to one of the most pivotal points in IBM's history. The CSC team, lead by Norm Rassmussen and Bob Creasy, a defect from Project MAC, to the development of CP/CMS. In the late 1960s, the CSC developed the first successful virtual machine operating system based on fully virtualized hardware, the CP-40. The CP-67 was released as a reimplementation of the CP-40, as was later converted and implemented as the S/360-67 and later as the S/370. The success of this platform won back IBM's credibility at MIT as well as several of IBM's largest customers. It also led to the evolution of the platform and the virtual machine operating systems that ran on them, the most popular being VM/370. The VM/370 was capable of running many virtual machines, with larger virtual memory running on virtual copies of the hardware, all managed by a component called the virtual machine monitor (VMM) running on the real hardware. Each virtual machine was able to run a unique installation of IBM's operating system stably and with great performance.

Other Time-Sharing Projects

IBM's CTSS and CP/CMS efforts were not alone, although they were the most influential in the history of virtualization. As time sharing became widely accepted and recognized as an effective way to make early mainframes more affordable, other companies joined the time-sharing fray. Like IBM, those companies needed plenty of capital to fund the research and hardware investment needed to aggressively pursue time-sharing operating systems as the platform for running their programs and computations. Some other projects that jumped onto the bandwagon included

- **Livermore Time-Sharing System (LTSS)** Developed by the Lawrence Livermore Laboratory in the late 1960s as the operating system for the Control Data CDC 7600 supercomputers. The CDC 7600 running LTSS took over the title of the world's fastest computer, trumping on the Atlas computer, which suffered from a form of trashing due to inefficiencies in its implementation of virtual memory.

- **Cray Time-Sharing System (CTSS)** (This is a different CTSS; not to be confused with IBM's CTSS.) Developed for the early lines of Cray supercomputers in the early 1970s. The project was engineered by the Los Alamos Scientific Laboratory in conjunction with the Lawrence Livermore Laboratory, and stemmed from the research that Livermore had already done with the successful LTSS operating system. Cray X-MP computers running CTSS were used heavily by the United States Department of Energy for nuclear research.

- **New Livermore Time-Sharing System (NLTSS)** The last iteration of CTSS, this was developed to incorporate recent advances and concepts in computers, such as new communication protocols like TCP/IP and LINCS. However, it was not widely accepted by users of the Cray systems and was discontinued in the late 1980s.

Virtualization Explosion of the 1990s and Early 2000s

While we have discussed a summarized list of early virtualization efforts, the projects that have launched since those days are too numerous to reference in their entirety. Some have failed while others have gone on to be popular and accepted technologies throughout the technical community. Also, while efforts have been pushed in server virtualization, we have also seen attempts to virtualize and simplify the data center, whether through true virtualization as defined by the earlier set of goals or through infrastructure sharing and consolidation.

Many companies, such as Sun, Microsoft, and VMware, have released enterprise-class products that have wide acceptance, due in part to their existing customer base. However, Xen threatens to challenge them all with their approach to virtualization. Being adopted by the Linux community and now being integrated as a built-in feature to most popular distributions, Xen will continue to enjoy a strong and steady increase in market share. Why? We'll discuss that later in the chapter. But first, back to the question… What is virtualization?

Configuring & Implementing…

Evolution of the IBM LPAR— More than Just Mainframe Technology

IBM has had a long history of Logical Partitions, or LPARs, on their mainframe product offerings, from System390 through present-day System z9 offerings. However, IBM has extended the LPAR technology beyond the mainframe, introducing it to its Unix platform with the release of AIX 5L. Beginning with AIX 5L Version 5.1, administrators could use the familiar Hardware Management Console (HMC) or the Integrated Virtualization Manager to create LPARs with virtual hardware resources (dedicated or shared). With the latest release, AIX 5L Version 5.3, combined with the newest generation of System p with POWER5 processors, additional mainframe-derived virtualization features, such as micro-partitioning CPU resources for LPARs, became possible.

IBM's LPAR virtualization offerings include some unique virtualization approaches and virtual resource provisioning. A key component of what IBM terms the Advanced POWER Virtualization feature, is the Virtual I/O Server. Virtual I/O servers satisfy part of the VMM, called the POWER Hypervisor, role. Though not responsible for CPU or memory virtualization, the Virtual I/O server handles all I/O operations for all LPARs. When deployed in redundant LPARs of its own, Virtual I/O servers provide a good strategy to improve availability for sets of AIX 5L or Linux client partitions, offering redundant connections to external Ethernet or storage resources.

Among the I/O resources managed by the Virtual I/O servers are

- **Virtual Ethernet** Virtual Ethernet enables inter-partition communication without the need for physical network adapters in each partition. It allows the administrator to define point-to-point connections between partitions. Virtual Ethernet requires a POWER5 system with either IBM AIX 5L Version 5.3 or the appropriate level of Linux and an HMC to define the Virtual Ethernet devices.

- **Virtual Serial Adapter (VSA)** POWER5 systems include Virtual Serial ports that are used for virtual terminal support.

Continued

■ **Client and Server Virtual SCSI** The POWER5 server uses SCSI as the mechanism for virtual storage devices. This is accomplished using a pair of virtual adapters; a virtual SCSI server adapter and a virtual SCSI client adapter. These adapters are used to transfer SCSI commands between partitions. The SCSI server adapter, or target adapter, is responsible for executing any SCSI command it receives. It is owned by the Virtual I/O server partition. The virtual SCSI client adapter allows the client partition to access standard SCSI devices and LUNs assigned to the client partition. You may configure virtual server SCSI devices for Virtual I/O Server partitions, and virtual client SCSI devices for Linux and AIX partitions.

The Answer: Virtualization Is...

So with all that history behind us, and with so many companies claiming to wear the virtualization hat, how do we define it? In an effort to be as all-encompassing as possible, we can define virtualization as:

> A framework or methodology of dividing the resources of a computer hardware into multiple execution environments, by applying one or more concepts or technologies such as hardware and software partitioning, time-sharing, partial or complete machine simulation, emulation, quality of service, and many others.

Just as it did during the late 1960s and early 1970s with IBM's VM/370, modern virtualization allows multiple operating system instances to run concurrently on a single computer, albeit much less expensive than the mainframes of those days. Each OS instance shares the available resources available on the common physical hardware, as illustrated in Figure 1.1. Software, referred to as a virtual machine monitor (VMM), controls use and access to the CPU, memory, storage, and network resources underneath.

Figure 1.1 Virtual Machines Riding on Top of the Physical Hardware

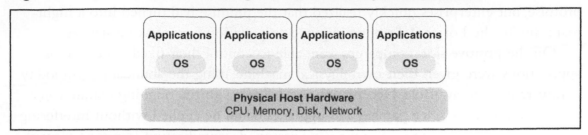

Why Virtualize?

From the mid-1990s until present day, the trend in the data center has been towards a decentralized paradigm, scaling the application and system infrastructure outward in a horizontal fashion. The trend has been commonly referred to as "server sprawl." As more applications and application environments are deployed, the number of servers implemented within the data center grows at exponential rates. Centralized servers were seen as too expensive to purchase and maintain for many companies not already established on such a computing platform. While big-frame, big-iron servers continued to survive, the midrange and entry-level server market bustled with new life and opportunities for all but the most intense use cases. It is important to understand why IT organizations favored decentralization, and why it was seen as necessary to shift from the original paradigm of a centralized computing platform to one of many.

Decentralization versus Centralization

Virtualization is a modified solution between two paradigms—centralized and decentralized systems. Instead of purchasing and maintaining an entire physical computer, and its necessary peripherals for every application, each application can be given its own operating environment, complete with I/O, processing power, and memory, all sharing their underlying physical hardware. This provides the benefits of decentralization, like security and stability, while making the most of a machine's resources and providing better returns on the investment in technology.

With the popularity of Windows and lighter-weight open systems distributed platforms, the promise that many hoped to achieve included better return on assets and a lower total cost of ownership (TCO). The commoditization of inexpensive hardware and software platforms added additional fuel to the evangelism of that promise, but enterprises quickly realized that the promise had turned into a nightmare due to the horizontal scaling required to provision new server instances.

On the positive side, companies were able to control their fixed asset costs as applications were given their own physical machine, using the abundant commodity hardware options available. Decentralization helped with the ongoing maintenance of each application, since patches and upgrades could be applied without interfering with other running systems. For the same reason, decentralization improves security since a compromised system is isolated from other systems on the network. As IT processes became more refined and established as a governance mechanism in many enterprises, the software development life cycle (SDLC) took advantage of the decentralization of n-tier applications. Serving as a model or process for software development, SDLC imposes a rigid structure on the development of a software product by defining not only development phases (such as requirements gathering, software architecture and design, testing, implementation, and maintenance), but rules that guide the development process through each phase. In many cases, the phases overlap, requiring them to have their own dedicated n-tier configuration.

However, the server sprawl intensified, as multiple iterations of the same application were needed to support the SDLC for development, quality assurance, load testing, and finally production environments. Each application's sandbox came at the expense of more power consumption, less physical space, and a greater management effort which, together, account for up to tens (if not hundreds) of thousands of dollars in annual maintenance costs per machine. In addition to this maintenance overhead, decentralization decreased the efficiency of each machine, leaving the average server idle 85 to 90 percent of the time. These inefficiencies further eroded any potential cost or labor savings promised by decentralization.

In Table 1.1, we evaluate three-year costs incurred by Foo Company to create a decentralized configuration comprised of five two-way x86 servers with software licensed per physical CPU, as shown in Figure 1.2. These costs include the purchase of five new two-way servers, ten CPU licenses (two per server) of our application, and soft costs for infrastructure, power, and cooling. Storage is not factored in because we assume that in both the physical and virtual scenarios, the servers would be connected to external storage of the same capacity; hence, storage costs remain the same for both. The Physical Cost represents a three-year cost since most companies depreciate their capital fixed assets for 36 months. Overall, our costs are $74,950.

Table 1.1 A Simple Example of the Cost of Five Two-Way Application Servers

Component	Unit Cost	Physical Cost	Virtual Cost
Server hardware	$7,500.00	$37,500.00	$7,500.00
Software licenses/CPU	$2,000.00	$20,000.00	$4,000.00
Supporting infrastructure	$2,500.00	$12,500.00	$2,500.00
Power per server year	$180.00	$2,700.00	$540.00
Cooling per server year	$150.00	$2,250.00	$450.00
Total three-year costs:		$74,950.00	$16,490.00
Realized savings over three years:	**$ 58,460.00**		

Figure 1.2 A Decentralized Five-Server Configuration

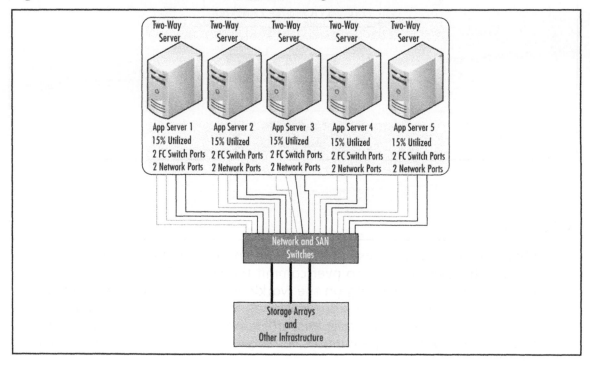

In contrast, the table also shows a similarly configured centralized setup of five OS/application instances hosted on a single two-way server with sufficient hardware resources for the combined workload, as shown in Figure 1.3. Although savings are realized by the 5:1 reduction in server hardware, that savings is matched by the savings in software cost (5:1 reduction in physical CPUs to license), supporting infrastructure, power, and cooling.

Figure 1.3 A Centralized Five-Server Configuration

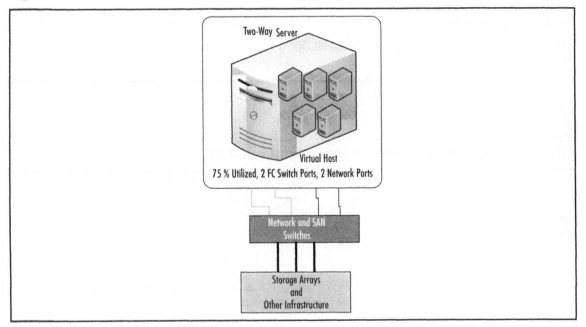

WARNING

When building the business case and assessing the financial impact of virtualization, be sure not to over-commit the hosts with a large number of virtual machines. Depending on the workload, physical hosts can manage as many as 20 to 30 virtualization machines, or as little as 4 to 5. Spend time upfront gathering performance information about your current work-loads, especially during peak hours, to help properly plan and justify your virtualization strategy.

Assuming that each server would average 15-percent utilization if run on physical hardware, consolidation of the workloads into a centralized virtual is feasible. The hard and soft costs factored into the calculations more closely demonstrate the total cost of ownership in this simple model, labor excluded. It is important to note that *Supporting Infrastructure*, as denoted in the table, includes rack, cabling, and network/storage connectivity costs. This is often overlooked; however, it is critical to include this in your cost benefit analysis since each Fibre-Channel (FC) switch port consumed could cost as much as $1,500, and each network port as much as $300. As illustrated in the figures, there are ten FC and ten network connections in the decentralized example compared to two FC and two network connections. Port costs alone would save Foo a considerable amount. As the table shows, a savings of almost 80 percent could be realized by implementing the servers with virtualization technologies.

Designing & Planning...

A Virtualized Environment Requires a Reliable, High-Capacity Network

To successfully consolidate server workloads onto a virtualized environment, it is essential that all server subsystems (CPU, memory, network, and disk) can accommodate the additional workload. While most virtualization products require a single network connection to operate, careful attention to, and planning of, the networking infrastructure of a virtual environment can ensure both optimal performance and high availability.

Multiple virtual machines will increase network traffic. With multiple workloads, the network capacity needs to scale to match the requirements of the combined workloads expected on the host. In general, as long as the host's processor is not fully utilized, the consolidated network traffic will be the sum of the traffic generated by each virtual machine.

True Tangible Benefits

Virtualization is a critical part of system optimization efforts. While it could simply be a way to reduce and simplify your server infrastructure, it can also be a tool to transform the way you think about your data center as a whole. Figure 1.4 illustrates the model of system optimization. You will notice that virtualization, or physical consolidation, is the foundation for all other optimization steps, followed by logical consolidation and then an overall rationalization of systems and applications, identifying applications that are unneeded or redundant and can thus be eliminated.

Figure 1.4 Virtualization's Role in System Optimization

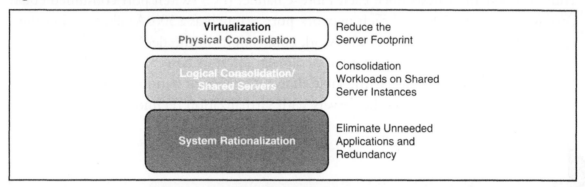

In Table 1.2 you will find a sample list of benefits that often help IT organization justify their movement toward a virtual infrastructure. Although each organization's circumstances are different, you only need a few of these points to apply to your situation to build a strong business case for virtualization.

Table 1.2 Benefits of Virtualization

Category	Benefit
Consolidation	Increase server utilization
	Simplify legacy software migration
	Host mixed operating systems per physical platform
	Streamline test and development environments
Reliability	Isolate software faults
	Reallocate existing partitions
	Create dedicated or as-needed failover partitions
Security	Contain digital attacks through fault isolation
	Apply different security settings to each partition

Consolidation

Three drivers have motivated, if not accelerated, the acceptance and adoption of virtualization technologies—consolidation, reliability, and security. The goal behind consolidation is to combine and unify. In the case of virtualization, workloads are combined on fewer physical platforms capable of sustaining their demand for computing resources, such as CPU, memory, and I/O. In modern data centers, many workloads are far from taxing the hardware they run on, resulting in infrastructure waste and lower returns. Through consolidation, virtualization allows you to combine server instances, or operating systems and their workloads, in a strategic manner and place them on shared hardware with sufficient resource availability to satisfy resource demands. The result is increased utilization. It is often thought that servers shouldn't be forced to run close to their full-capacity levels; however, the opposite is true. In order to maximize that investment, servers should run as close to capacity as possible, without impacting the running workloads or business process relying on their performance. With proper planning and understanding of those workloads, virtualization will help increase server utilization while decreasing the number of physical platforms needed.

Another benefit of consolidation virtualization focuses on legacy system migrations. Server hardware has developed to such levels that they are often incompatible with legacy operating systems and applications. Newer processor technologies, supporting chipsets, and the high-speed buses sought after can often cripple legacy systems, if not render them inoperable without the possibility of full recompilation. Virtualization helps ease and simplify legacy system migrations by providing a common and widely compatible platform upon which legacy system instances can run. This improves the chances that applications can be migrated for older, unsupported, and riskier platforms to newer hardware and supported hardware with minimal impact.

In the past, operating systems were bound to a specific hardware platform. This tied many organizations' hands, forcing them to make large investments in hardware in order to maintain their critical business applications. Due to the commoditization of hardware, though, many of the common operating systems currently available can run on a wide range of server architectures, the most popular of which is the x86 architecture. You can run Windows, Unix, and your choice of Linux distributions on the x86 architecture. Virtualization technologies built on top of x86 architecture can, in turn, host heterogeneous environments. Multiple operating systems, including those previously mentioned, can be consolidated to the same physical hardware, further reducing acquisition and maintenance costs.

Finally, consolidation efforts help streamline development and test environments. Rather than having uncontrolled sprawl throughout your infrastructure as new projects and releases begin or existing applications are maintained, virtualization allows you to consolidate many of those workloads onto substantially fewer physical servers. Given that development and test loads are less demanding by nature than production, consolidation of those environments through virtualization can yield even greater savings than their production counterparts.

Designing & Planning...

More Cores Equal More Guests... Sometimes

When designing the physical platform for your virtualization and consolidation efforts, be sure to take advantage of the current offering of Intel and AMD multi-core processors. Do keep in mind, though, that increasing your core count, and subsequently your total processing power, does not proportionally relate to how many virtual machines you can host. Many factors can contribute to reduced guest performance, including memory, bus congestion (especially true for slower Intel front-side bus architectures or NUMA-based four-way Opteron servers), I/O bus congestion, as well as external factors such as the network infrastructure and the SAN.

Carefully plan your hardware design with virtual machine placement in mind. Focus more on the combined workload than the virtual machine count when sizing your physical host servers. Also consider your virtualization product's features that you will use and how it may add overhead and consume resources needed by your virtual machines. Also consider the capability of your platform to scale as resource demands increase—too few memory slots, and you will quickly run out of RAM; too few PCI/PCI-X/PCI-e slots and you will not be able to scale your I/O by adding additional NICs or HBAs.

Finally, consider the level of redundancy and known reliability of the physical server hardware and supporting infrastructure. Remember that when your host fails, a host outage is much more than just one server down; all the virtual machines it was hosting will experience the outage as well.

Continued

Always keep in mind the key hardware traits required for any virtualization host:

- Performance
- Flexibility
- Reliability

Reliability

More than ever before, reliability has become a mandate and concern for many IT organizations. It has a direct relationship to system availability, application uptime, and, consequently, revenue generation. Companies are willing to, and often do, invest heavily into their server infrastructure to ensure that their critical line-of-business applications remain online and their business operation goes uninterrupted. By investing in additional hardware and software to account for software faults, infrastructures are fortified to tolerate failures and unplanned downtime with interruption. Doing so, though, has proven to be very costly.

Virtualization technologies are sensitive to this and address this area by providing high isolation between running virtual machines. A system fault in one virtual machine, or partition, will not affect the other partitions running on the same hardware platform. This isolation logically protects and shields virtual machines at the lowest level by causing them to be unaware, and thus not impacted, by conditions outside of their allocations. This layer of abstraction, a key component in virtualization, makes each partition just as if it was running on dedicated hardware.

Such isolation does not impede flexibility, as it would in a purely physical world. Partitions can be reallocated to serve other functions as needed. Imagine a server hosting a client/server application that is only used during the 8 A.M. to 5 P.M. hours Monday through Friday, another that runs batch processes to close out business operations nightly, and another that is responsible for data maintenance jobs over the weekend. In a purely physical world, they would exist as three dedicated servers that are highly utilized during their respective hours of operation, but sit idle when not performing their purpose. This accounts for much computing waste and an underutilization of expensive investments. Virtualization addresses this by allowing a single logical or physical partition to be reallocated to each function as needed. On weekdays, it would host the client/server application by day and run the batch processes at night. On the weekends, it would then be reallocated for the data maintenance tasks, only to return to hosting the client/server application the following Monday morning. This flexibility allows IT organizations to utilize "part-time" partitions to run core business processes in the same manner as they would physical servers, but achieve lower costs while maintaining high levels of reliability.

Another area that increases costs is the deployment of standby or failover servers to maintain system availability during times of planned or unplanned outages. While capable of hosting the targeted workloads, such equipment remains idle between those outages, and in some cases, never gets used at all. They are often reduced to expensive paperweights, providing little value to the business while costing it much. Virtualization helps solve this by allowing just-in-time or on-demand provisioning of additional partitions as needed. For example, a partition that has been built (OS and applications) and configured can be put into an inactive (powered-off or suspended) state, ready to be activated when a failure occurs. When needed, the partition becomes active without any concern about hardware procurement, installation, or configuration. Another example is an active/passive cluster. In these clusters, the failover node must be active and online, not inactive. However, the platform hosting the cluster node must be dedicated to that cluster. This has caused many organizations to make a large investment in multiple failover nodes, which sit in their data centers idle, waiting to be used in case of an outage. Using server virtualization, these nodes can be combined onto fewer hardware platforms, as partitions hosting failover nodes are collocated on fewer physical hosts.

Security

The same technology that provides application fault isolation can also provide security fault isolation. Should a particular partition be compromised, it is isolated from the other partitions, stopping the compromise from being extended to them. Solutions can also be implemented that further isolate compromised partitions and OS instances by denying them the very resources they rely on to exist. CPU cycles can be reduced, network and disk I/O access severed, or the system halted altogether. Such tasks would be difficult, if not impossible, to perform if the compromised instance was running directly on a physical host.

When consolidating workloads through virtualization, security configurations can remain specific to the partition rather than the server as a whole. An example of this would be super-user accounts. Applications consolidated to a single operating system running directly on top of a physical server would share various security settings—in particular, root or administrator access would be the same for all. However, when the same workloads are consolidated to virtual partitions, each partition can be configured with different credentials, thus maintaining the isolation of system access with administrative privileges often required to comply with federal or industry regulations.

Simply put, virtualization is an obvious move in just about any company, small or large. Just imagine that your manager calls you into the office and begins to explain his or her concerns about cost containment, data center space diminishing, timelines getting narrower, and corporate mandates doing more with less. It won't take too many attempts to explain how virtualization can help address all of those concerns. After realizing you had the answer all along, it will make your IT manager's day to learn this technology is the silver bullet that will satisfy the needs of the business while providing superior value in IT operations and infrastructure management and delivery.

NOTE

Most Virtual Machine Monitor (VMM) implementations are capable of interactive sessions with administrators through CLI or Web interfaces. Although secure, a compromised VMM will expose every virtual machine managed by that VMM. So exercise extreme caution when granting access or providing credentials for authentication to the VMM management interface.

How Does Virtualization Work?

While there are various ways to virtualize computing resources using a true VMM, they all have the same goal: to allow operating systems to run independently and in an isolated manner identical to when it is running directly on top of the hardware platform. But how exactly is this accomplished? While hardware virtualization still exists that fully virtualizes and abstracts hardware similar to how the System370 did, such hardware-based virtualization technologies tend to be less flexible and costly. As a result, a slew of software hypervisor and VMMs have cropped up to perform virtualization through software-based mechanisms. They ensure a level of isolation where the low-level, nucleus core of the CPU architecture is brought up closer to the software levels of the architecture to allow each virtual machine to have its own dedicated environment. In fact, the relationship between the CPU architecture and the virtualized operating systems is the key to how virtualization actually works successfully.

OS Relationships with the CPU Architecture

Ideal hardware architectures are those in which the operating system and CPU are designed and built for each other, and are tightly coupled. Proper use of complex system call requires careful coordination between the operating system and CPU. This symbiotic relationship in the OS and CPU architecture provides many advantages in security and stability. One such example was the MULTICS time-sharing system, which was designed for a special CPU architecture, which in turn was designed for it.

What made MULTICS so special in its day was its approach to segregating software operations to eliminate the risk or chance of a compromise or instability in a failed component from impacting other components. It placed formal mechanisms, called *protection rings*, in place to segregate the trusted operating system from the untrusted user programs. MULTICS included eight of these protection rings, a quite elaborate design, allowing different levels of isolation and abstraction from the core nucleus of the unrestricted interaction with the hardware. The hardware platform, designed in tandem by GE and MIT, was engineered specifically for the MULTICS operating system and incorporated hardware "hooks" enhancing the segregation even further. Unfortunately, this design approach proved to be too costly and proprietary for mainstream acceptance.

The most common CPU architecture used in modern computers is the IA-32, or x86-compatible, architecture. Beginning with the 80286 chipset, the x86 family provided two main methods of addressing memory: real mode and protected mode. In the 80386 chipset and later, a third mode was introduced called virtual 8086 mode, or VM86, that allowed for the execution of programs written for real mode but circumvented the real-mode rules without having to raise them into protected mode. Real mode, which is limited to a single megabyte of memory, quickly became obsolete; and virtual mode was locked in at 16-bit operation, becoming obsolete when 32-bit operating systems became widely available for the x86 architecture. Protected mode, the saving grace for x86, provided numerous new features to support multitasking. These included segmenting processes, so they could no longer write outside their address space, along with hardware support for virtual memory and task switching.

In the x86 family, protected mode uses four privilege levels, or rings, numbered 0 to 3. System memory is divided into segments, and each segment is assigned and dedicated to a particular ring. The processor uses the privilege level to determine what can and cannot be done with code or data within a segment. The term "rings" comes from the MULTICS system, where privilege levels were visualized as a set of concentric rings. Ring-0 is considered to be the innermost ring, with total control of the processor. Ring-3, the outermost ring, is provided only with restricted access, as illustrated in Figure 1.5.

Figure 1.5 Privilege Rings of the x86 Architecture

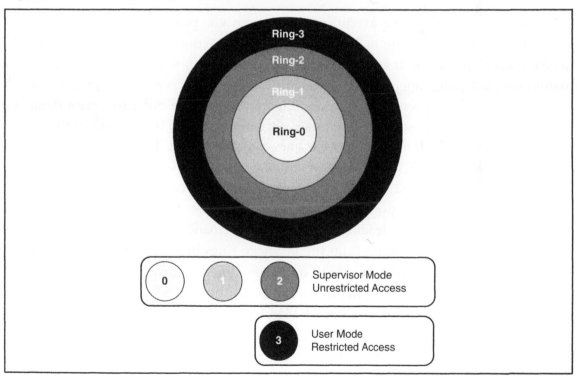

NOTE

The same concept of protection rings exists in modern OS architecture. Windows, Linux, and most Unix variants all use rings, although they have reduced the four-ring structure to a two-layer approach that uses only Rings 0 and 3. Ring-0 is commonly called *Supervisor Mode*, while Ring-3 is known as *User Mode*. Security mechanisms in the hardware enforce restrictions on Ring-3 by limiting code access to segments, paging, and input/output. If a user program running in Ring-3 tries to address memory outside of its segments, a hardware interrupt stops code execution. Some assembly language instructions are not even available for execution outside of Ring-0 due to their low-level nature.

The Virtual Machine Monitor and Ring-0 Presentation

The Supervisor Mode is the execution mode on an x86 processor that enables the execution of all instructions, including privileged instructions such as I/O and memory management operations. It is in Supervisor Mode (Ring 0) where the operating system would normally run. Since Ring-3 is based on Ring-0, any system compromise or instability directly impacts User Mode running in Ring-3. In order to isolate Ring-0 for each virtualized guest, it then becomes necessary to move Ring-0 closer to the guests. By doing so, a Ring-0 failure for one virtualized guest does not impact Ring-0, or consequently Ring-3, of any other guest. The perceived Ring-0 for guests can reside in either Ring-1, -2, or -3 for x86 architectures. Of course, the further the perceived Ring-0 is away from the true Ring-0, the more distant it is from executing direct hardware operations, leading to reduced performance and independence.

Virtualization moves Ring-0 up the privilege rings model by placing the Virtual Machine Monitor, or VMM, in one of the rings, which in turn presents the Ring-0 implementation to the hosted virtual machines. It is upon this presented Ring-0 that guest operating systems run, while the VMM handles the actual interaction with the underlying hardware platform for CPU, memory, and I/O resource access. There are two types of VMMs that address the presentation of Ring-0 as follows:

- **Type 1 VMM** Software that runs directly on top of a given hardware platform on the true Ring-0. Guest operating systems then run at a higher level above the hardware, allowing for true isolation of each virtual machine.

- **Type 2 VMM** Software that runs within an operating system, usually in Ring-3. Since there are no additional rings above Ring-3 in the x86 architecture, the presented Ring-0 that the virtual machines run on is as distant from the actual hardware platform as it can be. Although this offers some advantages, it is usually compounded by performance-impeding factors as calls to the hardware must traverse many diverse layers before the operations are returned to the guest operating system.

The VMM Role Explored

To create virtual partitions in a server, a thin software layer called the Virtual Machine Monitor (VMM) runs directly on the physical hardware platform. One or more guest operating systems and application stacks can then be run on top of the VMM. Figure 1.6 expands our original illustration of a virtualized environment presented in Figure 1.1.

Figure 1.6 The OS and Application Stack Managed by the VMM Software Layer

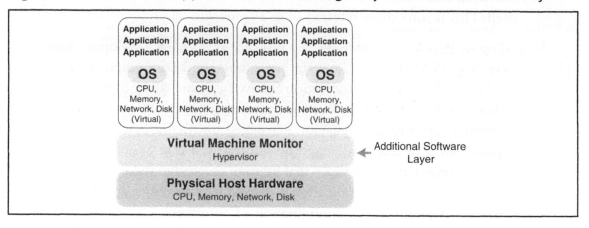

The VMM is the center of server virtualization. It manages hardware resources and arbitrates the requests of the multiple guest operating systems and application stacks. It presents a virtual set of CPU, memory, I/O, and Disk resources to each guest either based on the actual physical hardware or based on a standard and consistent selection of custom hardware. This section further discusses the role of the VMM and design considerations that are used when designing a VMM.

The Popek and Goldberg Requirements

Often referred to as the original reference source for VMM criteria, the Popek and Goldberg Virtualization Requirements define the conditions for a computer architecture to support virtualization. Written in 1974 for the third-generation computer systems of those days, they generalized the conditions that the software that provides the abstraction of a virtual machine, or VMM, must satisfy. These conditions, or properties, are

- **Equivalence** A program running under the VMM should exhibit a predictable behavior that is essentially identical to that demonstrated when running on the underlying hardware platform directly. This is sometimes referred to as *Fidelity*.

- **Resource Control** The VMM must be in complete control of the actual hardware resources virtualized for the guest operating systems at all times. This is sometimes referred to as *Safety*.

- **Efficiency** An overwhelming number of machine instructions must be executed without VMM intervention or, in other words, by the hardware itself. This is sometimes referred to as *Performance*.

According to Popek and Goldberg, the problem that VMM developers must address is creating a VMM that satisfies the preceding conditions when operating within the characteristics of the Instruction Set Architecture (ISA) of the targeted hardware platform. The ISA can be classified into three groups of instructions: privileged, control sensitive, and behavior. Privileged instructions are those that trap if the processor is in User Mode and do not trap if it is in Supervisor Mode. Control-sensitive instructions are those that attempt to change the configuration of actual resources in the hardware platform. Behavior instructions are those whose behavior or result depends on the configuration of resources.

VMMs must work with each group of instructions while maintaining the conditions of equivalence, resource control, and efficiency. Virtually all modern-day VMMs satisfy the first two: equivalence and resource control. They do so by effectively managing the guest operating system and hardware platform underneath through emulation, isolation, allocation, and encapsulation, as explained in Table 1.3.

Table 1.3 VMM Functions and Responsibilities

Function	Description
Emulation	Emulation is important for all guest operating systems. The VMM must present a complete hardware environment, or virtual machine, for each software stack, whether they be an operating system or application. Ideally, the OS and application are completely unaware they are sharing hardware resources with other applications. Emulation is key to satisfying the equivalence property.
Isolation	Isolation, though not required, is important for a secure and reliable environment. Through hardware abstraction, each virtual machine should be sufficiently separated and independent from the operations and activities of other virtual machines. Faults that occur in a single virtual machine should not impact others, thus providing high levels of security and availability.
Allocation	The VMM must methodically allocate platform resources to the virtual machines that it manages. Resources for processing, memory, network I/O, and storage must be balanced to optimize performance and align service levels with business requirements. Through allocation, the VMM satisfies the resource control property and, to some extent, the efficiency property as well.
Encapsulation	Encapsulation, though not mandated in the Popek and Goldberg requirements, enables each software stack (OS and application) to be highly portable, able to be copied or moved from one platform running the VMM to another. In some cases, this level or portability even allows live, running virtual machines to be migrated. Encapsulation must include state information in order to maintain the integrity of the transferred virtual machine.

The Challenge: VMMs for the x86 Architecture

Referring back to the IA-32 (x86) architecture, all software runs in one of the four privilege rings. The OS traditionally runs in Ring-0, which affords privileged access to the widest range of processor and platform resources. Individual applications usually run in Ring-3, which restricts certain functions (such as memory mapping) that might impact other applications. In this way, the OS retains control to ensure smooth operation.

Since the VMM must have privileged control of platform resources, the usual solution is to run the VMM in Ring-0, and guest operating systems in Ring-1 or

Ring-3. However, modern operating systems have been specifically designed to run in Ring-0. This creates certain challenges. In particular, there are 17 "privileged" instructions that control critical platform resources. These instructions are used occasionally in most existing OS versions. When an OS is not running in Ring-0, any one of these instructions can create a conflict, causing either a system fault or an incorrect response. The challenge faced by VMMs for the IA-32 (x86) architecture is maintaining the Popek and Goldberg requirements while working with the IA-32 ISA.

Types of Virtualization

Many forms of virtualization exist in modern information technology. The most common is server virtualization, which is what most people think of when the term "virtualization" is referenced. However, in addition to server virtualization, IT organizations use other types of virtualization, based on other connotations of the word. Many think of virtualization as meaning "partitioning" a computing resource into multiple entities. Virtualization can also mean just the opposite: presenting multiple entities as a single virtual entity, thus hiding or masking the true computing resources that are performing the work in the background. Many manufacturers and independent software vendors have developed products that utilize the latter approach to virtualization. Of the most common are virtualization products for storage, network, and applications. In Chapter 2 we'll discuss how to distinguish one type of virtualization from another in more detail.

Server Virtualization

Although the concepts we have discussed so far have been about virtualization in general, they are most exhibited in server virtualization products. Server virtualization has become the most successful form of virtualization today. Server virtualization is sometimes called full virtualization. Server virtualization abstracts both the hardware resources on the physical computer as well as the hosted guest operating systems that run on the virtualization platform. A virtual machine running on a virtualized server needs no special software in order to run on the virtualized server.

Implementations of server virtualization exist on, and for all, CPU platforms and architectures, the most popular being the IA-32 or x86. The challenges posed by the x86 architecture's ISA and the Popek and Goldberg requirements have led to several approaches to VMM development. Although there are many different implementations of a VMM for x86, they can be summarized into four distinct categories. Table 1.4 provides additional information about each category for server virtualization.

Table 1.4 Types of Server Virtualization

Type of Virtualization	Description	Pros	Cons
Full virtualization	A virtualization technique that provides complete simulation of the underlying hardware. The result is a system in which all software capable of execution on the raw hardware can be run in the virtual machine. Full virtualization has the widest range of support of guest operating systems.	Provides complete isolation of each virtual machine and the VMM; most operating systems can be installed without any modification. Provides near-native CPU and memory performance; uses sophisticated techniques to trap and emulate instructions in runtime via binary patching.	Requires the right combination of hardware and software elements; not quite possible on the x86 architecture in its pure form because of some of the privileged calls that cannot be trapped; performance can be impacted by trap-and-emulate techniques of x86 privileged instructions.
Paravirtualization	A virtualization technique that provides partial simulation of the underlying hardware. Most, but not all, of the hardware features are simulated. The key feature is address space virtualization, granting each virtual machine its own unique address space.	Easier to implement than full virtualization; when no hardware assistance is available, paravirtualized guests tend to be the highest performing virtual machines for network and disk I/O.	Operating systems running in paravirtualized virtual machines cannot be run without substantial modification; virtual machines suffer from lack of backward compatibility and are not very portable.

Continued

Table 1.4 Continued. Types of Server Virtualization

Type of Virtualization	Description	Pros	Cons
Operating System Virtualization	This concept is based on a single operating system instance.	Tends to be very lean and efficient; single OS installation for management and updates; runs at native speeds; supports all native hardware and OS features that the host is configured for.	Does not support hosting mixed OS families, such as Windows and Linux; virtual machines are not as isolated or secure as with the other virtualization types; Ring-0 is a full operating system rather than a stripped-down microkernel as the VMM, so it adds overhead and complexity; difficult to identify the source of high resource loads; also difficult to limit resource consumption per guest.
Native virtualization	This technique is the newest to the x86 group of virtualization technologies. Often referred to as hybrid virtualization, this type is a combination of full virtualization or paravirtualization combined with I/O acceleration techniques. Similar to full virtualization, guest operating systems can be installed without modification. It takes advantage of the latest CPU technology for x86, Intel VT, and AMD-V.	Handles non-virtualizable instructions by using trap-and-emulate in hardware versus software; selectively employs accelerations techniques for memory and I/O operations; supports x64 (64-bit x86 extensions) targeted operating systems; has the highest CPU, memory, and I/O performance of all types of x86 virtual machines.	Requires CPU architecture that supports hardware-assisted acceleration; still requires some OS modification for paravirtualized guests, although less than pure paravirtualization.

Designing & Planning...

Hardware-Assistance Enhances Virtualization

To maximize the performance of your x86-based physical platform and the hosted virtual machines, be sure to select processors that support hardware-assisted virtualization. Both Intel, providing Intel Virtualization Technology (Intel VT), and AMD, providing "Pacifica" (AMD-V), offer such technologies in their latest generation of processors available for servers as well as desktops and notebooks.

Hardware-assisting processors give the guest OS the authority it needs to have direct access to platform resources without sharing control of the hardware. Previously, the VMM had to emulate the hardware to the guest OS while it retained control of the physical platform. These new processors give both the VMM and the guest OS the authority each needs to run without hardware emulation or OS modification.

They also help VMM developers design a more simplified VMM. Since hardware-assisted processors can now handle the compute-intensive calculations needed to manage the tasks of handing off platform control to a guest OS, the computational burden is reduced on the VMM. Also, key state information for the CPU and guest OS can now be stored in protected memory that only the VMM has access to, protecting the integrity of the handoff process.

Finally, hardware-assisted processors, all of which support 64-bit processing, now allow the benefits of 64-bit computing to filter up to the guest OS and its hosted applications. This provides virtual machines with greater capabilities, headroom, and scalability.

Storage Virtualization

Storage vendors have been offering high–performance storage solutions to their customers for quite some time now. In its most basic form, storage virtualization exists in the assembly of multiple physical disk drives, or spindles, into a single entity that is presented to the host server and operating system, such as with RAID implementations. This can be considered virtualization because all the drives are used and interacted with as a single logical drive, although composed of two or more drives in the background.

The true storage tier and its components were further masked by the introduction and adoption of storage area network (SAN) technologies. Without any change to the operating system code responsible for managing storage subsystems, IT organizations are now sharing storage components between multiple servers, even though each server thinks it has its own dedicated physical storage, in actuality storage administrators have simply carved out a virtual quantity of drive space and presented it to the hosts for use.

More advanced technologies have begun to hit the market that take storage virtualization to the next level. Products exist that are capable of migrating storage in real time from one storage platform to another in the background based on rules and policies (such as retention policies, age of data, or last-time accessed) without any interruption or impact to the host. Software products exist that trap-and-emulate native SCSI commands and translate them to other storage instructions in the background, making it possible for a disk array to look like a suite of tape drives and tape libraries to back up software and operating systems without any modification.

Network Virtualization

As with storage vendors, manufacturers of network hardware have been in the virtualization arena for some time, although not always recognized as virtualization. The most popular forms of network virtualization are

- **Virtual LAN (VLAN)** Ratified in the IEEE 802.1Q standard, VLANs are a method of creating independent logical networks within a shared physical network. Network administrators incorporate VLANs into their network design to logically segment broadcast domains and control the interaction between devices on different network segments. VLAN technology has evolved and is a common feature in the application-specific integrated circuits (ASICs) of just about all modern-day Ethernet switches. Although multiple devices can be physically connected to the same network switch, VLANs allow network administrators to create multiple virtual networks that isolate each segment from the others. Each segment utilizes a portion of the available resources (CPU, memory, bandwidth, and so on) in the host switch.

- **Virtual IP (VIP)** An IP address that is not connected to a specific computer or network interface in a computer. VIPs are usually assigned to a network device that is in-path of the traversing network traffic. Incoming packets are sent to the VIP but are redirected to the actual interface of the receiving host(s). VIPs are mostly used for redundancy and load-balancing scenarios, where multiple systems are hosting a common application and are capable of receiving the traffic as redirected by the network device.

- **Virtual Private Network (VPN)** A private communication network used to communicate confidentially over a public network. VPN traffic is often carried over highly insecure network mediums, such as the Internet, creating a secure channel for sensitive and confidential information to traverse from one site to another. It is also used as a means of extending remote employees home networks to the corporate network. Although special software is usually needed to establish the connection, once established, interaction with other resources on the network is handled the same way it would be on a true physical network, without requiring any modification of the network stack or operating system.

Application Virtualization

Administrators have always been plagued with the deployment and maintenance of desktop applications. Web applications and dynamically updated applications have been popular solutions to application distribution. Application virtualization seeks to tackle the problem by encapsulating a virtualization layer and all components of an application into a single file that can be run on a user's desktop. Application packages can be instantly activated or deactivated, reset to their default configuration, and thus mitigate the risk of interference with other applications as they run in their own computing space.

Some of the benefits of application virtualization are:

- **It eliminates application conflicts** Applications are guaranteed to use the correct-version files and property file/Registry settings without any modification to the operating systems and without interfering with other applications.

- **It reduces roll-outs through instant provisioning** Administrators can create pre-packaged applications that can be deployed quickly locally or remotely over the network, even across slow links. Virtual software applications can even be streamed to systems on-demand without invoking a setup or installation procedure.

■ **It runs multiple versions of an application** Multiple versions can run on the same operating system instance without any conflicts, improving the migration to newer versions of applications and speeding the testing and integration of new features into the environment.

Common Use Cases for Virtualization

Now that we have discussed the concept, history, and types of virtualization in depth, the last thing to review before diving into virtualization with Xen's hypervisor, or VMM, is the use cases for virtualization. As mentioned earlier, not every scenario can appropriately be implemented using virtualization technologies. Some workloads are large enough and consistent enough to warranty their own dedicated computing resources. Others are so large it takes a farm of resources just to be able to handle the workload, as is the case with high-performance clusters (HPCs). However, most workloads, regardless of the size of your company, are great candidates for virtualization; and by doing so, you can realize substantial benefits.

If you have not already adopted virtualization technologies as part of your infrastructure strategy, the following are some examples where you can put virtualization to work for you:

■ Technology refresh

■ Business continuity and disaster recovery

■ Proof of concept (POC) deployments

■ Virtual desktops

■ Rapid development, test lab, and software configuration management

Technology Refresh

Asset life-cycle management is an area that gets many CFOs and CIOs attention because of the cost imposed to the business. As one phase of the life cycle, a technology refresh, or the replacement of older fixed assets with newer ones, can stand out on a department or corporate profit and loss statement, even with the lower prices of technology today. In many cases, it makes more sense to replace them than to pay to maintain aging and often obsolete equipment. But what if you could reduce the cost further?

During a technology refresh, the opportunity to virtualize and consolidate some of your existing workloads is great. There are some basic questions you should ask before undertaking any technology refresh, as represented in Table 1.5. If you could answer to one or more of these questions, then virtualization should be the answer you have been looking for.

Table 1.5 Factors to Consider When Choosing Virtualization for a Technology Refresh

Factor to Consider	How Virtualization Addresses It
Q: Is the server that is being refreshed hosting an application that is still valuable to the company rather than being deprecated or obsolete?	If the application still provides value to the company, then it is a good strategy to make sure the application and operating system are hosted on a reliable, supported hardware environment. Virtualization can help by reducing the costs, both hard and soft, of refreshing your infrastructure.
Q: Is current performance acceptable to the business?	New servers can be several times more powerful than the servers you are planning on refreshing. If you did a physical-to-physical refresh, that would lead to underutilized servers and considerable waste of processing power. If you deem current performance to be satisfactory, then a virtual machine is perfect for your application, especially since virtual machines can often perform at near-native levels.
Q: Is there a trend that shows that additional resources will be needed in the short term?	Upgrading server resources can be a costly and time-consuming effort with considerable downtime. A virtualized environment is flexible, and upgrade can often be performed dynamically on some platforms. For others, it is as simple as taking a few minutes to power down the virtual machine, reconfigure resource allocation, and then power the virtual machine up.

Continued

Table 1.5 Continued. Factors to Consider When Choosing Virtualization for a Technology Refresh

Factor to Consider	How Virtualization Addresses It
Q: Can legacy applications be migrated easily and cost-effectively to a newer operating system or hardware?	Many legacy operating systems and applications are difficult to migrate to new hardware platforms with substantial modification. The hardware environment presented by the VMM, on the other hand, often has simple hardware with drivers available for all operating systems supported, making migrations much simpler.
Q: Will there be issues or complications either restoring applications and data to a new server or reinstalling and configuring the applications and data from the ground up?	A process known as physical-to-virtual (P2V) allows you to make an image of your servers and convert them to virtual machines, eliminating the need to restore from backup or possibly reinstall the application from scratch. In some cases, this can happen without any downtime.
Q: Is the application one that requires higher availability and recoverability from failure or some other system compromise?	Features such as live migrations allow single-instance virtual machines to achieve higher availability than on a physical platform. Or if a clustered or load-balanced environment is desired but is not possible because of the hardware investment, making your failover node(s) virtual machines can incur minimal up-front costs that equate to substantial savings down the road.

Business Continuity and Disaster Recovery

Business continuity and disaster recovery initiatives have picked up over the past few years. Customer demand and federal regulations have helped accelerate those efforts and give them the attention they have needed for some time. However, business continuity plans (BCPs) can often require a large investment in standby technology in order to achieve the recovery point and time objectives. As a result, IT disaster recovery can be a slow moving, never-ending process.

Virtualization is an ideal platform for most cases since it eliminates the need to purchase an excessive amount of equipment "just in case." Most software vendors of backup/recovery products support the restoration of operation systems and applications of physical servers to virtual machines. And if you currently use a recovery service provider because hosting your own hot site was too costly, virtualization may make that option more achievable by substantially reducing the investment your company needs to make.

For example, if your company has identified 50 servers that comprise your mission-critical applications and must be brought back online within 72 hours of a disaster, you would need 50 servers available and all the supporting data center and network infrastructure to support them (space, HVAC, power, and so on) at your recovery site. However, establishing your recovery site with virtualization technologies, you could reduce that number to five physical servers, each targeted to host ten virtual machines, a modest quantity based on what most companies achieve currently. That is a 90 percent reduction in acquisition costs for the servers as well as the environment costs to support them. Just think of the space reduction going from 50 to 5 servers!

Proof of Concept Deployments

Business managers often get frustrated with IT's inability to provision an environment to host a proof of concept (POC) for a proposed application that is intended to add value to the business. Most IT organizations do not have spare assets (at least any that are viable) laying around, nor have the time to spend to provision an application that is not associated with an approved "move-forward" project. As a result, most POCs are either set up on inadequate equipment, such as desktops, or not established at all, presenting a risk of missed opportunity for the business.

Virtual machines find their strength in situations such as this. Rapid provisioning, no hardware investment needed, safe, secure, and reliable... all the qualities needed to quickly build a POC environment and keep it running during the time it is needed. Even better, if the POC is successful and you decide to go to production with the application, you can migrate your virtual machine from your test infrastructure to your production virtual infrastructure without having to rebuild the application, saving lots of time in the end.

Virtual Desktops

Companies often have huge investments in client PCs for their user base, many of which do not fall into the category of power users. Similar to server hardware, client PC hardware continues to improve and get more powerful, often being underutilized.

If you have users that run a CRM application, e-mail, a Web browser, and some productivity applications such as spreadsheets and word processing, those users are well suited for a virtual desktop environment. Placing a thin client with keyboard, mouse, and monitor on their desk, the computing power can safely and securely be moved into the data center, hosted as a virtual machine on server hardware. In environments requiring desktop hardware encryption, PC firewalls, and other security devices, this can lead to a substantial reduction in complexity and software licensing as well.

If you are planning on rolling out a new wave of PCs for hundreds of call center agents or in a manufacturing environment (just think of how dirty those shiny new, underutilized PCs will get in just a few days on the shop floor), consider instead creating a virtualized desktop infrastructure in your data center and saving your company lots of money while you are at it.

Rapid Development, Test Lab, and Software Configuration Management

Development teams have always been good candidates for virtualization. Whether it's a desktop-based virtualization product or hosting some development servers as virtual machines in the data center, virtualization has proven to be effective in increasing the productivity of developers, the quality of their work, and the speed at which they complete their coding. In the same way, virtualization can speed up the testing cycles and also allow a higher density of automated testing, thus accelerating the time to release or to market.

Virtualization enables companies to streamline their software life cycle. From development and testing, through integration, staging, deployment, and management, virtualization offers a comprehensive framework for virtual software life-cycle automation that streamlines these adjacent yet often disconnected processes, and closes the loops between them. In addition to these obvious benefits, you can creatively design solutions around a virtual infrastructure to help your software development and test teams to:

- Provide remote lab access and desktop hosting for offsite or offshore development resources, minimizing duplication of lab equipment at each site.

- Close the loop between software development and quality assurance—capturing and moving defect state configurations.

- Reproduce and resolve defects on demand.

- Clone or image a production virtual machine and host it in your QA test infrastructure for security patch, service pack, or maintenance release testing.

- Push a staged configuration into production after successful testing is completed, minimizing errors associated with incorrect deployment and configuration of the production environment.

Summary

Virtualization is an abstraction layer that breaks the standard paradigm of computer architecture, decoupling the operating system from the physical hardware platform and the applications that run on it. As a result, IT organizations can achieve greater IT resource utilization and flexibility. Virtualization allows multiple virtual machines, often with heterogeneous operating systems, to run in isolation, side-by-side, on the same physical machine. Each virtual machine has its own set of virtual hardware (CPU, memory, network interfaces, and disk storage) upon which an operating system and applications are loaded. The operating system sees the set of hardware and is unaware of the sharing nature with other guest operating systems running on the same physical hardware platform. Virtualization technology and its core components, such as the Virtual Machine Monitor, manage the interaction with the operating system calls to the virtual hardware and the actual execution that takes place on the underlying physical hardware.

Virtualization was first introduced in the 1960s to allow partitioning of large, mainframe hardware, a scarce and expensive resource. Over time, minicomputers and PCs provided a more efficient, affordable way to distribute processing power. By the 1980s, virtualization was no longer widely employed. However, in the 1990s, researchers began to see how virtualization could solve some of the problems associated with the proliferation of less expensive hardware, including underutilization, escalating management costs, and vulnerability.

Today, virtualization is growing as a core technology in the forefront of data center management. The technology is helping businesses, both large and small, solve their problems with scalability, security, and management of their global IT infrastructure while effectively containing, if not reducing, costs.

Solutions Fast Track

What Is Virtualization?

☑ Virtualization technologies have been around since the 1960s. Beginning with the Atlas and M44/44X projects, the concept of time-sharing and virtual memory was introduced to the computing world.

☑ Funded by large research centers and system manufacturers, early virtualization technology was only available to those with sufficient resources and clout to fund the purchase of the big-iron equipment.

☑ As time-sharing evolved, IBM developed the roots and early architecture of the virtual machine monitor, or VMM. Many of the features and design elements of the System370 and its succeeding iterations are still found in modern-day virtualization technologies.

☑ After a short quiet period when the computing world took its eyes off of virtualization, a resurgent emphasis began again in the mid-1990s, putting virtualization back into the limelight as an effective means to gain high returns on a company's investment.

Why Virtualize?

☑ As virtualization technology transitioned from the mainframe world to midrange and entry-level hardware platforms and the operating systems that they ran, there was a shift from having either a decentralized or a centralized computing model to having a hybrid of the two. Large computers could now be partitioned into smaller units, giving all of the benefits of logical decentralization while taking advantage of a physical centralization.

☑ While there are many benefits that companies will realize as they adopt and implement virtualization solutions, the most prominent ones are consolidation of their proliferating sprawl of servers, increased reliability of computing platforms upon which their important business applications run, and greater security through isolation and fault containment.

How Does Virtualization Work?

☑ The operating system and the CPU architecture historically have been bound and mated one to the other. This inherent relationship is exemplified by secure and stable computing platforms that segregate various levels of privilege and priority through rings of isolation and access, the most critical being Ring-0.

☑ The most common CPU architecture, the IA-32 or x86 architecture, follows a similar privileged model containing four rings, 0 to 4. Operating systems that run on x86 platforms are installed in Ring-0, called Supervisor Mode, while applications execute in Ring-3, called User Mode.

☑ The Virtual Machine Monitor (VMM) presents the virtual or perceived Ring-0 for guest operating systems, enabling isolation from each platform. Each VMM meets a set of conditions referred to as the Popek and Goldberg Requirements, written in 1974. Though composed for third-generation computers of that time, the requirements are general enough to apply to modern VMM implementations.

☑ While striving to hold true to the Popek and Goldberg requirements, developers of VMMs for the x86 architecture face several challenges due in part to the non-virtualizable instructions in the IA-32 ISA. Because of those challenges, the x86 architecture cannot be virtualized in the purest form; however, x86 VMMs are close enough that they can be considered to be true to the requirements.

Types of Virtualization

☑ Server Virtualization is the most common form of virtualization, and the original. Managed by the VMM, physical server resources are used to provision multiple virtual machines, each presented with its own isolated and independent hardware set. Of the top three forms of virtualization are full virtualization, paravirtualization, and operating system virtualization. An additional form, called native virtualization, is gaining in popularity and blends the best of full virtualization and paravirtualization along with hardware acceleration logic.

☑ Other areas have and continue to experience benefits of virtualization, including storage, network, and application technologies.

Common Use Cases for Virtualization

☑ A technology refresh of older, aging equipment is an opportune time to consider implementing a virtual infrastructure, consolidating workloads and easing migrations through virtualization technologies.

☑ Business can reduce recovery facility costs by incorporating the benefits of virtualization into the BCP and DR architectures.

☑ Virtualization also gives greater levels of flexibility and allows IT organizations to achieve on-demand service levels. This is evident with easily deployed proof-of-concept, pilot, or mock environments with virtually no overhead to facilitate or manage it.

☑ The benefits of virtualization can be driven beyond the walls of the data center to the desktop. Desktop virtualization can help organizations reduce costs while maintaining control of their client environment and providing additional layers of security at no additional cost.

☑ Virtualization is, and has been, at home in the software development life cycle. Such technologies help streamline development, testing, and release management and processes while increasing productivity and shortening the window of time from design to market.

Frequently Asked Questions

Q: What is virtual machine technology used for?

A: Virtual machine technology serves a variety of purposes. It enables hardware consolidation, simplified system recovery, and the re-hosting of earlier applications because multiple operating systems can run on one computer. One key application for virtual machine technology is cross-platform integration. Other key applications include server consolidation, the automation and consolidation of development and testing environments, the re-hosting of earlier versions of applications, simplifying system recovery environments, and software demonstrations.

Q: How does virtualization address a CIO's pain points?

A: IT organizations need to control costs, improve quality, reduce risks and increase business agility, all of which are critical to a business' success. With virtualization, lower costs and improved business agility are no longer trade-offs. By enabling IT resources to be pooled and shared, IT organizations are provided with the ability to reduce costs and improve overall IT performance.

Q: What is the status of virtualization standards?

A: True open standards for getting all the layers talking and working together aren't ready yet, let alone giving users interoperable choices between competitive vendors. Users are forced to rely on de facto standards at this time. For instance, users can deploy two different virtualization products within one environment, especially if each provides the ability to import virtual machines from the other. But that is about as far as interoperability currently extends.

Q: When is a product not really virtualization but something else?

A: Application vendors have been known to overuse the term and label their product "virtualization ready." But by definition, the application should not be to tell whether it is on a virtualized platform or not. Some vendors also label their isolation tools as virtualization. To isolate an application means files are installed but are redirected or shielded from the operating system. That is not the same as true virtualization, which lets you change any underlying component, even network and operating system settings, without having to tweak the application.

Q: What is the ideal way to deploy virtualization?

A: Although enterprises gain incremental benefits from applying virtualization in one area, they gain much more by using it across every tier of the IT infrastructure. For example, when server virtualization is deployed with network and storage virtualization, the entire infrastructure becomes more flexible, making it capable of dynamically adapting to various business needs and demands.

Q: What are some of the issues to watch out for?

A: Companies beginning to deploy virtualization technologies should be cautious of the following: software costs/licensing from proliferating virtual machines, capacity planning, training, high and unrealistic consolidation expectations, and upfront hardware investment, to name a few. Also, sufficient planning upfront is important to avoid issues that can cause unplanned outages affecting a larger number of critical business applications and processes.

Chapter 2

Choosing the Right Solution for the Task

Solutions in this chapter:

- **Issues and Considerations That Affect Virtualization Implementations**

- **Distinguishing One Type of Virtualization from Another**

☑ **Summary**

☑ **Solutions Fast Track**

☑ **Frequently Asked Questions**

Introduction

Virtualization has grown to mean many things, but at its core it is really just another name for abstraction. Abstraction is what computer people have been using for years as a method to represent real world objects in the digital realm of the computer. Abstraction is used to provide a common interface through which components can interact. One example of abstraction would be the use of telephone numbers. These days the number has little bearing on the location of the user. We take for granted the complexity of locating a device across a wide variety of physical mediums. We as humans trust that if we dial the number, the person we're looking for will answer.

Virtualization is an implementation of a standard interface that applications can trust to behave in a familiar manner. This interface may mask significant complexity, or it may merely be a direct channel to the underlying system. Some virtual environments are implemented as simply as replacing a library that an application uses with another similar library which provides similar functionality and additional features. Other virtual environments go so far as to implement an entire "virtual hardware" environment which is impossible to detect from within.

Still other virtual environments are designed to provide "run anywhere" functionality. A programmer need not concern himself with the intricacies of the current platform. He is presented with a common interface and standardized functions both of which he can trust to perform key behaviors.

This chapter describes the various levels of virtualization. It attempts to present the advantages and disadvantages of the various levels of abstraction. This information should help you choose the correct level of virtualization to meet a variety of project requirements.

Issues and Considerations That Affect Virtualization Implementations

Choosing the virtualization technology that is most applicable for your task can vary greatly. If you just want to conduct some rudimentary testing, you might want to use a simple form of operating system virtualization such as Linux-VServer. If you just want to improve the operation of a particular line of business application, you might use VMware's ThinApp. Or if you are a tad braver, you might be architecting the virtualization infrastructure your whole company will operate on some day. Whatever your mission, the pressures that shape your virtualization usage can range from performance goals to policy issues so making sure your solution fits the right problems is very important.

Performance

Performance is usually the most important metric for deciding how to structure your virtualization environment. If you see large changes in usage between different applications throughout a day then you may need a different virtualization structure than if your usage model is fairly static. In addition, your performance requirements can also drive what type of hardware will host the virtualization platform. Some hardware platforms were created solely with virtualization in mind whereas other types of hardware can run a virtualization platform just as well as a standard operating system. In addition, some applications may require considerable CPU processing power whereas other applications may have significant I/O requirements. Understanding what your current needs are as well as your future growth is extremely important.

Redundancy

As soon as the first major government or financial organization began to rely on data processing systems they wanted to make sure that if the system went down there was another system picking up the workload. Why buy one when you can buy two for twice the price? The good news is that virtual machines are dramatically less expensive and simpler to setup than the super computers of yore. In fact, some virtualization platforms such as Microsoft Hyper-V and VMware ESX have attempted to make virtual machines highly available by clicking a check box in a GUI. Some virtualization platforms have multiple levels of high availability. You need to figure out if your systems must be fault tolerant and, if so, to what degree. Some virtualization platforms offer multiple levels of fault tolerance. Basic fault tolerance capabilities simply move a virtual machine to a new host if the primary host fails. You need to decide if your application can tolerate thirty to sixty seconds of downtime for a virtual machine servicing the application. If not, you may need to investigate even stronger forms of fault tolerance, which reduce downtime from one to three seconds. Marathon Technologies provides this type of fault tolerance in its everRun product and VMware Fault Tolerance is a new feature for the VMware platform that is scheduled for release in 2009. Please refer to Chapter 11 for a more thorough discussion of high availability.

Operations

There are also several operational issues that can influence your virtualization deployment. Hardware maintenance windows, software upgrades, change control, virtual machine lifetimes, and licensing constraints can potentially change what type of virtualization you use. For example, moving virtual machines from one hardware system to another—installing new upgraded hardware and then moving those virtual machines back with little or no downtime—is extremely practical and should be included n your planning process. In addition, if you just want a second system for testing and won't be using it in production, then that can drastically change how you use virtualization.

Backups

Disaster recovery requirements can significantly change your virtualization deployment. A solution that can backup 10 virtual machines might be very different than a system that can backup 400 virtual machines. The VMware platform offers a feature called Snapshots that stores a binary diff of a virtual machine image and stores it on disk. This solution might work fine in a smaller environment but can begin to strain if you need to backup hundreds of virtual machines. By the same token, a solution that can easily backup hundreds of virtual machines may not scale to an environment where you need to backup thousands of virtual machines. Some larger environments use deduplication technology to significantly reduce the amount of data stored within a virtualization infrastructure.

Security

One of the best ways to improve the performance of your virtualized environment is to move a virtual machine from one host system to another where there are more hardware resources available. The movement can be done on-demand or dynamically using automation features of the virtualization platform. The dynamic movement of virtual machines from one physical host system to another has become the blood pumping through the veins of many IT organizations offering optimal use of hardware resources.

Taking advantage of virtual machine movement has some important impacts on security. Moving a virtual machine running the corporate web site to the same physical hardware system that also processes the company payroll may introduce a policy problem. Designing proper segmentation and change control policies must be considered when designing your infrastructure.

Evolution

The question most people have these days is not if virtualization will be adopted within their organization but instead when and how those deployments will occur. At the time of writing many organizations have adopted a policy that all new physical servers will be purchased as virtualization servers and any older systems that go through a hardware refresh will undergo a physical-to-virtual (P2V) conversion onto virtualized hardware. There are many stages in this virtualization adoption process that are worth discussion so you have an idea of what you are in for and what possibilities exist.

Discovery

One of the first phases of virtualization adoption is learning about all of the different options that are available out there. There is a whole host of choices ranging from library emulation all the way up to full grid computing capabilities. There are lots of challenges in between and understanding as many potential problems up front can significantly help you avoid problems in the future.

Testing

The birth of many virtualization deployments usually begins with an IT engineer who wants to test out a theory for how something will work but there isn't any hardware available to run the test. You may want to test out a new version of software or you may want to upgrade a running system to a new patch and see if everything still works. Whatever the case may be you might install UML, VMware Workstation, or Bochs to run the new system on your existing computer. These are virtualization solutions that run certain types of virtual machines on top of an existing operating system. This type of virtualization isn't dual booting but instead running an entirely new operating system at the same time as the parent operating system. The new virtual machine can have its own IP address that can be contacted from the network.

Production

After a while that new virtual machine you created to test out a theory may become useful. You may find yourself relying on the services provided by that virtual machine on a consistent basis. In fact, there may be other people in the organization that start using the system as well. At this point you may need to move the system into a production environment where the virtual machine is always running. The next step might be to move the system to something like VMware Server, which will run the virtual machine as a background service in your host operating system. Another option is to move the virtual machine to a full-fledged virtualization host system. Some options in this category include VMware ESX/ESXi, Hyper-V, XenServer, or Parallels. These systems are considered mature virtualization platforms and the pricing options have also become very economical or even free.

Mobility

Once you have several virtualization platforms running in a production environment, you might notice how simple it is to bring down a virtual machine on one host, move the virtual disks for the virtual machine to a new host, and bring the virtual machine back up on the new host. The time required to complete this type of virtual machine move is largely dependent on the speed of storage transfer across a network. A solution for improving this manual process includes yet another layer of abstraction and some specialized features of the virtualization platform. If the host platform accesses its file storage over the network as opposed to a local disk, then transferring the new virtual machine to a new host system is largely a matter of just telling the new host system to start up a new virtual machine where the virtual hard disk for the new virtual machine is located on the network. Using this technique, the disks required to run the virtual machine don't need to be transferred across the network thereby dramatically speeding up the move to just a few seconds. There are several cost effective storage solutions that you can use to gain this capability including openfiler or FreeNAS in addition to commercial offerings such as 3Par, NetApp, EMC Clariion, or HP StorageWorks.

Grid

At this point you may have installed a storage area network to enable fast movement of virtual machines in your environment. You may find yourself powering on more web servers just before noon and then powering them off late in the afternoon so the CRM application can process sales data during the evening on the same host systems. Instead of manually instigating these virtual machine moves, you could use a feature such as VMware Distributed Resource Scheduler (DRS). DRS can detect when a virtual machine becomes starved for resources and instigate moving the virtual machine to a new host system that could better satisfy the resources needed by the virtual machine. These new automation capabilities within virtualization platforms offer the type of utility computing that drastically decreases cost and improves the performance and reliability of IT environments.

Distinguishing One Type of Virtualization from Another

The hype surrounding the word virtualization has become so overblown that it can be difficult to distinguish one type of virtualization from another. In some cases the abstractions offered by different types of virtualization platforms overlap. In other cases, virtualization capabilities might abstract a portion of IT resources in completely different ways. Figure 2.1 attempts to depict the different types of virtualization, how they are similar, how they are different, and what portion of the IT structure they abstract.

Figure 2.1 Different Types of Virtualization

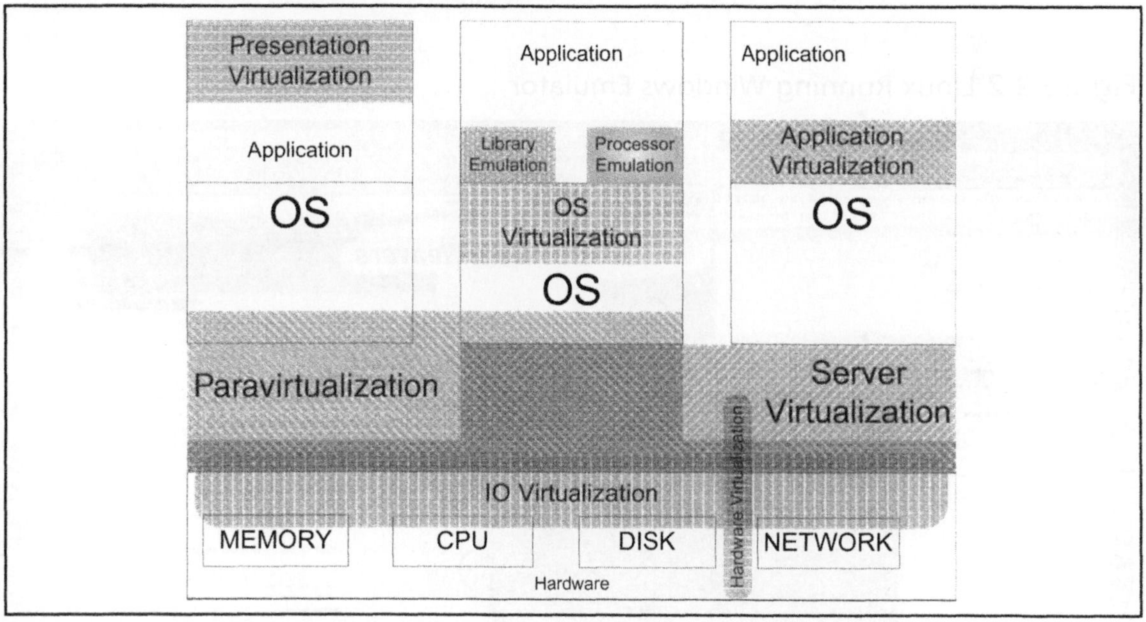

Library Emulation

One of the most basic forms of virtualization is emulation. Library emulation solutions run a particular guest application built for one type of operating system on a different type of host operating system. The emulator will provide the same API as the original operating system environment within the context of the host operating system. Library emulation has the performance advantage of not requiring an entire guest operating system to run. Unfortunately, it does not work in every situation since operating system application programming interfaces can be quite expansive and complex potentially introducing inconsistencies between the original guest operating system and the emulated interface.

Wine

The Windows emulator is a software package that allows you to run Windows programs on various Unix platforms. The software emulates the native Windows API and translates those calls into Unix, X Windows, and OpenGL API calls. Using the Wine software, you can run popular Windows programs such as Microsoft Office and Excel as well as games like Counter Strike, EVE Online, and World of Warcraft. Figure 2.2 shows a Linux system running a Microsoft PowerPoint application.

Figure 2.2 Linux Running Windows Emulator

Cygwin

Cygwin is a software package that allows you to run certain Linux programs on a Microsoft Windows operating system. One of the most popular uses of Cygwin is to run a Linux shell such as bash on a Windows system. As the bash program makes Linux API calls, the Cygwin software translates the API calls into native Windows API calls (see Figure 2.3).

Figure 2.3 Linux Running Windows Emulator

Processor Emulation

Emulating hardware processor instructions is another type of virtualization. Processor emulators translate CPU instructions received from a hosted guest operating system into native CPU instructions. The advantage of this type of an approach is that a guest operating system can be run on numerous types of native processors. The disadvantage is that performance suffers due to the real-time interpretation that occurs. Bochs and QEMU are different flavors of processor emulation platforms.

Operating System Virtualization

Operating system virtualization abstracts operating system components to guest operating systems such as memory access, file system, and network access. One key component of this type of virtualization is that the kernel of the parent operating system is the same kernel used in each guest operating system. This type of virtualization avoids emulation since the same system call interface is shared by each guest. Memory and CPU resources can be managed very effectively because load balancing is more efficient since there is not a hypervisor boundary that must be crossed to perform process execution.

Since all guests hosted using OS virtualization share the same kernel, they also share any problems within the shared kernel including stability or security problems. Upgrades can be problematic because upgrading one virtual machine requires updating all virtual machines on the same host system, which can cause logistical problems. Examples of OS virtualization platforms include Linux-VServer, Paralleles Virtuozzo Containers, OpenVZ, and Solaris Containers.

Application Virtualization

Some application virtualization solutions such as VMware's ThinApp offer the ability to stream the application to a user's desktop from a file server. By using this approach administrators can update a single file on a centralized file server so that the next time users start the application, they will get the latest version of that application. By encapsulating an entire application into a single file, the administrator also enables the user to run multiple versions of an application at the same time on the same desktop. Another application virtualization solution is the Microsoft App-V product.

Presentation Virtualization

Another technique for solving the problem of application distribution is to abstract the presentation layer of the application usage experience. Presentation virtualization requires a small application to be run locally on your desktop that connects over a network to a server where the application is running. The communication between the desktop and the server transfers all keyboard, video, and mouse data over a specialized protocol such as the Microsoft Remote Desktop protocol or the Citrix XenApp Independent Computing Architecture protocol.

Server Virtualization

The virtualized server can run completely different operating systems without each guest knowing that another guest is running on the same physical system. The virtualized server does the job of sharing the physical hardware with each guest operating system running.

One of the most critical components of a server virtualization platform is the hypervisor. A hypervisor is software that allows multiple virtual machines to share access to physical CPU, memory, disk, and network resources. Initially, hypervisors ran on top of an existing operating system. This type of hypervisor is sometimes called a hosted hypervisor. Examples of hosted hypervisors include VMware Workstation/Server, Microsoft Virtual PC/Server, and Parallels Workstation. Another type of hypervisor is sometimes called a bare-metal hypervisor. Examples of bare-metal hypervisors include VMware ESX, Microsoft Hyper-V, and Citrix XenServer. Even though these hypervisors are classified as bare-metal hypervisors, they don't actually run directly on bare-metal but instead run inside of a parent operating system.

Dedicated Hardware

A hypervisor that does not have a parent operating system is sometimes referred to as an embedded hypervisor or an integrated hypervisor. The VMware ESXi virtualization platform is an example of a hypervisor that runs directly on actual hardware without an underlying operating system. The ESXi hypervisor can boot from a local disk or over the network. The only thing the hypervisor does is run virtual machines. The ESXi virtualization platform is completely managed from an application programming interface. The lack of a parent operating system reduces maintenance and the attack surface area of the platform. If there is no parent operating system, then you don't need to patch it and you can't attack it. Another example of an embedded hypervisor is the Hitachi Virtage platform.

Hardware Compatibility

Hypervisor virtualization has become more popular than emulation largely for performance reasons. Some hypervisors do not emulate CPU instructions but instead only modify the portions of the virtual machine execution that need to be modified in order to share the physical hardware across multiple virtual machines. The job of the hypervisor or an emulation layer is largely to get instructions from virtual machines to the physical hardware. For example, if you wanted to get from one side of a river to another an emulation approach would use a ferry to get across the river whereas a hypervisor would use a bridge.

The performance gains that hypervisors offer over emulation do not come for free. The ability to run virtual machines at near native hardware speeds requires giving up a certain amount of flexibility in your choice of hardware. Most hypervisors have specific hardware requirements that require the type of x86 hardware that they can run on. At the time of writing the Microsoft Hyper-V product not only requires a 64-bit processor but also specialized virtualization instructions as discussed in the section titled "Hardware Virtualization" to follow in this chapter. The more hardware systems your virtualization platform supports, the more flexibility you gain in your virtualization deployment.

Hypervisors require specialized hardware for deployment, and certain features within a hypervisor might even mandate certain hardware specifications. Since hypervisors don't emulate every CPU instruction from a virtual machine for performance reasons, the virtual machine has a small amount of dependency on the actual physical processor of the host system. If the physical processor does not support the instruction set used by the running applications on a virtual machine, then the hypervisor will not be able to run the virtual machine. This is normally not a problem but vendors such as Intel and AMD continue to innovate x86 processors so they usually include new features. The culprit here is that x86 is not always x86. These processors define a class, and different types within the class support different instruction sets. So just because you can run a virtual machine on one VMware ESX host does not necessarily mean you can run that same virtual machine on another VMware ESX host system.

Chapter 11 describes how virtual machines can dynamically move between a pool of host systems called a cluster. Given that hypervisors have specific hardware requirements, creating a cluster necessitates that the hardware specification of all hosts in the cluster be similar. For example, a virtual machine that requires the use of Intel x86 instruction set SSE4.1 cannot be migrated to a host that has an x86 processor that is running the Intel quad core CPU with the Kentsfield core. The hypervisor vendors are working to mitigate these types of problems.

Paravirtualization

A server virtualization platform attempts to present a generic hardware interface to a guest virtual machine, whereas a paravirtualized platform requires the guest virtual machine to use virtualization specific drivers in order to run within the virtualized platform. In certain circumstances paravirtualization can offer performance benefits, but some administrators consider the requirement of specialized drivers within the operating system as invasive. Examples of paravirtualized platforms include the Xen and TRANGO hypervisors.

Even though paravirtualization offers some unique advantages, there are many problems with the technology in general. Before you can use a particular operating system within a paravirtualized environment, you must first make sure that the virtualization platform offers drivers for the guest operating system. This means that the platform may support Linux kernel version 2.4 but it does not necessarily support kernel version 2.6. What it also means is that one development group from company 'A' has a version of the drivers but open source group 'B' also has a set of drivers. It can become confusing to an administrator which drivers should be used depending on the pros and cons of each implementation. And those differences can be very complex. Different operating systems may have vastly different methods for transferring data to and from hardware devices. This can make paravirtualization extremely complex and thus prone to errors.

I/O Virtualization

As physical x86-based host systems continue to increase processing power, there is a growing need to abstract the flow of data in and out of these systems. At the time of writing there are x86-based servers that can host 1000 virtual machines. Even if the host systems have multiple physical network adapters to provide the I/O needs of those virtual machines, the logistical problems surrounding cabling, port density, rack space, cooling, and other data center issues begin to heat up.

Virtualized I/O solutions abstract physical network interfaces such as Ethernet, FibreChannel, or Infiniband to a host server system. Most virtualized I/O solutions involve some type of software driver that runs within the host operating system itself. This software driver has the ability to present a single physical network interface as multiple physical network interfaces to the operating system running on the host. For example, you could have a HP server with a single 20Gbps Infiniband host channel adapter running VMware ESX with the virtualized I/O driver. The virtualized I/O driver could present the hypervisor with one 10Gbps Ethernet adapter and four host bus adapters for SAN connectivity. The ESX server would then further split up those virtualized I/O fabric adapters into hypervisor virtualized network adapters attached to the virtual machines themselves. The physical hardware ends up virtualized twice. Even though the method for virtualized I/O is complex, the end result is a much simpler environment to manage. Some vendors offering compelling solutions in this area include 3Leaf Systems and Xsigo Systems.

Hardware Virtualization

Computer processing chips that offer capabilities to run multiple virtual machines simultaneously are considered a form of hardware virtualization. These capabilities improve a virtualization platform's ability to switch from running one virtual machine to another. Examples of hardware virtualization technologies include Intel's Virtualization Technology (VT) and AMD Virtualization (AMD-V). Some virtualization platforms such as Microsoft Hyper-V require virtualization extensions in order to run.

Tools & Traps...

Management

Development of virtualization technology began in the early 1960s but has skyrocketed in the past 10 years as it has been applied to the ubiquitous x86 line of processing technology. In that time there has been a renaissance of virtualization technology such as hypervisors and hardware virtualization, but what has become increasingly apparent is that management technology is the largest driver of virtualization solutions. The more you work with virtualization, the more you will want to script, automate, and manage virtualization deployments. When you are considering what type of virtualization technology to use, make sure that there is a strong programmatic interface to the platform. A virtualization platform with a strong application programming interface allows you to customize how the solution works and enables open source projects as well as third party vendors to develop new and innovative solutions for the platform.

Summary

The breadth and depth of virtualization solutions has significantly evolved over the last 40 years. The development of virtualization technology has continued to improve the solutions for age old information technology problems. In order to effectively use the virtualization solutions that exist, it is important to understand your immediate and future needs. Some people view virtualization as a more efficient use of resources but at the same time might think that using a virtualization platform will not produce the same performance as using a single operating system on a single hardware platform. This may be true, but the real challenge is knowing how computing resources need to be used in your organization. IT organizations with the fastest performing systems understand the core business drivers behind the organization. Once those goals are well understood, virtualization can be a powerful weapon in realizing them.

When the phone rings at 3 a.m. because an IT system is not functioning properly, sleep is lost, people get yelled at, and life at home can be less than enjoyable. Ensuring that a machine failure is not a failure of the IT organization but instead a lane change on the road to operations bliss becomes much simpler in a virtualization environment. Providing stellar uptimes, quick backups, and secure computing environments can not only eliminate angry users but also produce gold stars on your report card. Understanding the different types of virtualization gives you powerful tools in building a resilient and productive IT organization.

As shown in Figure 2.1 near the beginning of the chapter, the different flavors of virtualization abstract almost every angle of the computing stack. Server virtualization solutions abstract hardware resources such as CPU, memory, disk, and network interfaces to virtual machines. In addition virtualization solutions can abstract software interfaces, GUI interfaces, portions of operating systems, portions of applications, and even low level kernel drivers.

Solutions Fast Track

Issues and Considerations That Affect Virtualization Implementations

☑ Performance fluctuations.

☑ Application tolerance.

☑ Software upgrades and change control.

☑ Understanding the stages of virtualization adoption.

Distinguishing One Type of Virtualization from Another

☑ Server virtualization is the most popular form of x86 virtualization.

☑ Emulation provides better hardware and software compatibility than hypervisor based solutions.

☑ Hypervisors provide significant performance advantages over emulation solutions.

☑ Hardware compatibility is an ongoing challenge with hypervisor based solutions.

Frequently Asked Questions

Q: I've never installed any type of virtualization. What is the best way to start learning about the technology?

A: Download VMware Server and install it. Create a virtual machine and install an operating system on it.

Q: Isn't virtualization slower than real hardware?

A: A single virtual machine running on a single physical server is negligibly slower than not using a virtualization platform.

Q: Why do I need a storage area network?

A: A storage area network improves the ability to move virtual machines between physical hosts.

Q: Can my application detect if I am running in a virtual machine?

A: On some virtualization platforms it has been possible to issue low level CPU instructions within a virtual machine whose output might indicate whether or not the machine is running on a virtualization platform.

Q: I am running software whose license is tied to the hardware. Can I install that software in a virtual machine?

A: Most of the major licensing vendors have adopted their software to allow licensed applications to run in a virtualization platform. Check with the application vendor to make sure there are no problems.

Chapter 3

Building a Sandbox

Solutions in this chapter:

- Sandbox Background
- Existing Sandbox Implementations
- Describing CWSandbox
- Creating a Live DVD with VMware and CWSandbox

☑ Summary

☑ Solutions Fast Track

☑ Frequently Asked Questions

Introduction

There are several ways to obtain information about malware and in particular bot applications, as seen in the book, *Botnets—The Killer Web App* (Syngress 2007). Much of this chapter has been adapted from the contribution of Carsten Willem to the Botnet book. One approach is to analyze suspected malware by executing them in a so-called *sandbox*. Through this analysis we hope to learn more about its internals, the underlying communication method and infrastructure. Sandboxes are a common concept in computer security and are used for executing program code that comes from unverified or untrusted sources.

In the following sections of this chapter we describe sandbox technology and its application to malware analysis. First, we introduce the general sandbox architecture and its components. Then we will discuss several implementations of malware analysis sandboxes, followed by a more detailed explanation of one of these products, the CWSandbox. A sample analysis report for a very simple bot application is presented and explained. After that a detailed description of how to use the sandbox in real malware analysis is given, and a lot of useful and real examples of many different malicious actions that usually are performed by a bot are shown. This part of the chapter will give you the knowledge and ability to *read* an analysis report and identify the important malicious internals of the analyzed bot software. We will present some results that we have achieved on our live sandbox systems by successfully analyzing more than 10,000 malware samples. Finally, we have included instructions on how to build a Live DVD containing a VM with Windows XP Pro and the CWSandbox for use in the field or in the classroom.

Sandbox Background

A sandbox offers a monitored and controlled environment, such that the unknown software cannot do any harm to the real hosting computer system. This can be achieved by only blocking some critical operations or by implementing a complete virtual environment, where the processor, memory, and the file system are simulated and the real system is not accessible by the tested application. In malware analysis the main objective of the sandbox is to monitor the accesses to system resources, not to block them. A virtual machine or some other mechanism is used so that the system can be brought back into a clean and uninfected initial state after an analysis run. Consequently, the protection of the underlying system is not so important. This form of analysis is called *behavior analysis*. This form of analysis is in contrast to *code analysis*, where the program instructions are examined with the help of a disassembler or a debugger.

The Visible Sandbox

To illustrate the functionality and the components of sandbox technology, the architecture and operation of CWSandbox is described. Different sandbox applications will implement sandbox technology differently. In our example, the host computer is running Ubuntu, which is running VMware, which is running Windows XP Pro, which is running the sandbox application, cwsandbox, which is running the malware application.

In our example, the sandbox itself consists of two different executables: cwsandbox. exe and cwmonitor.dll. The first one is the main application, which starts the malware and controls the whole analysis process, and the second one is a Dynamic Link Library (DLL), which is injected into all monitored processes in the malware. The sandbox is executed with the malware and associated command line parameters as its arguments. It is the sandbox that actually executes the malware.

During the execution of the malware, the DLL intercepts each critical API call and informs the main application about the call. Depending on the type of the system call, it either waits for the sandbox to decide how to continue, delegates control to the called API function, or simply returns with a simulated or error result. Besides the monitoring, the DLL also has to ensure that whenever the malware starts a new process or injects code into an already running process, the sandbox is informed about that. In that case a new instance of the DLL is injected into that newly created or already existing process, such that this process also can be monitored. A schematic of this architecture is given in Figure 3.1.

Figure 3.1 A Transparent Sandbox Instance Using CWSandbox

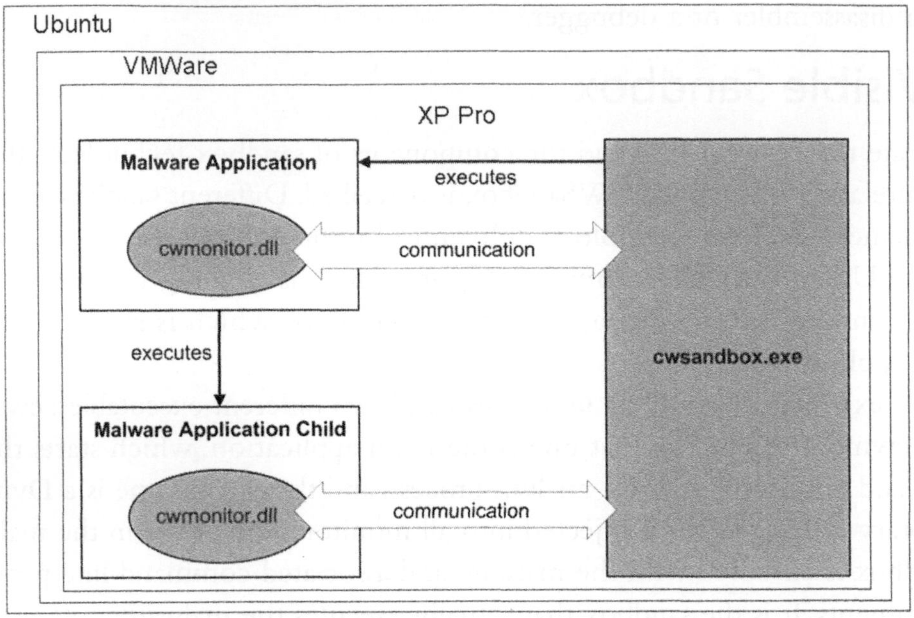

As mentioned, the monitoring DLL informs the sandbox about each performed API call, which in fact is done by sending a *notification* to it. These notifications include a lot of information, like the name of the API function, the used parameters, or the time when the call occurred. Depending on the type of the called function, a different *TNotification* class is used. Subclasses for the following categories exist:

- *TNotification_COM*: Used for API calls that create COM objects

- *TNotification_DLLHandling*: Used for API calls that load/unload a DLL or that dynamically determine the entry points of API functions (used during explicit linking)

- *TNotification_FileSystem*: Used for API calls that access the file system

- *TNotification_ICMPPacket*: Used for API calls that send ICMP packets

- *TNotification_INIFile*: Used for API calls that use the Windows built-in methods to access *.ini* files

- *TNotification_Mutex*: Used for API calls that create or access mutex objects

- *TNotification_Network*: Used for API calls that use the Windows built-in network methods; for example, for accessing Windows shares

- *TNotification_Process*: Used for API calls that perform actions on processes; for example, creating, terminating, or opening a process

- *TNotification_ProtectedStorage*: Used for API calls that perform accesses on the *Protected Storage*, which is a Windows Service for storing authentication data of applications or Web sites

- *TNotification_Registry*: Used for API calls that access the registry

- *TNotification_Service*: Used for API calls that access Windows Services

- *TNotification_System*: Used for API calls that perform system functions; for example, rebooting the system

- *TNotification_SystemInfo*: Used for API calls that query system info; for example, querying the current user

- *TNotification_Thread*: Used for API calls that perform actions on threads; for example, creating or terminating

- *TNotification_User*: Used for API calls that use the Windows built-in user management functions; for example, creating or deleting a user

- *TNotification_VirtualMemory*: Used for API calls that access another process's virtual memory

- *TNotification_Window*: Used for API calls that access the currently existing windows; for example, to find a window with a given title or class name

- *TNotification_WinSock*: Used for API calls that perform WinSock operations

There is a focus on analyzing the network connections and the traffic data. For that reason the transferred data is inspected and the underlying web protocol is trying to be determined. At the moment the following protocols are understood: *Hypertext Transport Protocol (HTTP), File Transfer Protocol (FTP), Simple Mail Transfer Protocol (SMTP), Internet Relay Chat Protocol (IRC)*, and the *Ident Protocol (IDENT)*. Connections that use the RFC-conform messages and slightly modified versions are automatically detected and all the protocol dependent data is extracted (e.g., the login information, downloaded Web sites, or performed FTP commands). If an SMTP connection is detected, the CWSandbox can be instructed to trick the malware such that only informational requests are sent to the remote SMTP server instead of real mail delivery. The malware thinks that it is working with a proper SMTP server and that all the information about outgoing mails can be monitored, but actually no single mail is sent at all.

cwsandbox.exe

The cwsandbox.exe is a noninteractive console application, as it expects—and needs—no user input during its execution. The only possible input is CTRL+C, which is the standard Windows shortcut for terminating console applications. If termination is not ended prematurely by using this shortcut, the sandbox runs until all malware processes have terminated, a custom timeout is reached, or some critical event has occurred that requires an instant termination of the malware processes. During its runtime the following tasks are performed:

- The malware process is started in suspended mode, such that the process object is created and all modules are loaded, but no single instruction is executed yet

- The cwmonitor.dll is injected into this new process

- Runtime options and information are exchanged with this DLL

- Throughout the execution notifications are received from the DLL inside of each monitored process; depending on the received notification, some decisions have to be made by the sandbox; the DLL then waits for this decision and continues in the way the sandbox decided; however, in most cases no decision is needed and the DLL simply routes the call to the original API function after sending the notification

- After all processes have terminated or a given timeout is reached, all still running processes are terminated or the created malicious threads are stopped if their parent processes cannot be terminated safely, as it is the case with essential Windows processes like winlogon.exe

- Under some circumstances the malware is terminated before the timeout occurs, for example to prevent serious harmful actions

- A high level analysis report is created from the collected data

- Optionally, a .cab file archive is created from all the monitored data and some additional files

Besides the monitoring of the relevant API function calls, the sandbox also offers some helpful features for a manual postprocessing step of the results. Some of the most important features are enabled with the configuration options STORE_CREATED_FILES and DUMP_PROCESSES. The first one provides that a copy of all newly created files is written into the *.cab* file. By this, you can get the data of temporary files, which often are used as a source for encryption and then contain the plain text of data, which is transmitted only in an obfuscated version over the network. Furthermore this includes copies of all downloaded files, which may contain code updates or other malware files. The second option enables a functionality that creates process dumps of all monitored processes shortly before they are terminated or suspended. So, if a malware sample is compressed or encrypted, you will get a decompressed and decrypted version of the binary code by that. All process dumps are also stored in the mentioned .cab file.

WARNING

Please keep in mind that the main purpose of CWSandbox is to monitor and not to block the actions of the analyzed file. This means that your local system as well as other remote systems may be infected by it and that sensitive data may be retrieved and sent to the malware operator. Furthermore there may remain active malicious code also after the analysis process has finished. The sandbox tries to terminate all created processes and to stop all malicious threads that have been injected into running system services. But as this is not possible in any case, you always should reset your system back to a clean state after a performed analysis.

---

cwmonitor.dll

The cwmonitor.dll is injected into each monitored process by the sandbox application. This is automatically done, if a new process is started by the malware, or an existing process is infected with malicious code. If a monitored process wants to perform either of these operations, the sandbox application controls this creation/injection as described in the following. If a new application should be started, the sandbox intercepts directly after creating the process and before executing any single operation of it. Then, the monitoring DLL is injected and the newly created process is only resumed, if the initialization routine of the DLL can be successfully performed. The infection of an already running process works in an analog way: if a monitored process injects code into an already running one, CWSandbox intercepts this before any single operation of the injected code is allowed to be executed. Then, the monitoring DLL is injected and completely initialized. If the initialization of the DLL fails for some reason, the created process or infected thread is terminated automatically without being able to perform any single instruction.

In its initialization routine the DLL first collects some information about the hosting process, like username or security context information. Then it sets up an inter-process communication (IPC) object to communicate with the sandbox application. Via this mechanism, the collected process information is sent to the sandbox and some configuration settings are received in turn. Function hooks are installed for all relevant API functions, which are used to intercept their calls. The technique used for realizing the hook functions is called Inline Code Overwriting and is described in detail in the following. There are several other approaches like Import Address Table (IAT) Patching, Export Address Table (EAT) Patching, or using Proxy DLLs. Every hooking technique has its disadvantages and advantages, but for CWSandbox the currently used one seems to fit best.

The inline patching performed in CWSandbox works in the following way. Each Windows API function that is being used in an application is implemented in one of the Windows DLL files like kernel32.dll, advapi32.dll, or ntdll.dll. These DLLs either are loaded automatically on process initialization or can be reloaded manually during runtime by one of the functions LoadLibrary, LoadLibraryEx, or LdrLoadDll. No matter how and when the DLL is loaded, at runtime the code of each API function that is called needs to reside in the virtual memory of the calling process. Accordingly, the cwmonitor.dll is able to locate these functions in memory, either by using the API function GetProcAddress or by manually parsing the EAT of the containing Windows DLL module. For catching all calls to the particular function, a JMP instruction is written to its code location as the first operation. This JMP operation is used to reroute the execution to a customized hook function.

As an example, Figure 3.2 shows an extract of the CreateFileA function from kernel32.dll, which is used to open an existing file or to create a new file. In the upper part of the figure the original and unmodified version of this function is shown. The first three instructions are displayed in a light gray box, the following ones in a dark gray box. The operations from the light gray one are those that are overwritten by the JMP instruction after the hook is installed. You can see that in the lower part of the figure: the first light gray box is completely missing, because it has been overwritten. The following bytes from the dark gray box are not modified at all.

Figure 3.2 Inline Code Overwriting

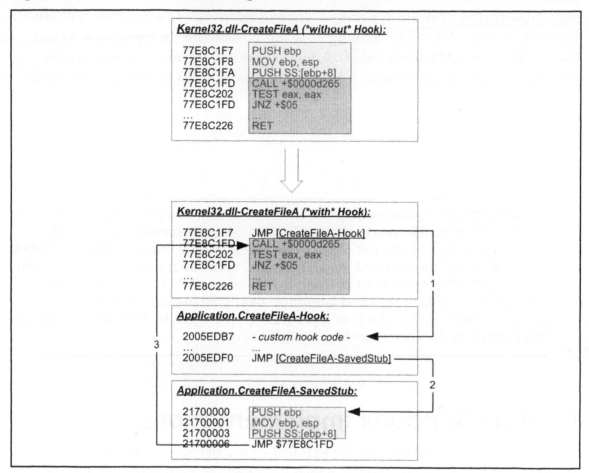

At hook installation, before the introducing bytes of a function are overwritten, these have to be saved to some other memory location as they later may be needed to perform the original API function. In the lowest box of the figure you can see that these bytes are copied to a location called SavedStub. Now, each time the CreateFileA function is called, first the JMP operation is executed and control is delegated to the hook function (shown in the middle box of the lower figure-part). If the original API should be called from inside of the hook function, first the SavedStub is executed and then control is transmitted back to the original API function. In fact the operations from the dark gray box are executed then, which have not been modified by the hook. This form of API Hooking is the most effective and comfortable one, which can be done from user mode. But as it is detectable by the malware application, coming releases of CWSandbox will use some form of kernel mode hooking. It is also possible for an application to not use the Windows API functions at all, but to perform the relevant system calls directly. Because this technique is hard to and laborious to implement, usually it is not done in malware.

WARNING

CWSandbox will deliver no false positives, as all contents of a produced analysis report reflect operations that actually have been performed. In contrast, there always will be the risk of false negatives, as only the explicitly monitored operations will be reported. As an example, applications are able to perform system calls directly instead of using the Windows API. Nevertheless, since this is rather complicated and laborious, nearly all malware uses the API. But you never can be sure that a program is clean, just by finding no malicious operations in the corresponding analysis report.

Existing Sandbox Implementations

There are several software tools that perform such a behavior analysis by executing a sample in some form of sandbox, which monitors the performed actions and afterward creates an analysis report of these actions. One candidate is the Norman SandBox, which was developed by Norman ASA, a Norwegian company that specializes in data security. Norman simulates a whole computer system and a connected network. The implementation details and a description of the underlying technology can be found in their *Sandbox Whitepaper*.[1] A live version of their sandbox is available online at http://sandbox.norman.no/live.html, where everyone can submit malware samples and get an analysis report by e-mail later. Another product is TTAnalyze, which was developed by Ulrich Bayer, Ikarus Software GmbH, in cooperation with the Technical University of Vienna. TTAnalyze uses the PC emulator *QEMU* to run a complete Windows operating system inside of it. In this emulated system the technique of API Hooking (a technique described later in this chapter) is used to monitor the interesting system calls of the malware. The decoupling from the network has the advantage that the malware is not able to infect other computers, but there also is the disadvantage that less information can be collected, as no real outgoing connection can be established.

Chas Tomlin has chosen a different approach with his Sandnet. There, the malicious software is executed on a real Windows system, not on an emulated or simulated one. After 60 seconds of execution, the host is reset and forced to reboot from a Linux image instead of its actual Windows OS. For that purpose Preboot Execution Environment (PXE) is used: a mechanism for booting a computer via its network interface independently of an available data storage device or operating system. After booting Linux, the Windows partition is mounted and the registry hives are extracted as well as the complete file list. Both are sent to a different analysis host for further examination. After that, the Windows partition is reverted back to its initial clean state using *PartImage*.[2] As Chas Tomlin's Sandnet focuses on the network activity, several dispositions are made. During the execution of the malware, the Windows host is connected to a virtual Internet with an IRC server running that positively answers all incoming IRC connection requests. Furthermore, all packets are captured to examine all other network traffic afterward. The collected packets are parsed using perl scripts for known protocols such as IRC, DNS, and HTTP, and the relevant information is extracted.

A similar method is used in *Truman—The Reusable Unknown Malware Analysis Net*, which is provided by Joe Stewart from LURHQ. It consists of a PXE bootable Linux client based on Chas Tomlin's PXE Windows Image Using Linux [Tomb] and a set of additional tools. The malware sample is also executed on a real Windows system, which is connected to a virtual Internet. After the sample's execution, the Truman tools are used to dump the system's memory and its file system contents. By that, a different analysis machine is able to examine the dumps and compare them against the initial system state. More information on Truman can be found at www.lurhq. com/truman.

Finally, there is CWSandbox, which results from the diploma thesis of Carsten Willems and is being further improved and still under development (see Figure 3.3). A free research version as well as a commercial version can be retrieved from Sunbelt Software. More information and also a live sandbox, where anyone is able to submit suspicious software samples and get an analysis report by mail later, can be found at www.cwsandbox.org and www.sunbeltsandbox.com.

Figure 3.3 Running CWSandbox

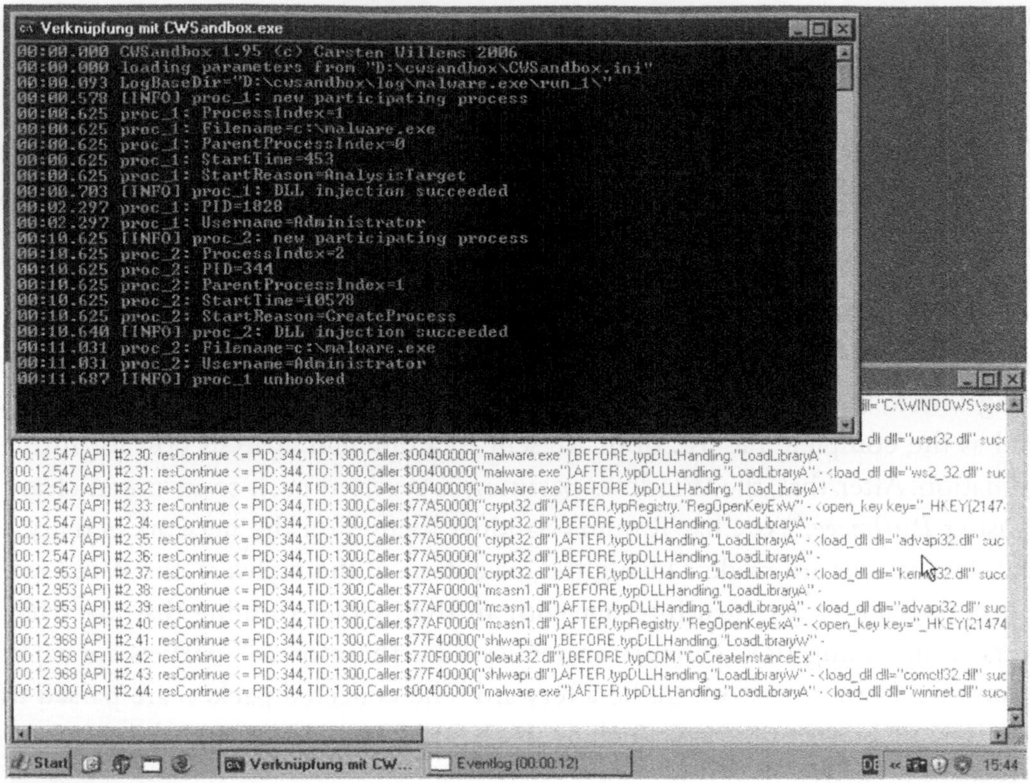

Describing CWSandbox

CWSandbox is an application for the automatic behavior analysis of malware. This dynamic analysis is performed by executing the malicious application in a controlled environment and catching all relevant calls to the Windows API. These API calls are used for accessing the Windows system resources like files, the registry, or the network, so all the malware's actions can be examined by that. In a second step a high level summarized report is generated from this monitored data. One focus lies on the analysis of bots, and a big effort is spent on extracting and evaluating the network traffic data. To give an intuitive image of the sandbox in advance, a short example is presented first. It shows the analysis of a bot application that was collected by a honeypot. We will use this bot as a basic example in this chapter, because it is a simple one, but comprises most of the techniques and actions characteristic for most of the bots currently available. It is named *Backdoor.IRCBot.S* by BitDefender, *BackDoor.Generic4.VT* by AVG, and *Backdoor.Win32.IRCBot.yc* by Kaspersky.

Due to the nature of its origin the name we chose is based on its MD5 hash value, therefore it is 82f78a89bde09a71ef99b3cedb991bcc.exe. For starting its analysis in CWSandbox the following command is used:

```
c:\cwsandbox.exe TARGET_FILENAME=82f78a89bde09a71ef99b3cedb991bcc.exe
```

The sandbox then starts the malware and monitors its actions by inspecting the performed API calls performed by it. Figure 3.2 shows an example output of this execution. The upper main console window prints out information about the malware process and about all new processes that were started or injected. The lower event log window gives information about each monitored API function that was called by one of them. After a customizable time, all participating malware processes are terminated or stopped. Then a summarized and high level XML analysis report is created from the collected data. The analysis report contains a separate section for each process that was involved, and for each of them several subsections that contain actions of a particular type; for example, there is one subsection for accesses to the file system, one for accesses to the registry, and another one for the performed network operations. Figure 3.4 shows an extract of such an XML report.

Figure 3.4 Analysis Report

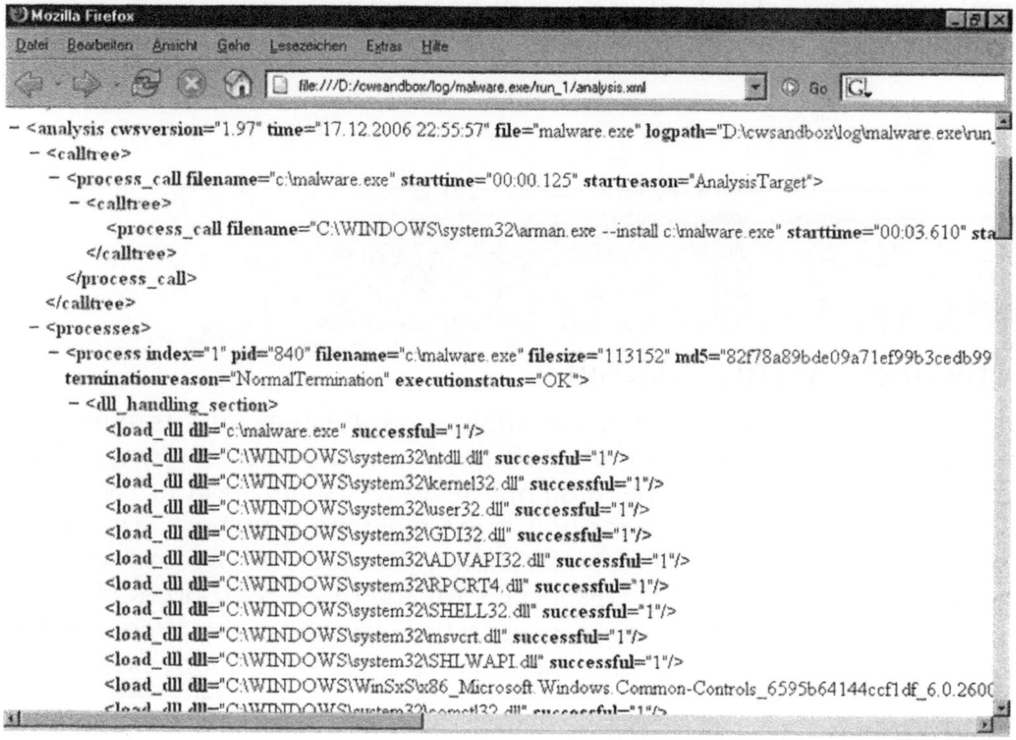

CWSandbox is used to create analysis reports for single malware samples, and it is integrated into a bigger system, the Automated Analysis Suite (AAS). This suite consists of several software components and is used to collect and analyze malware automatically and provides a database repository. You can see a schematic overview of the AAS in Figure 3.5. All its components are arranged around a central database, which holds the malware sample files and the resulting analysis reports. This database is filled by manual malware submission via a Web interface or by automatic collection via Nepenthes sensor hosts. Of course, the malware submission interface can also be used by other collecting mechanisms, but currently this is done only via Nepenthes. One or more CWSandbox hosts are where the actual analysis is performed (see Figure 3.5). On such a host an instance of the CWSandbox is running, which periodically queries the database for new samples. If a new one is found, it is downloaded and an analysis is started on it. Afterward the resulting report is written back to the database and the host is brought back into a clean state. Therefore, on our live systems most of the CWSandbox hosts are realized as virtual machines, which run under VMware, but this is only for convenience reasons. All you need is a mechanism to reset the CWSandbox host back to a clean initial state after a performed analysis. Accordingly, this also can be done by using applications like DeepFreeze,[3] a hardware restore solution, or by using a dual-boot or network-boot system as well.

Notes from the Underground…

Detecting a Virtual Machine

Using virtual machines for malware analysis has become very popular today. Due to that fact a lot of malicious applications try to detect if they are running in a virtual environment. Depending on the used virtualization software, there exist different characteristics for which the malware can check. This includes specific registry entries, the list of running processes or system services, or typical behavior of the system. Especially for the often used product VMware there exist a lot of publicly known detection methods. The Web site www.trapkit.de presents a lot of them and also offers the tools *scoopy doo* and *jerry*

Continued

for that purpose. A generic approach to VM detection has been presented by Joanna Rutkowska under the name redpill. It is based on the fact that retrieving the address of the Interrupt Descriptor Table (IDT) is a nonprivileged instruction that also can be called from user mode applications. Because the IDT address retrieved when running in a virtual machine is different from that in a real system, we can easily use this for VM detection. The best thing about this trick is that it works with any virtualization software. As newer CPU generations offer real virtualization support, we can only hope that in the future, VM detection will become impossible or at least (and most probably) much more difficult.

Figure 3.5 Automated Analysis Suite (AAS)

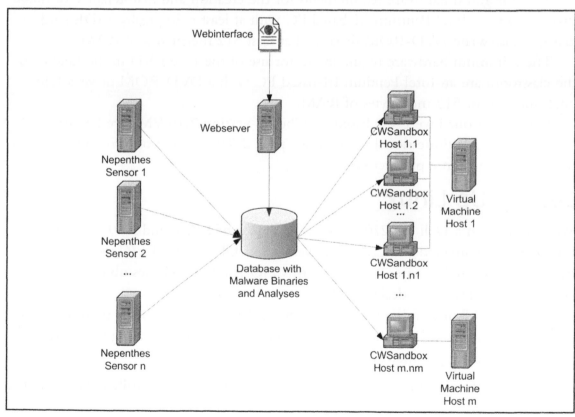

Creating a Live DVD with VMware and CWSandbox

While working at Portland State University, two students, Fred Shore and Andreas Turriff, created a bootable DVD containing VMware, a virtual Windows XP Pro instance, and the CWSandbox. The following sections contain that report and will help you build your own instance. Even though these instructions use the CWSandbox, the skills described will permit you to substitute the sandbox tool of your choice.

This project began as the brainchild of Craig Schiller, the CISO at Portland State University. The idea was to create a bootable Linux Live DVD that included a virtual version of Windows XP and CWSandbox for use in the classroom and in the field for the manual analysis of malware. We created a Live DVD because the necessary files would not fit on a CD.

The minimum hardware requirements for the creation and maintenance of the Live DVD is an Intel Pentium III-based PC with at least a 20 gigabyte IDE hard drive, a read/write DVD-ROM drive, and at least 512 megabytes of RAM.

The minimum hardware requirements for use of the Live DVD in the field or in the classroom are an Intel Pentium III-based PC with a DVD-ROM drive, a USB port, and at least 512 megabytes of RAM.

We created our Live DVD based on Ubuntu version 7.10, VMware Server v1.05, and Windows XP Professional with service pack 2. The version of Windows XP Pro used a volume license product key.

Setting Up Linux

We started with a Dell GX270 with 1.5 gigabytes of RAM and a 40 GB IDE HDD. We downloaded the Live DVD version of Ubuntu v7.10 (Gutsy Gibbon) from the Ubuntu Web site. The link to this ISO is http://releases.ubuntu. com/7.10/ubuntu-7.10-desktop-i386.iso.

We set up Ubuntu using the default settings. When we got to the partitioner we selected manual setup.[4] We chose to use a 3 partition scheme, creating the partitions with the following parameters:

1. Boot Partition (must be established in the first 1024 tracks, usually within first 8G):

    a. Mount point: /boot

    b. Size: 128 megabytes

    c. File System: ext2

2. Swap Partition:

   a. Mount point: N/A

   b. Size: 2000 megabytes

   c. File System: swap

3. Root Partition

   a. Mount point: /

   b. Size: whatever space is left

   c. File System: ext3

After the setup is complete we installed all the updates to Ubuntu 7.10. After restarting and logging in to Ubuntu for the first time, we fired up Firefox and went to the Ubuntu community forums to get the documentation to change the unsafe default settings in Ubuntu. The page is https://help.ubuntu.com/community/UnsafeDefaults.

There is also a change to make in /etc/init.d/mountdevsubfs.sh:

1. Open a terminal window located in the launch bar under Applications/ Assessories.

2. Type the following line into the terminal window:

   ■ gksudo gedit /etc/init.d/mountdevsubfs.sh

   ■ and press **Enter**.

3. Enter your password.

4. Remove comments (#) from the following four lines starting with mkdir -p /dev/bus/usb/.usbfs line.

   ■ # Magic to make /proc/bus/usb work

   ■ #

   ■ mkdir -p /dev/bus/usb/.usbfs

   ■ domount usbfs "" /dev/bus/usb/.usbfs -obusmode=0700,devmode=0600, listmode=0644

   ■ ln -s .usbfs/devices /dev/bus/usb/devices

   ■ mount --rbind /dev/bus/usb /proc/bus/usb

5. Save the file, then restart the computer.

Next we need to set up an instance of VMware.

Setting Up VMware Server v1.05

The first step in setting up VMware server is to download the tar.gz package from the VMware Web site, www.vmware.com/download/server. You should register your copy of VMware Server at http://register.vmware.com/content/registration.html to receive a serial number for VMware server. The application is free but still requires a serial.

We chose to set up VMware server with the default settings. Just remember to run all the terminal commands with sudo in front of it. When you extract the VMware server package to your HDD, be sure to check the All Files radio button. It will create a directory called vmware-server-distrib. The script you need to run is sudo ./vmware-install.pl.

1. As you are prompted by the script, just select the default settings and let the script start the configuration script. The configuration script will compile a version of VMware for your kernel.

2. Finally enter your serial number and the VMware server set up is complete.

3. Run the server by typing **sudo vmware** and typing your password.

4. Click connect to complete the connection to the host VMware server.

5. Click **Create a new virtual machine**.

Next, we will set up the virtual machine.

Setting Up a Virtual Machine in VMware Server

1. Click the **Next** button to move to the next step in the setup wizard.

2. On the Virtual Machine Configuration page, select the **Custom** radio button and then click **Next**.

3. On the Guest Operating System page, select the **1. Microsoft Windows** radio button and choose Windows XP Professional from the **Version** drop-down box. Click **Next**.

4. On the Name the Virtual Machine page, choose the **Name** and **Location** for your virtual machine and click **Next**.

5. On the Processor page, use the default, **One** processor and click **Next**.

6. On the Access Rights page, uncheck the **Make this virtual machine private** checkbox and click **Next**.

7. On the Memory page, type **256** in the **MB** input box and click **Next**.

8. On the Network Connection page, select the **Use network address translation (NAT)** radio button and click **Next**.

9. On the I/O Adapter Types page, use the default, the **BusLogic** radio button, and click **Next**.

10. On the Disk page, choose the **Create a new virtual disk** radio button and click **Next**.

11. On the Virtual Disk Type page, choose the default, the IDE (Recommended) radio button, and click **Next**.

12. On the Disk Size page, leave the default Disk size (GB): 8.0 but uncheck both the **Allocate all disk space now** checkbox and the **Split disk into 2GB files** checkbox and click **Next**.

13. On the Disk File page, choose the name of your virtual disk file, and click **Finish**.

14. Once you are back to the VMware Server Console, click **Edit virtual machine settings**.

15. We need to add a USB device so click the **+ Add** button, select the USB Controller under Hardware Types, and click **Next**.

16. On the Device Status page it gives instructions on how to use the 2 port USB 1.1 controller (VMware Server does *not* support USB v2.0) and click **Finish**.

17. Click **OK** to close the Virtual Machine Settings window.

Next, you will need to set up Windows XP in the virtual machine you just created.

Setting Up Windows XP Professional in the Virtual Machine

Setting up Windows XP Professional in the virtual machine we just created is a straightforward process, just like setting it up on a regular PC. You need a Volume Licensed version of Windows XP Professional with service pack 2 and a product key for it. We set up XP using all the default settings. It is not until after XP is set up that the real configuration begins. First, install the VMware Tools, click **VM** on the VMware Server Console, and select **Install VMware Tools** from the drop-down menu.

We used a simple set of requirements to ready XP for the CWSandbox installation:

1. Create a user account with administrative privileges.

2. In System Properties:

   a. Turn off System Restore

   b. Turn off Error Reporting

   c. Set Performance to Adjust for best performance

   d. Set the page file to 384–384

3. Turn on the Windows Firewall.

4. Run Windows Updates, however many times it takes to bring XP up to date (we haven't tested the installation with SP3).

5. Set up a dummy e-mail account using Outlook Express.

6. Using Add/Remove Programs/Windows Setup, remove all unnecessary components such as Games, Windows Themes, and so on.

Finally, we are ready to set up CWSandbox.

Setting Up CWSandbox v2.x in Windows XP Professional

We set up the Live DVD to do manual malware analysis with CWSandbox. This means that we require only eight of the files in the WinXP Binaries.zip distributed by Sunbelt Software:

- CWSandbox.exe

- CWSandbox.ini

- CWMonitor.dll

- CWSandboxConfigTool.exe

- HTMLReport.xslt

- CWSandbox_EULA.pdf

- Sunbelt CWSandbox User Guide V2.pdf

- Botnets_10_excerpt.pdf

These files should be put into a directory on the C-drive; we used C:\CWSandbox. Then we made short-cuts on the desktop to CWSandbox.exe, CWSandboxConfigTool. exe, and each of the pdf files. The CWSandboxConfigTool was especially helpful because it provides a simple explanation for every option available for running CWSandbox. The HTMLReport.xslt file worked very well in formatting the analysis. xml for viewing after running a malware analysis. The path to the HTMLReport.xslt should be set to three levels above the analysis.xml—..\..\..\ HTMLReport.xslt—using the CWSandboxConfigTool.

Now that we have a fully functioning instance of CWSandbox we are ready to create a Live DVD with this instance.

Configuring Linux and VMware Server for Live DVD Creation

1. Install Remastersys (see www.remastersys.klikit-linux.com)

   a. Open a terminal, become root by typing **sudo su** and press **Enter**.

   b. The Remastersys repository needs to be added to your /etc/apt/sources. list; type: gedit /etc/apt/sources.list

   c. Paste the following into the sources.list: # Remastersys, deb http://www. remastersys.klikit-linux.com/repository remastersys/.

   d. Then simply either reload in Synaptic or you can "sudo apt-get update" and install remastersys.

   e. To install remastersys, in the terminal window, type apt-get install remastersys and press **Enter**.

   f. Type **exit** and press **Enter** in the terminal window to leave super user.

2. Edit the Virtual Machine definition file (.vmx, usually in /var/lib/vmware/ Virtual Machines). In a terminal window, type:

   cd /var/lib/vmware/Virtual\ Machines**/theNameOfYourVirtualMachine/** (replace the bold text in the preceding line with the name of your virtual machine)

   a. Use your favorite text editor to edit the file: **theNameOfYourVirtual-Machine**.vmx.

   b. Remember to insert **sudo** before the command.

    c. Add the following three lines to the end of the file and save it:

- disk.Locking = "FALSE"
- workingDir = "/tmp"
- uuid = "KEEP"

3. Use your favorite editor to add the following line to the end of /etc/vmware/config file: mainMem.useNamedFile = "FALSE"

4. Set disk to independent-nonpersistent** mode:

    a. Select the Virtual Machine in the VMware Server console.

    b. Click '**Edit virtual machine settings**, select the Hard Disk entry on the Hardware tab, and click **Advanced** in the lower right corner.

    c. On the Virtual Device Node page, click the **Independent** checkbox, the **Nonpersistent** radio button, and under **Other** click the **Disable write caching** checkbox.

    d. Click **Okay** on each of the configuration pages and exit the VMware.

Now the Windows XP instance is set to be nonpersistent; whatever changes that are made to the Windows XP instance after this will be lost after a restart.

To make changes to the Windows XP instance, set the radio button from nonpersistent to persistent on the Virtual Device Node page and save the changes.

5. Run "sudo remastersys dist cdfs". This command gathers all the files necessary for the Live DVD and stores them in /home/remastersys/. You will be prompted for your ubuntu cd during this process so put it in **now**.

6. (Optional) If necessary, modify the files in /home/remastersys to suit your requirements (e.g., change the banner and boot options in /home/remastersys/ISOTMP/isolinux/isolinux.cfg).

7. Run "sudo remastersys dist iso". This command creates the Live DVD in iso format and places it in /home/remastersys.

8. Burn the .iso file located in /home/remastersys to DVD.

Updating Your Live DVD

Updating your Live DVD is a relatively simple process if you use the machine already configured for creating a Live DVD. The process has three steps (two steps are optional).

1. (Optional) Update your Linux Installation.

2. (Optional) Update VMware Server.

3. (Optional) Update Windows XP (including the CWSandbox Files). Remember, you need to make the hard drive in your virtual machine persistent. Make your changes to Windows XP, then make the drive nonpersistent again.

4. Run the command 'sudo remastersys clean' in a terminal window. This command cleans the /home/remastersys/ directory completely by deleting all the files. So if you have done the optional customization of your Live DVD via step 8 of the previous section, save copies of your customizations before running this command.

5. Repeat steps 5 through 8 from the previous section.

Summary

Sandbox technology is used to protect the local system while executing unknown or malicious code. They achieve this protection by either blocking critical operations (e.g., the sandbox provided in Java) or by executing the suspect code in a virtual environment. The virtual environment permits you to instrument and observe malware with impunity to its effects. You can choose to permit or block communications with other computers. You can configure the sandbox to respond as if it has transmitted spam while in reality it has sent nothing. Sandbox technology in a virtual environment is ideal for analyzing unknown or malicious code. Using the sandbox to isolate the real operating system, a sandbox can reveal valuable information about the behavior of malicious or unknown code. It can reveal decompressed and decrypted versions of packaged code, connections attempted, files opened, userids, passwords, and much more.

For those occasions when you must perform malware analysis in the field, we have described the process for building a Live DVD with built-in VMware, Windows XP and the CWSandbox. We described an application of sandbox technology as the central server and automated malware analysis tools that can work in conjunction with malware collectors like Nepenthes. Finally we cautioned investigators about the rise of VMware aware techniques. Using the sandbox, the alert investigator may be able to see attempts by VMware aware code attempting to check for VMware's presence.

Solutions Fast Track

Sandbox Background

☑ Sandboxes are a common tool in security/malware research; they allow the execution of unknown software in a controlled, restricted and monitored environment

☑ CWSandbox is example of a sandbox tool for automatic behavior analysis of Windows executables; the functionality of a sandbox is achieved by taking the following steps:

1. The initial malware process is created by the starter application cwsandbox.exe.

2. cwmonitor.dll is injected into each monitored process.

3. The DLL installs API hooks for all important functions of the Windows API.

4. If a new process is started by the malware or an existing one is infected, this process is also monitored.

5. After a customizable time all monitored processes are terminated/stopped.

6. A high-level summarized analysis report is created of all the monitored actions.

7. The network traffic is examined, important Web protocols (HTTP, FTP, IRC, and so on) are recognized and all relevant protocol data is reported (username, password, and so on).

Existing Sandbox Implementations

☑ Norman SandBox was developed by Norman AS. at http://sandbox.norman.no.

☑ TTAnalyze was developed by Ulrich Bayer, Ikarus Software GmbH, in cooperation with the Technical University of Vienna.

☑ In Chas Tomlin's Sandnet the malicious software is executed on a real Windows system, not on an emulated or simulated one.

☑ Truman is tThe Reusable Unknown Malware Analysis Net, by Joe Stewart from LURHQ.

☑ *CWSandbox* is from the diploma thesis of Carsten Willems.

Describing CWSandbox

☑ CWSandbox is an application for the automatic behavior analysis of malware. This dynamic analysis is performed by executing the malicious application in a controlled environment and catching all relevant of its calls to the Windows API

☑ CWSandbox is designed to attach reporting tools to malware. It is not designed to block malicious activity of the malware. You are responsible for blocking any outbound traffic that may result from executing the malware.

☑ Malware may be able to detect the presence of a virtual environment by checking specific registry entries, the list of running processes or system services, or typical behavior of the system. Many detection methods are known for the popular VMware product. The website *www.trapkit.de* describes a lot of them and also offers the tools *scoopy doo* and *jerry* for that purpose. Joanna Rutkowska described a generic approach to VM detection which she called *redpill*. Redpill checks the IDT address retrieved when running in a virtual machine since it is different to that in a real system. This trick works with any virtualization software.

☑ Sandbox technology can be extended to serve as a tool for automatic collection and analysis of malware, as in *Automated Analysis Suite (AAS)*.

☑ AAS uses a database to store malware samples and the corresponding created analysis reports.

☑ AAS integrates the honeypot tool *Nepenthes* for automatic malware collection.

☑ Additionally, malware can be submitted via a PHP-based Web interface.

☑ AAS embeds CWSandbox for automatic analysis.

Creating a Live DVD with VMware and CWSandbox

☑ Once you have created a sandbox, you can turn that implementation into a bootable DVD so that you can take the sandbox into the field.or distribute the tool to a classroom of students to give them hands-on malware analysis experience.

Frequently Asked Questions

Q: What kind of things can you find using sandbox technology?

A: You are only limited by the instruments that you attach to the malware. You can learn the ip addresses of FQDN of different members of a botnet, the identity of command and control servers, malicious code download servers, the nickname, userid and password of bot command and control servers, unpacked and unencrypted versions of stealth malware, the filenames of files that are part of the malicious system, a list of all files opened by the malware, and more.

Q: I really like the Live DVD idea. How can I create my own Live-CDs and DVDs using other content?

A: Instructions for creating your own Live-CDs and DVDs can be found on howto-forge. We used a how-to written by Falko Timme, "Creating Your Own Custom Ubuntu 7.10 Or Linux Mint 4.0 Live-CD With Remastersys," Copyright © 2008 HowtoForge.

Q: What does virtualization do for Sandbox technology?

A: Virtualization makes it possible for a security investigator to try multiple tests on a malware sample without having to wipe the test system's hard drive between test sessions. Without virtualization, the measures to ensure integrity could be provided using reverting tools such as DeepFreeze, Partimage, or hardware restore solutions. The virtual environment permits investigators to create several members of a network to examine the interaction of a botnet.

Q: I don't want to give away my licensed copies of Windows or Cwsandbox. How do I create a Live DVD that doesn't include my license keys?

A: You can use SYSPREP and the process located http://www.uea.ac.uk/itcs/software/xp/xp-sysprep.html to remove the product keys so that a new owner of the DVD can use their own product keys. If you created the image file after you install the sandbox but before you enter the license, then the new owner of the DVD will need to provide their own license or add a different sandbox product.

Notes

1. For more information go to http://sandbox.norman.no/pdf/ 03%20sandboxwhitepaper.pdf.

2. This utility saves/restores hard disc partitions in many formats to an image file (see www.partimage.org).

3. This tool is for resetting your computer to its original state (see www.faronics. com/html/deepfreeze.asp).

4. Right-click on free space on /dev/sda or /dev/had to create partitons in the free space.

Bibliography

Falco. *Creating Your Own Custom Ubuntu 7.10 or Linux Mint 4.0* Live-CD with Remastersys, HowtoForge.

Unsafe Defaults, https://help.ubuntu.com/community/UnsafeDefaults. Ubuntu community forums, user documentation, last edited 2007-10-03 20:31:48 by Joel Goguen.

Willems, Carsten. *Botnets, the Killer Net App*, Chapter 10 Excerpt. Syngress, 2007. ISBN: 1597491357.

Willems, Carsten. *Portions of CWSandbox User Guide v2*. Sunbelt Software, 2007.

Chapter 4

Configuring the Virtual Machine

Solutions in this chapter:

- Hard Drive and Network Configurations
- Physical Hardware Access
- Interfacing with the Host

☑ Summary

☑ Solutions Fast Track

☑ Frequently Asked Questions

Introduction

This chapter will cover common configuration tasks which apply to many of the previously mentioned scenarios. It will highlight areas where virtualization can provide resources to the security professional that would be difficult or impossible to accomplish using traditional methods.

Many of these configuration options will be specific to the virtual machine implementation chosen, but where possible methods of accomplishing these tasks in the popular implementations will be presented.

Resource Management

Appropriately limiting resource usage by applications and guest operating systems not only provides cost savings but also is necessary to ensure that potential security outbreaks do not deny service to other guests running on the same host. The original Morris Worm released onto the Internet in 1988 was one of the first major computer security breaches in history. The worm proliferated to thousands of computers on the Internet. The worm would have continued to spread unabated if it had not wastefully consumed resources to the point of slowing the infected systems to a crawl. The resulting denial-of-service condition caused the phones of system administrators to ring off the hook. The system administrators swiftly diagnosed and eventually repaired the problem.

Limiting resource usage involves setting appropriate limits for CPU and memory consumption by a virtual machine. You edit the CPU and memory resources for a virtual machine in the *Virtual Machine Properties* dialog on the Resources tab. These fields allow you to set minimums (Reservation), maximum (Limit), and shares for resource allocation. Shares are used to set relative weights between different VMs for the allocation between minimum and maximum. You can also control the resources used by groups of virtual machines using resource pools. Once you set resource usage suitably, you can mitigate any effects that a security breach may induce within your environment.

Hard Drive and Network Configurations

Two of the most basic configuration elements for any virtual machine are the hard drive and network configurations. Almost all virtualization vendors provide a number of different types of hard drives as well as a number of network configuration scenarios that should be taken into consideration not only just for general purposes, but also for consideration in any security related implementation.

Hard Drive Configuration

Both VMware and Virtual PC provide great flexibility in ways to configure hard disks. Fundamentally there are two types of hard disks that most vendors support. The first is a virtual disk, which is typically a file that is configured in such a manner as to emulate a physical hard disk. Indeed, from the perspective of the virtual machine the virtual disk looks, acts, and feels just like a real hard disk. The other option is to use a physical disk. In this case, instead of creating a file (or set of files) that appear to be a hard disk, you actually use a real physical hard disk as the disk that the virtual machines will use.

In the case of some enterprise virtualization products, such as VMware ESX, the "physical disk" can be a LUN that has been configured on SAN storage. This is referred to as raw device mapping (RDM). With an RDM the virtual machine is configured with a virtual disk that is simply a pointer or forwarder to the mapped LUN. One of the reasons for using both physical drives and RDMs is a potential performance increase over using a virtual disk.

Growing Disk Sizes

By using virtualization, and, in particular, virtual disks, you can dynamically increase the amount of space a virtual disk consumes on the underlying hardware as it is needed. For example, you may create a virtual disk that is 20GB in size; however, once you install the OS and applications in the virtual machine, you may only be using 5GB of the 20GB total. Rather than having a disk on the physical host that is using up 20GB of space (and effectively wasting 15GB), the virtual disk can be configured to only use the space required, in this case 5GB. This can be very helpful in the event that you are constrained for space in your storage, however you need to be mindful of this fact since if the virtual machine suddenly needs more than the 5GB and it is not available, it could cause problems in running the virtual machine.

Virtual Disk Types

Most vendors support creating virtual disks that are either IDE or SCSI type of disks. You will need to consult with your virtualization vendor to determine with certainty, but in most cases selecting a SCSI disk type is the recommended choice since it typically provides for better performance than a similarly created IDE disk type.

Using Snapshots

Another consideration to factor in the hard drive configuration of your virtual machines is the ability to snapshot the hard disk. Disk snapshots are one of the most compelling reasons for virtualization. With disk snapshots you are able to save the disk contents and state at a moment in time (called a snapshot) which in turn allows you to revert the disk (and thus the entire virtual machine) to whatever state the disk was in at the time the snapshot was created. For example, you may make a snapshot prior to applying any patches so that if the patches do not work or cause problems with the virtual machine you can simply roll back to the snapshot, as if the patches had never been applied. This is a great method for testing malicious software and code. You can configure a snapshot, then introduce the malicious software or code the virtual machine for testing, and once the testing is finished, revert to the saved snapshot, thus removing the malicious software and code completely. In fact, it is as if you had never run the software at all.

Network Configuration

Computers without network interfaces while significantly more secure, also lose a lot of their potential. Fortunately, the virtualization software currently available offers some very interesting options that can add significant value to a single computer. As we go through these configuration options, we will also suggest some of the various uses for them.

Creating an Interface

Adding interfaces to a virtual machine is in general a simple process. In VMware workstation the task can be accomplished from the virtual Machine Settings dialog. Clicking **Add Hardware** and selecting **Ethernet Adapter** will bring up the dialog box shown in Figure 4.1. Select one and click **Finish**.

Figure 4.1 Selecting the Type of Network Interface to Add

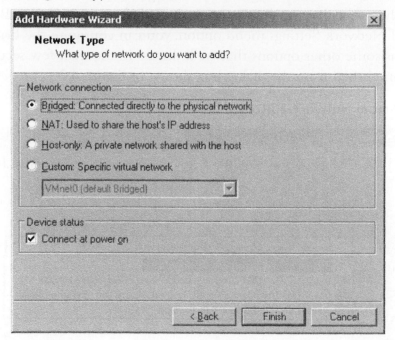

Bridged

This is one of the more interesting options available in a virtual machine. A bridged interface appears on the guest as just another interface. The bridging interface of the host is used to provide physical network connectivity for the virtual machine as if the virtual machine was directly connected to the network. The virtual machine receives its own IP address on the network, etc.

One item that you should be aware of is the interaction between a firewall on the host and the packets being sent to the virtual machine(s). To the firewall these packets can often appear to have been sent incorrectly because the virtual machine has a different IP address than the physical machine. They will likely be blocked. This can be a very frustrating scenario. It is recommended that the firewall be tuned, if possible, to allow incoming packets to the IP address of the virtual interface. It should also be noted that the firewall can block certain forms of traffic that do not depend on IP addresses such as DHCP packets. In some cases it may be necessary to disable the firewall entirely or use another interface type such as natted.

By default, VMware will choose the bridging interface automatically. It makes a decision based on factors such as which interfaces have routable IP addresses, and which interfaces are currently assigned as default gateways. This choice can be made manually in the event that the default is not optimal for your scenario. By using the Edit->Virtual Network Settings menu option, you can configure the bridging interface (as well as some other options that we'll discuss in the next few sections. These tasks are accomplished from the dialog box shown in Figure 4.2.

Figure 4.2 Virtual Network Editor

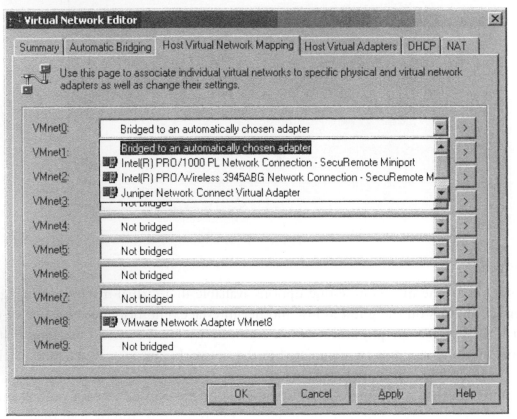

Host-Only

The host-only network can be used in a number of scenarios, most commonly when you do not want the virtual machine to communicate with anything on the physical network. The host-only network does not have access to external machines. In addition, the guest machine is not subject to the same network "noise" that it might be on an internal network. This feature allows the security professional two distinct scenarios. First, it is ideal for malware testing. This topic will be covered further in Chapter 6. One issue to keep in mind is whether the host should have access to the same network as the guest machine. In the case of malware analysis, this is not advised.

The second instance in which a host-only network adapter might be used is for testing older software. Older software can be susceptible to worms. Ideally, older worms would not still infect things on the Internet. Unfortunately, however, this is not always the case. By using a host-only network adapter, you have significantly more control over what goes onto the network (note that if the host has an adapter on the network, then it can still communicate with the guest machine [for better or worse]).

There is an option for setting up the subnet for the host-only machine, as well as whether the host will provide DHCP services. DHCP allows for the guest machine to query for an IP. Note that because it is a host-only network, no default gateway will be assigned, and no DNS servers will be offered.

Natted

This option allows the virtual machine to be on a network that exists only in the host and yet to be able to communicate with systems on the physical network by way of NAT. It is different from the host-only networks primarily because of the additional NAT service that the host provides; for example, in VMware workstation the "VMware NAT Service." This service allows the host to route to and from multiple guest machines, translating between the IP addresses the virtual machines use and the IP addresses used on the physical network via a NAT process. The traffic from the guests will appear to be coming from the IP address of the host machine, and the host will pass along any packets in response to requests initiated by a guest, thereby allowing all of the machines to "share" the same IP address as the host. One should be aware that certain protocols do not function well in natted environments. This is also true of certain security tools.

Tools & Traps...

Natted Interfaces Can Interfere with Security Tools

One should be aware that certain protocols do not function well in natted environments. This is also true of a number of security tools. Although some tools are able to detect that they are in a natted environment, security tools are especially prone to being disabled in a natted environment. Be sure to test your tool against a known target to baseline your results before using the tool in the field. The category I've had the most difficulty with has been certain high-speed network scanners. The natted environment doesn't seem to be able to track the number of connection requests, and the responses don't seem to appear correctly.

When in doubt, a bridged interface should be used for any network scanning. Note that the sudden appearance of a new MAC address on a port can have undesirable side effects at the switch level such as disabled ports. If you suddenly lose connectivity through a switch for no apparent reason, this "feature" might be the culprit. In some cases this can be avoided by creative use of MAC cloning and firewalls, although this solution should be considered hit and miss at best.

Multiple Interfaces

The final configuration to mention is the ability for a guest machine to have multiple interfaces. If the VMware NAT Service doesn't provide you with the desired natting functions, you can replicate the function using a "routing" guest with multiple interfaces. This is particularly handy if you have multiple virtual machines on a host-only network that need to communicate with each other and you want all traffic for external sources from those guests to go through a specific virtual machine that is acting as a firewall (and thus is configured with two interfaces, one of which is on the host only network). This virtual machine could even be configured to proxy and manipulate the traffic from the other guests and potentially the host computer as well. To do this one sets the IP address of the host machine's physical adapter to a nonroutable IP address (for example, 192.168.200.50). The guest machine that will be doing the routing needs a "bridged" interface (eth0) associated with the physical interface of the host machine. Its IP will likely be assigned by DHCP. A host-only network should then be set up. The host-only interface of the guest (eth1) should be set as a default gateway (such as 192.168.10.1), and the host-only interface of the host should be something on the same network (192.168.10.10, for example). The default route on the hosting server should then be set to 192.168.10.1. Finally, the host needs to be configured to pass along the traffic to the bridged interface. If the guest is running Linux, the following rules will accomplish this:

```
iptables –A FORWARD –i eth1 –j ACCEPT
iptables –A POSTROUTING –t nat –o eth0 –j MASQUERADE
```

These rules will allow the host to use the guest to provide network services. They can include both firewalling and packet manipulation, depending on the guest.

Physical Hardware Access

In some cases the virtual machine can also be given access to the physical hardware such as a physical disk or a USB device. This type of access allows the virtual machine an even greater range of capabilities. This option should suffice for most virtual hardware requirements. If full native hardware is desired for some specific scenarios (such as wireless penetration testing), we would recommend using a scenario in which the same machine can be booted both on native hardware and in a virtual environment. This dual booting scenario will be discussed in Chapter 12.

Physical Disks

A physical partition can be used for a native machine. This option is often used when data is needed from an old hard drive. The simple solution to this problem is to put the drive into a computer as a secondary drive and copy data from the drive to the primary drive. However, this procedure may not be feasible in some circumstances. The file system of the secondary drive may not be compatible with the operating system that is installed on the primary drive. The required data may only be retrievable in a program installed on the secondary disk. It might be annoying, difficult, or even impossible to install the required software on the primary partition. The secondary drive might even be infected by malware. Virtualization can often be used to gain access to the secondary physical drive, complete with its installed operating system without having to assemble an additional computer.

Using VMware makes creating a virtual machine with access to physical hard drives a relatively simple task. The first step is to use the Add Hardware Wizard shown in Figure 4.3. Select **Hard Disk** and click the **Next** button.

Figure 4.3 Add Hardware Wizard

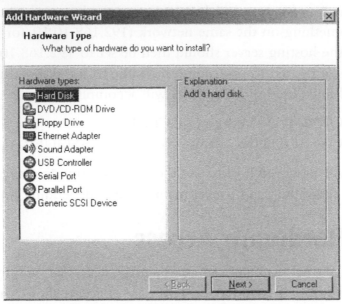

A wizard will appear where you can choose what type of disk to create (see Figure 4.4). The various options are explained on the dialog box, but we will choose **Use a physical disk**. Select this option and continue by clicking the **Next** button.

Figure 4.4 Choosing the Type of Hard Disk

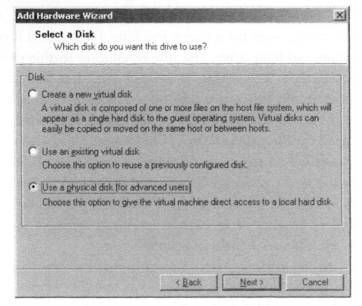

After you choose to use a physical hard disk, your next step is to determine which hard drive to use. Choose the disk that is not in use by the primary operating system. Ideally, VMware would at a minimum indicate the disk sizes (or even better a disk ID of some sort) so that you could choose the correct disk; unfortunately, however, this is not the case. The disk order is determined at the BIOS level. You can get an idea of which disk is first in Windows by going into the Properties of one of your fixed disks and clicking the **Hardware** tab, as shown in Figure 4.5. Note that if you choose the Windows disk that is already mounted, you can cause the host operating system to crash with a Blue Screen of Death or similar dangerous scenarios. The Hardware tab will show you in which order your disks are connected to the operating system.

Figure 4.5 Windows Disk Properties Hardware Tab

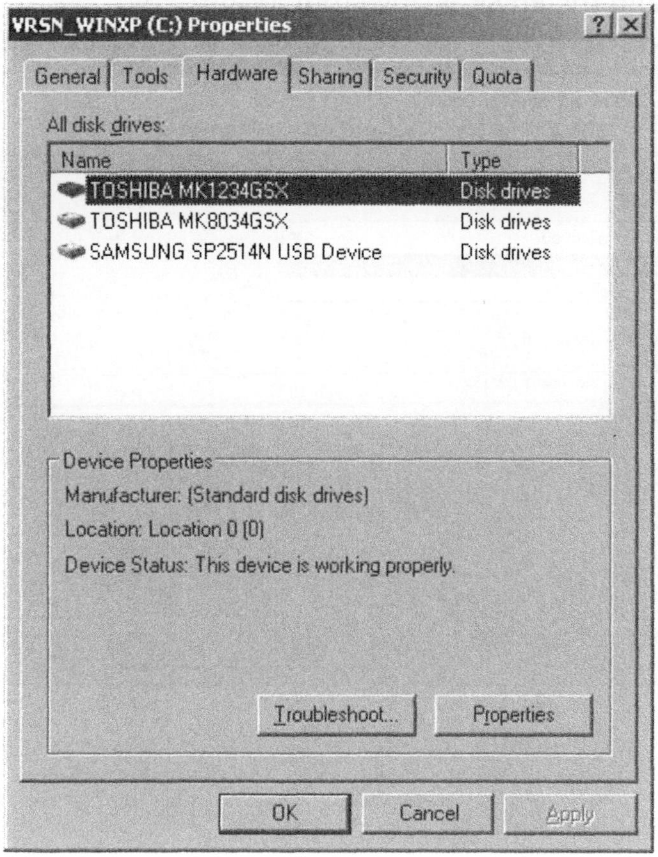

You know the first disk is the one that you want to work with because of the name of the disk. Because the numbering begins at zero (something C programmers are used to, but much of the world would consider strange), you will choose the option for **Physical Drive 0** on the wizard that is shown in Figure 4.6. Note the options to Use the Entire disk or to use individual partitions. If you choose to allocate specific partitions, you can block the virtual machine from even seeing other partitions of the disk. It should be noted, however, that if the virtual machine can't "see" the partition, then its number may change, causing issues with an operating system that was already installed. If you are using a disk that has been created in a native (nonvirtualized) hardware scenario, we recommend that you allocate all partitions that pertained to that operating system. Using the entire disk is the most simple option, and this is the recommended option if your requirements permit choosing it.

Figure 4.6 Choosing the Physical Drive to Allocate

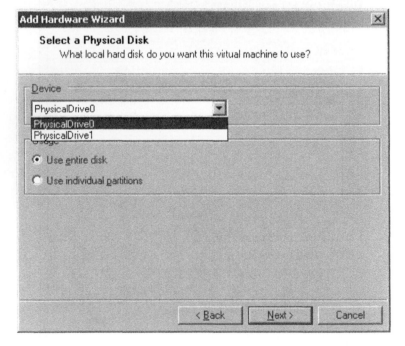

When the virtual machine is started, the partition you just allocated will be available in the same way a virtual hard disk would be available. If this new disk is set up as the primary disk, the operating system installed on the disk can be booted (assuming hardware compatibility with the virtual machine). This arrangement should allow the disk to come up, and you should be able to use and interact with the machine as if it were any other machine. Note that this arrangement should not be used to forensically examine the hard drive. The process of mounting the hard drive (whether on virtual or native hardware) will modify the disk, and crucial information may be lost as a result.

USB Devices

USB disks can also be used for storage in a virtualized environment. In fact, most USB devices can be connected to a virtual machine and function very well. To connect a USB device to the virtual machine in VMware workstation, choose the following menu options: **VM->Removable Devices->USB Devices** (see Figure 4.7). From there a list of USB devices known to the system will be displayed. The devices that are already connected to the virtual machine will have a check mark next to them. Clicking a device that is not connected will connect it, and clicking a checked item will disconnect it. Note that this will disconnect it from the host rather abruptly. Devices should be disabled or unmounted at the operating system level before disconnecting them from a machine in much the same way that they should be before removing them in the physical world.

WARNING

If you are running a virtual machine from a removable disk, do not attempt to connect that device to the virtual machine. The virtual machine will likely crash because its source files are no longer available.

Figure 4.7 Connecting a USB Device

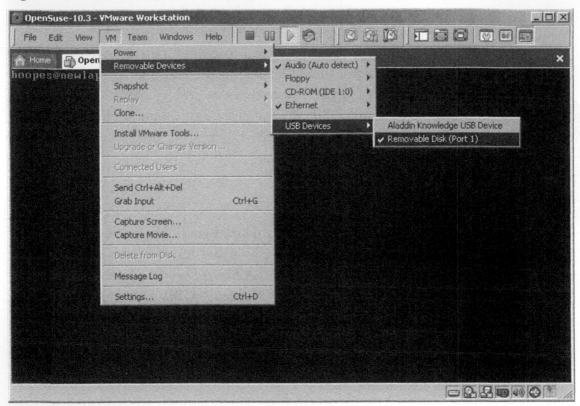

Interfacing with the Host

Both VMware and Microsoft Virtual PC provide utilities that simplify and improve the performance of Virtual machines. VMware tools install drivers, as well as additional configuration options. In the case of VMware ESX, VMware tools also enable the balloon driver, which allows for VMware to improve memory utilization and performance. Both of the suites provide the ability for the mouse to "engage" and "disengage" as it hits the boundaries of the window. This function allows a more natural interaction with machines in a window.

You should install the vendor tools and utilities and keep them up-to-date, in most if not all instances.

Cut and Paste

One additional feature that is enabled as a result of installing the utilities is the ability to cut and paste information between the host and the guest operating systems.

This ability is as simple as highlighting something in the host operating system (or another guest machine), and then activating the virtual machine window, and pasting using the native functionality of the guest operating system.

Notes from the Underground…

Security Implications of Virtual Machine Utilities

The virtual machine utility functionality is supported using an internal interface which allows communication between the guest and the host machines. This interface is present whether or not the utilities have been installed in the guest operating system and should be considered an additional attack surface when evaluating the security of the virtual machine. In addition, special notice should be given to cut-and-paste functionality. Guests can "examine" the clipboard at any time, and as a result nothing confidential should be put into the clipboard while a virtual machine running possibly malicious code (or a remote connection to a virtual machine console) is enabled.

How to Install the VMware Tools in a Virtual Machine

Click the **VM menu option** in the virtual machine console and choose **Install VMware Tools**. This should bring up a dialog similar to Figure 4.8.

Figure 4.8 Recommendation to Install VMware Tools

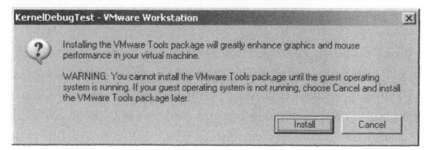

Clicking **Install** will connect a CD image that in Microsoft Windows will automatically run the installation program. In Linux and a number of other operating systems, a CD that has a compressed archive file containing the tools will be mounted. In a Windows guest the following wizard is brought up (see Figure 4.9).

Figure 4.9 VMware Tools Installation Wizard

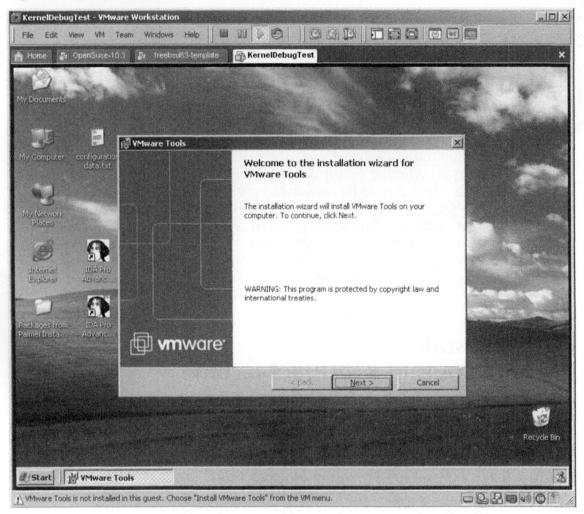

Clicking **Next** will bring up the choices shown in Figure 4.10. Clicking **Next** will bring up a dialog about configuring the tools installation. Although the Typical installation will probably suffice for most people, you'll choose the **Custom** installation to illustrate some of the available options. You can always "modify" the type of installation at a later date using the same steps you used to begin this process.

Figure 4.10 Choosing the Type of VMware Tool Setup

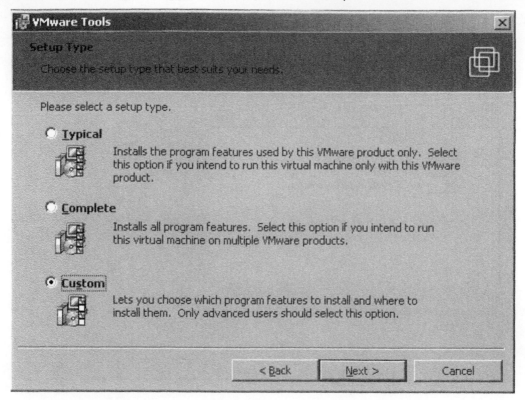

Clicking the **Next** button will bring up a wizard similar to the one shown in Figure 4.11. This dialog allows you to choose which portions of the tools package you would like to install. The toolbox enables features such as Cut and Paste, as well as time synchronization. The shared folders option enables SMB connections between the host and guest. If you put a file into a shared folder, it "appears" on the shared folder of the guest system as well. This is a very handy mechanism for sharing files between the host and guest, but it can also be a security concern and thus should be given consideration before enabling it.

Figure 4.11 VMware Toolbox Installation Options

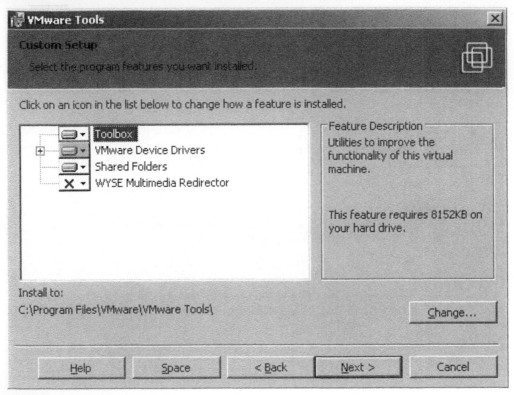

Expanding the VMware Device Drivers menu allows you to choose which device drivers will be installed. Using these drivers is recommended, assuming they meet the requirements for the server, because they will increase the performance and stability of the virtual machine. If you are using this server for a device driver level test, these drivers may not be appropriate or desired. Figure 4.12 shows the options available when the **Device Drivers** tree is expanded.

Figure 4.12 VMware Device Driver Installation Options

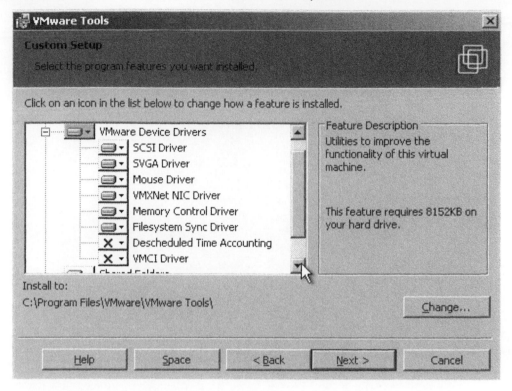

A final confirmation menu (shown in Figure 4.13) is brought up to allow any last-minute changes to the configuration settings. If any changes are desired, you can hit the **Back** button and return to the previous menus.

Figure 4.13 Installation Confirmation Screen

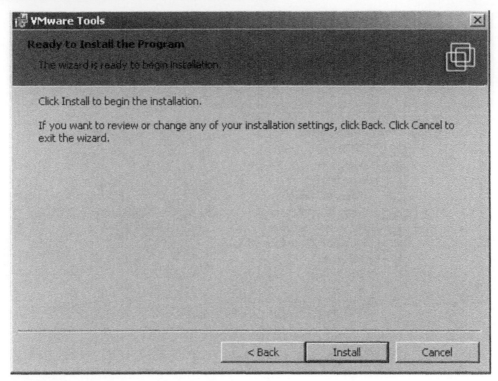

Clicking **Install** will start the installation process. Because this process is being carried out from a CD "image" that is installed on a hard drive, the installation actually goes significantly faster than it would from a native CD. The installation process has a status screen (show in Figure 4.14) that shows a progress bar moving across the screen. It is normally a very swift process.

Figure 4.14 Status of VMware Tools Installation

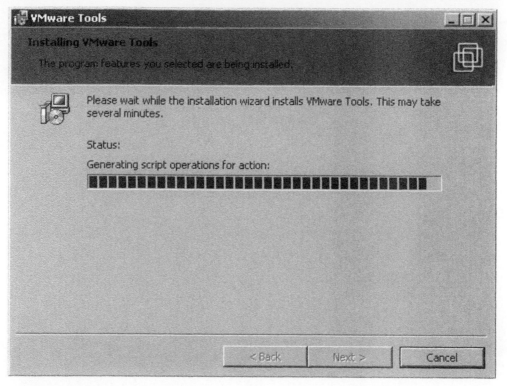

Finally, assuming all has gone well (which it usually does), you should be presented with a screen similar to the one shown in Figure 4.15. This screen confirms that the wizard has completed the installation correctly. At this point it will direct you to reboot your machine to gain the advantages of the newly installed drivers. This is an expected behavior (unlike some software reboots that are forced on Windows users). The fundamental device drivers have been changed and need to be activated during the boot process.

Figure 4.15 VMware Tools Installation Completion

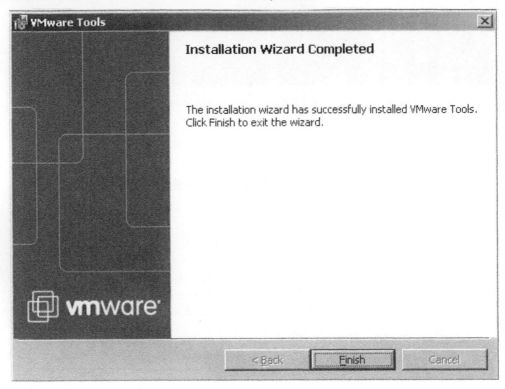

Following the installation you will want to restart the guest so that the new device drivers are enabled. You should note that at this point when you click on the virtual machine window (while a graphical user interface is activated), it will capture your mouse, and moving the physical mouse will move the mouse pointer within the virtual window. A new ability has been introduced because of the tools. When you move the mouse to the edge of the virtual desktop, the mouse will "release," and you can click on other windows on the hosting machine. The cut-and-paste functionality should allow the clipboards of the guest and host operating systems to behave as if they are connected.

How to Install the Virtual Machine Additions in Virtual PC

Installing the Virtual Machine Additions in Virtual PC is also very easy to do. When the option to **Install/upgrade Virtual Machine Additions** is chosen, a CD will be mounted that contains the installation package. The options are very similar to the VMware tools options, and they won't be covered in detail in this chapter.

Summary

The options available for configuring a virtual machine are varied and rich. Using these options enables you to gain significant advantage over using physical hardware in a number of situations. As you read the remainder of this book, these configuration scenarios will come up repeatedly. We hope this chapter has highlighted some of the flexibility available in virtualized environments. We have just scratched the surface, and a number of advanced techniques will be covered throughout the book.

Solutions Fast Track

Hard Drive and Network Configurations

☑ Virtual disks and physical disks can be used for the virtual machine hard drive

☑ Virtual disks can be configured to dynamically grow as required by the virtual machine, up to the limit of the disk size configuration

☑ Snapshots can be used to save the disk at a point in time so that the virtual machine can be reverted to that time, thus undoing anything that occurred subsequent to the snapshot

☑ Virtual machines can be configured with single or multiple network interfaces

☑ Host Only: This option allows for local communication only. No connection to the host's network interfaces is managed by the virtual machine monitoring package.

☑ Natted: This option allows for communication using the host's network interfaces. All traffic will appear to be sourced from the hosts IP address.

☑ Bridged: This option allows the Guest to appear on the network as an additional machine. It will have its own MAC address and IP address and be able to send and receive its own packets.

Physical Hardware Access

☑ In some cases the virtual machine can also be given access to the physical hardware such as a physical disk or a USB device. This type of access allows the virtual machine an even greater range of capabilities.

☑ USB disks can also be used for storage in a virtualized environment. In fact, most USB devices can be connected to a virtual machine and function very well.

☑ If you are running a virtual machine from a removable disk, do not attempt to connect that device to the virtual machine. The virtual machine will likely crash because its source files are no longer available.

Interfacing with the Host

☑ Most vendors provide a set of tools and utilities, such as VMware Tools, which allow for interfacing between the guest and the host

☑ The utilities provide functionality such as allowing copy-and-paste functionality between the guest and the host as well as providing for the transfer of files between the guest and host regardless of external network connectivity

☑ The utilities also provide drivers and functions that increase the performance and stability of the virtual machine, and potentially the host as well

Frequently Asked Questions

Q: Should I install vendor tools and utilities such as VMware tools?

A: Yes, in almost all cases you should. The utilities typically provide drivers and applications that improve the performance, stability, and functionality of the virtual machines.

Q: Can I use a physical disk for the hard drive of the virtual machine?

A: Yes you can. This is an advanced configuration, however, and should be approached with caution and understanding of the implications of using a physical disk.

Q: What network configuration options are available?

A: Most virtualization software supports three types of network configurations. The first is a simple bridged connection that allows the virtual machine to be connected directly to the underlying physical network topology. The second is a host-only connection that limits the virtual machine to only being able to communicate on the virtual network on the host. The third is a NAT connection that causes the virtual machine to use the same IP address as the underlying host, with the host providing NAT functionality between the guest and the rest of the physical network.

Chapter 5

Honeypotting

Solutions in this chapter:

- **Herding of Sheep**
- **Detecting the Attack**
- **How to Set Up a Realistic Environment**

☑ **Summary**

☑ **Solutions Fast Track**

☑ **Frequently Asked Questions**

Introduction

Honeypots are used to attract would be attackers in the interest of learning something about them. The honeypot appears to be a server with one or more vulnerabilities that the attacker can exploit. They can be as simple as a default installation of your favorite operating system or a complex network involving multiple servers and full implementations of fake traffic to make it appear as though the environment is as real as possible.

Honeypots can be set in a variety of locations. They are often set up as Internet accessible boxes. University projects often set them up as stand-alone environments. They can also be deployed amongst corporate servers in order to divert the attention of an attacker away from the true production machines. They are sometimes even deployed internally to detect the inquisitive insider before they can cause serious problems.

The organization setting up the honeypot normally also sets up intrusion detection/ monitoring software to observe the activities that the attacker undertakes. The goal is normally to determine what the attacker is after, what methods they use once they've compromised a box, and what tools are they using.

Virtualization brings whole new dimensions to the sophistication of honeypots. Instead of individual boxes requiring their own dedicated hardware whole clusters of juicy looking targets can be deployed. A honeypot and the infrastructure to monitor any attacks on it can be deployed on the same hardware. Multiple operating systems can be used to give the appearance of an extensive environment with minimal investment.

Herding of Sheep

Honeypots are a powerful and flexible technique for not only positively identifying attacks to hosts on a network but also monitoring and recording how the attacks were carried out. Honeypots can work in conjunction with intrusion detection systems (IDS), but unlike an IDS, they have an advantage in a much lower rate of false positive alerts. This is because honeypots do not provide any legitimate network services, nor have they any legitimate users, but instead are idle devices on the network. As a result, any network traffic seen entering or leaving a honeypot is by definition suspicious and a pretty good indication that your network is under attack.

By learning how to combine honeypots and virtualization together, you can quickly create almost any type of virtual infrastructure with minimal resources or effort, effectively creating a virtual world to distract and misdirect attackers away from the real network servers. This is an environment that you control, and, through the power of virtualization you can pause, reset, and duplicate at will.

By using virtualization techniques you can build up a whole array of different virtual honeypots and virtual networks in your virtual toolbox. These can be quickly put together in different configurations to solve many different security problems. Furthermore, once a honeypot has been compromised, and you've collected the information you need, just roll back the honeypot to the last good snapshot and start again. With virtualization there's no need to manually rebuild every compromised honeypot.

This chapter will guide you through creating different virtual honeypots and the virtual networking that supports them. It will start with some simple but useful practical examples and will end by recreating some of the latest honeypot techniques in redirecting traffic from remote sensors to a central honeynet under your control.

Firstly, there are some widely accepted distinctions or classifications between the different types of honeypots and how they are positioned within a network.

Honeypots can be classified as either high interaction or low interaction. This classification distinguishes between honeypots that emulate operating systems or services and honeypots that are genuine operating systems or services. This classification gives an indication as to the depth of interactivity or fidelity of the honeypot.

Low interaction honeypots that emulate systems or services are usually implemented as an application running on a secure server. The attackers interact with the application and not the hosting server itself. The depth to the service depends upon how much intelligence has been manually programmed into the application or script. An example of a low interaction honeypot is a Linux host running a honeypot application or a Windows host running the KFSensor honeypot application.

In comparison high interaction honeypots do not run any service emulation applications but instead are full operating systems with real services. So a Windows 2008 virtual machine placed on a network configured as a mail server could be considered a high interaction honeypot.

Both types of honeypots have their advantages, disadvantages, and complexities; however, the choice between the different classifications of honeypots is most often based on risk versus potential gains. High interaction honeypots can pose the greatest security risk because when they are compromised the attacker has full control of a complete operating system. This can then be used fully to participate in further malicious activity. However, the potential gains could be in securing production systems against a sophisticated and motivated hacker by observing his *modus operandi* through such a honeypot.

Honeynets

"To really get in touch with the dark side, one needs a honeynet: a real machine connected to a network, which can be probed, attacked, 'owned', and abused."[1]

A honeynet is a collection of high interaction honeypots on a tightly controlled and highly monitored network. The use of these was pioneered by the Honeynet Project www.honeynet.org along with their recommended technique of using a layer 2 bridge to provide the required tight control and monitoring. This control and monitoring is necessary as high interaction honeypots are, after all, full operating systems.

The layer 2 bridges when used with honeypots are known as honey walls and are an essential part of any honeynet. Rather than installing servers with dual network adaptors and their associated networking, virtualization makes installing honey walls incredibly easy. In fact a pre-built honey wall template makes an excellent addition to anybody's virtualization toolkit allowing them to reuse their honey wall time and time again as they build different honeynets.

The honey wall is a virtually undetectable bridge into a honeynet network. The honey wall monitors and restricts the amount and type of data entering or leaving the honeynet. By using the honey wall, the damage a compromised honeypot can cause to networks external to the honeynet can be limited. In this way the risks associated with implementing a honey wall can be reduced and controlled.

Depending on how the honeynet architecture has been implemented, honeynets are either described as GenI, GenII, or GenIII honeynets.

Gen I

GenI honeynets were the first implementations of honeynets with the defining feature of a honey wall that was assembled by hand. Even though these honey wall implementations varied considerably, many of them were constructed from a host with two or more network interfaces for bridging the traffic between network segments. As described in "Know Your Enemy: Honeynets" (The Honeynet Project, May 2006), the main of aim of these honey walls was to provide the following:

- Data control
- Data capture
- Data analysis
- Data collection

Gen II

GenII honeynets were defined by utilizing a CDROM for installation to overcome the difficulties in building consistent, secure layer 2 bridges that contained an effective range of monitoring tools. The honey wall CDROM was created by the Honeynet Project and was a complete prebuild bootable honey wall environment. It was capable of controlling both the rate and type of data flowing through a bridge by using both iptables and snort inline. Snort inline dynamically changes the content of packets as signatures are detected to neutralize the payload of an attack.

Network alerts were also facilitated via snort signature matching. The honey wall was also capable of capturing Sebek UDP packets sent from a honeypot with the Sebek kernel module. This module—which is very similar to a rootkit in that it is undetectable on the host—captures an attacker's keystrokes within the honeypot. In this way the keystrokes of an attacker are captured even if an encrypted channel such as SSH was used.

Gen III

GenIII honeynets are architecturally the same as Gen II honeynets, however they offer improvements to the web interface in the display of network statistics and alerts as well as deployment and management improvements.

Where to Put It

Once a decision has been made to implement a honeypot, the next logical question is where to put it. Fundamentally there are two places that a honeypot can be located: a single local network or a distributed network. There are pro's and con's to each approach.

Local Network

One obvious option for the location of a honeypot is to install it completely on a local and self-managed network. This has the benefit of ensuring that the honeypot is in an environment that you are 100% in control of. There are no external dependencies in any way. You can configure the systems as you require without needing to worry about how they interact with other systems.

While this can be appealing you must undertake steps to ensure that a honeypot system installed on a local network cannot be compromised or used to gain access to your legitimate network resources. This can most easily be accomplished by separating the networks that the honeypots reside on from the rest of your network through the use of firewalls and similar devices.

NOTE

A drawback of using a single local network is that it impedes the ability to host honeypots throughout your organization. All the honeypots have to be in the same location, however, if you have multiple internet points of presence or if you want to monitor multiple potential internal environments, using a single local network can be impractical.

Distributed Network

Some of the most exciting projects currently underway with honeypots are based around the idea of collecting and collating data from arrays of distributed honeypots. These distributed systems allow you to gain valuable insights into malicious activity happening on a number of other remote networks in real time. Some of these projects even allow you to redirect hacker activity across the Internet to your local virtual honeypots without ever having to install a honeypot into the remote location. The attacker is unable to detect the redirection and as such will attack the local one believing it is part of the remote network.

There are a number of distributed honeypot projects which greatly ease the configuration of distributed honeypots. Some are supplied as preconfigured virtual machines to download and start using immediately.

Honeymole, www.honeynet.org.pt/index.php/HoneyMole, is a project that makes the creation of layer 2 bridges over encrypted TCP/IP tunnels easy. For more information go to the following Web sites:

www.honeyathome.org

www.leurrecom.org

http://ids.surfnet.nl/wiki/doku.php

SURFids is an open source distributed intrusion detection project. It is a well developed and sophisticated package that uses databases for event management and a sophisticated GUI for management. It utilizes open source components to redirect malicious network traffic to a central honeypot. OpenVPN and tap interfaces are used to provide layer 2 bridging over TCP/IP into a Nepenthes honeypot. A demonstration VMware image is available from the SURFids website so that you can be up and running with this in no time at all.

SURFids has many noteworthy features such as automatic geo-location and mapping of an attacker's source IP address, passive TCP fingerprinting of the attacker's host, and antivirus scanning and sandboxing of captured binaries. However of particular interest is SURFids's bootable USB memory stick. This memory stick can be used on any low specification host with only one network card to boot it up into a remote sensor/redirector. This has been thoughtfully implemented as the remote device will query the server for updates every hour and automatically upload any available. The aim of this is to make administration of a large number of remote sensors as simple as possible.

Layer 2 Bridges

Layer 2 bridges are a very useful networking capability in the area of honeypots. Not only are they used extensively to create honey walls and other network monitoring points, they can also be used to undetectably redirect network traffic for use in distributed honeynets. When properly implemented, they act as a basic mechanism through which control of all network traffic can occur.

To understand how layer 2 bridges work, here is a quick recap of TCP/IP. TCP/IP is a suite of layered protocols used by network devices to send and receive data on a network. The protocols are layered on top of each other, as can be seen in Table 5.1. The highest layer is the Application Layer, and the lowest is the Physical Layer.

Table 5.1 TCP/IP Layers

OSI Layer Number	OSI Layer Name	TCP/IP Layer Number	TCP/IP Layer Name	Transmission Unit
7	Application	4	Application	Application Data (i.e., HTTP web traffic, SMTP email)
6	Presentation			
5	Session			
4	Transport	3	Transport	Segment/Datagrams
3	Network	2	Internet	IP Packets
2	Data Link	1	Network/Link	Frames
1	Physical			Electrical pulses

As you can see layer 1 is the network layer, and it is very far down the TCP/IP stack. To interconnect different networks together, IP routing is used. IP routing relies upon routers to route packets based upon their IP addresses to the correct network. This is very effective and is used extensively throughout the Internet. Remote redirectors or probes can be easily created on remote networks that will redirect all IP packets to the local honeypot based upon layer 3 routing (layer 3 refers to layer 3 of the OSI model, not the TCP/IP model or layers).

Even though layer 3 IP redirection would effectively redirect packets, it would be fundamentally flawed for the redirection of honeypot data. This is because layer 3 redirection alerts hackers that the host they are attacking is not within the correct network and could indeed be a honeypot. This can be tested quickly by using traceroute to see the number of routers or "hops" to the remote system, with the redirection showing up in the final hop. Furthermore when the attacker gains access to the honeypot, it has a different IP profile and be on the wrong network to what he was trying to break into.

Finally, layer 3 redirection is limited to only IP packets. As a result the protocols below layer 3—which are local to the network segment—are not redirected. This would limit the effectiveness of the honeypot or honeyfarm as these other protocols may be what the attacker or scripts have exploited in order to compromise the honeypot.

It is much more difficult to redirect layer 2 protocols since by definition they are not routable and are only local to a particular network segment. So Linux iptables firewall could not redirect this layer as it operates at only layer 3, the IP layer, and above. One method to redirect layer 2 traffic is to encapsulate as the layer 2 data and above within a layer 3 packet. This layer 3 packet can then be routed over the internet as normal and then unencapsulated on the receiving end. This is effectively what the honeymole project achieves.

Honeymole

Honeymole, www.honeynet.org.pt/index.php/HoneyMole, is a small program developed by the Brazilian Honeynet Project for securely redirecting remote network traffic to a local honeypot. It achieves this by creating encrypted layer 2 bridges over TCP/IP using the SSL libraries. The great advantage to using honeymole is that it allows you to securely host your honeynets in one central location, greatly reducing the risk and overhead of running multiple remote honeypots. Furthermore by being able to run your honeypots centrally you can take full advantage of virtualization by hosting all of your honeypots in a central virtualization host. This would not be possible if they were dispersed through multiple remote networks (at the very least it would require virtualization hosts in all locations).

The first honeymole 1.0 release was in 2005. It is still under active development with the current 2.0.2 released in 2008. A typical honeymole configuration is shown in Figure 5.1. In this configuration both the honeymole server and the honeypot have been virtualized and reside on a single VMware Server.

Figure 5.1 Typical Honeymole Configuration

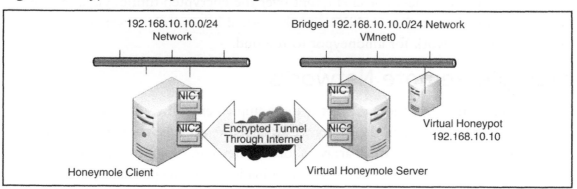

Virtualization can be used further by creating a small Linux honeymole virtual machine as a template. This can then be easily copied and then uploaded to the remote hosts, which can execute it with either VMware player or VMware Server.

As honeymole relies upon SSL certificates for authentication between the honey-mole client and the honeymole server, your first stage to installation is to generate certificates for the Certificate Authority, the Server Certificate, and the Client Certificate. This is aided by the inclusion of scripts within the honeymole tar file for their creation. The second stage is to compile both the honey wall server and the honey wall client on their respective hosts and edit their configuration files.

Both the client and server configuration files contain options for compression and encryption algorithms, but crucially they both contain a mandatory entry for a Berkeley Packet Filter (BPF). This is instrumental to the operation of honeymole and it is used to instruct honeymole as to which packets to capture and send over the layer 2 bridge.

These BPF filters entry within the honeymole configurations for the remote client at 192.168.10.10.1 is as follows:

```
FILTER = "dst host 192.168.10.10.1 and not src host 20.30.40.50"
```

For the local server at 20.30.40.50 the filter is as follows:

```
FILTER = "src host 192.168.10.10.1 and not dst host 20.30.40.50"
```

As can be seen, both the remote honeymole client and the local honeymole server have two network cards. This results in a much more robust implementation without network loops. In both the client and server the TCP/IP stack is removed from the first network interfaces and labelled NIC1 on each. This is achieved by entering ifconfig eth0 0.0.0.0 on each host. In this way packets can be 'sniffed' from NIC1 on the honeymole client, sent over the encrypted tunnel via interface NIC2, and then 'injected' from NIC1 on the virtual honeymole server onto the local honeynet network for a honeypot to respond.

Multiple Remote Networks

The organization where the honeynet is to be implemented may have a small number of remote networks. As such the honeynet architecture must be capable of redirecting appropriate network traffic to an array of local honeypots. Not only must this be achieved in a secure manner, but cross contamination of honeypot data and also accidently bridging two remote networks together must be avoided. Therefore local honeypots that are responding to different network ranges must be physically isolated on different network segments to avoid bridging.

One solution is to add another network interface card (NIC) to the honeymole server for each remote network. In this way network separation is achieved by physical means as remote packets are injected onto different physical segments through their dedicated NICs. This can be seen in Figure 5.2, where NIC3 has been added to the honeymole server for use by the 90.100.100.0 network.

Figure 5.2 Providing Network Isolation via Additional NICs

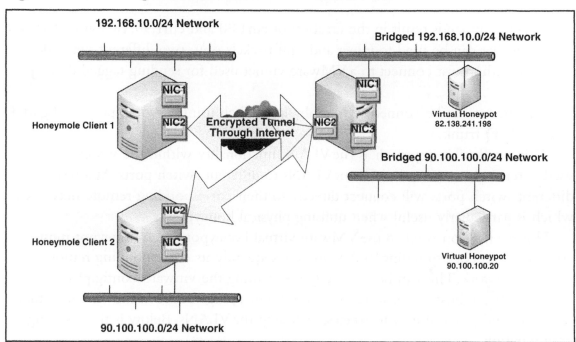

Even though the approach shown in Figure 5.2 fulfils the security and separation requirements initially, it is somewhat limited as it would not scale to host honeypots on many different networks. This is because it would require a prohibitive number of networks. Furthermore, if the honeymole server is implemented with VMware server, there is a limitation of four virtual network interfaces per virtual machine.

Therefore, in the architecture shown in Figure 5.2 only one more network could be redirected before the four network card limitation was reached and another virtual honeymole server would be needed.

An alternative and more flexible approach is to have the output of the honeymole server as a VLAN trunk port. In this way many different network segments can be carried through one network interface.

To create two VLANs numbered 80 and 90 to be carried through the eth1 interface on the honeymole VMware virtual machine, the following commands are issued within the virtual machine and also on the VMware host.

```
Ifconfig eth0 add 80
Ifconfig eth0 add 90
```

These commands result in the creation of eth1.80 and eth1.90, two virtual VLAN interfaces that can be used to inject and sniff packets onto two different network segments. Eth1 must connect to a VMware vmnet used for sending tagged 802.1q packets.

The vmnet can be connected to a physical switch using a switch port configured as an 802.1Q trunk.

This is a flexible approach as the VLAN functionality within the switch can be used extensively to present different VLANs to different switch ports. As a result different switch ports will connect directly to their corresponding remote networks, which is particularly useful when utilising physical honeypots.

However, if you want to use VMware virtual honeypots, each honeypot must connect to its corresponding VLAN and consequently its corresponding remote bridged network. This can be achieved by executing the vmware-config.pl script on the VMware host server to reconfigure the mappings between the vmnet virtual networks and physical host interfaces, including the VLANs. Below is the resulting configuration.

```
Vmnet0 is bridged to eth0
Vmnet1 is bridged to eth0.80
Vmnet2 is bridged to eth0.90
```

As can be seen in Figure 5.3, vmnet1 is mapped to eth0.80, which is one of the virtual Linux VLAN interfaces which were created in the step above. The final step is to map the virtual network interface of all the honeypots and the honeymole to the correct vmnetwork.

Figure 5.3 Mapping Virtual Network Interfaces to Correct vmnet Networks

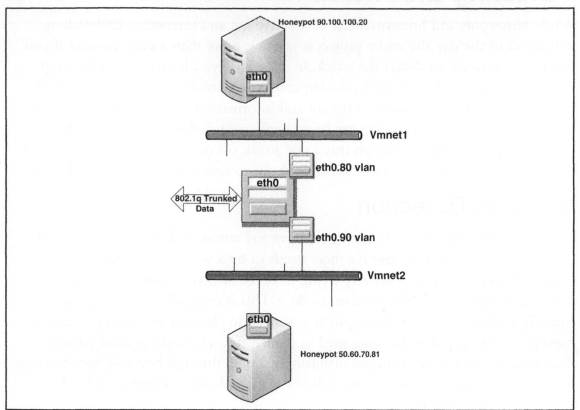

The architecture shown in Figure 5.3 is both scalable and flexible for implementing a large number of honeypots to respond to remote attacker activity through a honeymole server. Each additional honeypot only requires another VLAN to vmnet mapping to be created to which a honeypot can be attached. By combining together virtual networks and VLANs great flexibility is achieved as physical switches can introduce physical honeypots into the infrastructure. Furthermore virtual networks with their corresponding virtual honeypots can be reassigned to different VLANs very quickly.

Detecting the Attack

While honeypots and honeynets can be a pretty fun and interesting undertaking, at the end of the day the entire project is nothing more than a geek exercise if you don't have a means to detect the attack. In a lot of ways a honeypot is a learning exercise in a safe and controlled environment. A well implemented honeypot will provide a tremendous amount of insight and information with regard to how attacks are executed, what compromises are being performed, and what impact of the attack is. If you are unfortunate enough that a real attack occurs on your production environment, you know where and what to look for to restore functionality and security.

Intrusion Detection

Honeypots are a great way of luring attackers and automated malware away from your production systems, however there needs to be a way of being aware of when somebody or something is actively trying to break into your honeypot, and, even better, how many times they've tried to do it. This is especially important if you're running a high interaction honeypot as you need to monitor the compromise and prevent the honeypot from being used to launch further attacks at third parties. This monitoring can be achieved manually by going through host and network logs, but it would soon become tedious, will not scale, and, once compromised, a host's logs may not be reliable.

This is where intrusion detection systems (IDS) come in, to automate the monitoring, reporting, and alerting of honeypot attacks. IDS are a great complement to honeypots and they can even be built as virtual machines straight into your virtual environment. As with other examples in this chapter, once an IDS has been built as a virtual machine, it can be cloned and installed into other parts of your environment for further monitoring with very little further effort.

SNORT, www.snort.org, is a very popular open source IDS system often used alongside honeypot installations. It works by inspecting network packets for "signatures," which are known data patterns within packets indicating malicious behavior. It is included in the honeynet's project honey wall bridge as the IDS capability. SNORT Inline is another feature of SNORT which is able to change the packet payload of any packets that have been identified as malicious. This is particularly useful as the payload of an attack can be neutralized before it ever reaches the intended recipient.

Getting up and running with SNORT should be very easy as there is a whole range of pre-built virtual appliances you can download from the VMware website, www.vmware.com. Virtual appliances of particular note are SmoothWall Express, Untangle 5.0, and the Backtrack Live CD. Even though these are great appliances and well worth the time, the best tool for monitoring honeypots is still the Honeynet Project's honey wall.

Network Traffic Capture

There are primarily three different ways to capture the malicious traffic destined for your honeypot. These are

- Span port from a switch
- Honey wall bridge
- Network tap

A span port on a managed switch copies or mirrors all of the data entering or leaving a switchport on a switch to another switchport. This other switchport would then have a packet capture device, the simplest of which could be a Linux host running tcpdump, connected to it collecting packets. This is an effective way to capture packets quickly or on a small scale and is a valuable technique. However this approach soon runs into scalability problems as you try to monitor more than a couple of honeypots.

When using virtualization and especially virtual networks there is a further problem with span ports that also applies to network taps. This is the difficulty in spanning or tapping a virtual network because network packets do not physically leave the virtualization server. In order to perform this network traffic capture the tap or span must be placed where the network data is accessible in the physical network. This may be quite difficult to achieve in some scenarios where virtualization is used extensively especially if vpns are terminated on a virtual host. If you are using VMware ESX server, however, you can configure the virtual switch (vSwitch) to operate in promiscuous mode allowing you to connect a virtual machine running your sniffing software to the vSwitch and thus sniff and capture all the traffic on that vSwitch.

A physical network tap is also a good device to aid in honeypot packet capture. They work by being an inline physical device that sits in the middle of either a copper or fibre optic cable. In this way all network data must pass through the network tap, where a copy is sent out of a third interface to your packet capture device. Just like the span port, they are undetectable, and just like the span port they are difficult to scale and cannot capture virtual network traffic.

By design a honey wall bridge is also an excellent device for packet capture. The Honeynet Project's honey wall is a prebuilt honey wall which is not only fully capable of packet capture but also packet flow analysis. It is virtually undetectable, but arguably its biggest advantage over the other two options is that it can also be fully virtualized. This means it is able to capture packets from within the virtual networks themselves. This leads to greater virtualization and cleaner network monitoring designs.

Monitoring on the Box

While monitoring the network to see the data being transmitted and received is valuable, you also want to be able to monitor the application and systems on the box itself regardless of whether it is a physical or virtual system. This allows you to monitor things like exactly what the attacker is doing to the applications and operating system, which provides information about how you can protect your production resources from the same kinds of attacks.

One option for monitoring the box is to implement some form of host based intrusion detection. The benefits of this are similar to network based IDS. Another option is to use a configuration management and baselining tool such at NetIQ Secure Configuration Manager, ConfigurSoft, or Tripwire. These applications allow you to define a specific configuration and then report on any variances or differences from the defined baseline. This can be helpful in illustrating files and configurations that the attacker may have changed.

Something that must be kept in mind is that attackers typically try to identify applications such as anti-virus and IDSand disable them to prevent them from notifying you of an attack. Another option for an attacker is to try to spoof or deceive the monitoring application so that it provides false information. Consequently you must take the information provided by any particular box with a grain of salt.

Tools & Traps...

Leveraging VMware VMsafe

VMware VMsafe is a program by VMware that is promising to provide low level security APIs and functionality to security vendors. While most of the functionality for VMsafe will not be available until the next release of VMware ESX server, it's worth being aware of in the context of monitoring the box. VMsafe APIs (in particular the VIPER and Introspect APIs) have the potential to provide out of guest monitoring of all memory and processing occurring in a virtual machine. This has the potential to allow a honeypot that is running as a virtual machine to have all memory and processing to be monitored completely externally via a special security virtual machine, and, most importantly, in a manner that is undetectable to an attacker.

How to Set Up a Realistic Environment

Honeypots can be used in a variety of different ways to collect information from the different sources of attacks. When building honeypots to collect and correlate trends across different networks to investigate automated scanning and attacks, a high degree of realism is not needed. This is because the automated tools used for scanning are typically just searching for vulnerabilities and rarely check for realism. However if your honeypots are purely for intrusion detection and are situated deeper into your secure network to detect sophisticated, manual hacking attempts, then your honeypots must be realistic so that the attacker actually attempts to compromise the system.

This realism could be achieved through careful configuration to make the honeypot appear to be similar to any other legitimate neighboring server on the network. Virtualization, in particular VMware, is widely used in enterprise production environments and should not be an immediate indication of a honeypot. Attempting to disguise a server as virtual is rarely necessary and also very difficult to achieve successfully.

Plausibility is important and an attacker would be suspicious of your honeypot if it doesn't reflect the general security level of the network you're trying to protect. So installing a honeypot with too many vulnerabilities in a generally well secured and patched network may well raise suspicions. Therefore generally apply the same security practices such as patching and firewalling to the honeypots but with slightly less rigor to ensure that the honeypot is typical of the network but still the most vulnerable host.

Configuring honeypots to appear to be systems that are still in development or under test is another good ruse for creating plausibility as to why a honeypot is different or less secure to other hosts on the network. Pitfalls can also come through the power of virtualization and copying virtual machines. If you move a host to a different network or clone a host from another network without cleaning up old configurations, then you may alert the attacker that he's on a recycled honeypot.

Nepenthes

Nepenthes, http://nepenthes.mwcollect.org, is a modular low interaction honeypot designed to emulate vulnerabilities worms use to spread across networks. Nepenthes does have a different approach from other honeypots in that it only aims to emulate the vulnerable parts within a service such as vulnerabilities within SMTP servers rather than emulating the service as a whole.

Furthermore Nepenthes also has a shellcode processor which is able to extract the shellcode from an exploit and execute it in order to fetch malware. In this way a large collection of worms can be automatically downloaded for further analysis. Currently the vulnerabilities emulated are only specific to Windows platforms, and, as of August 2008, it was still under active development with the latest release being February 2008. It is designed for the Linux/BSD platform, and it will also run on Windows under Cygwin. Installation on Debian-based systems can be performed using apt-get install nepenthes.

Setting Up the Network

Virtualization is as much about creating virtual networks and joining them together in unique ways as it is about creating stand alone virtual hosts. Furthermore if you can master creating virtual networks you are able to build more and more of your infrastructure virtually inside a single host. This section will cover creating two virtual networks using VMware server. This will be used as the building blocks for creating much more complicated networks later such as honeynets with honey walls but the principles will remain exactly the same.

Firstly in the creation of the network architecture, VMware makes it possible to create separate and distinct virtual networks inside a single server. Since these networks are virtual they can be reconfigured quickly in software rather than the time consuming alternative or rewiring physically switches and hubs. Honeypots can be moved quickly from one virtual network to another without even having to shut them down by using a very simple administration GUI.

Figure 5.4 shows two virtual networks and four virtual machines; one of which is in a prime position to be a honey wall. All networks and machines are within a single VMware host shown in blue.

Figure 5.4 Using a Virtual Machine as a Honey Wall

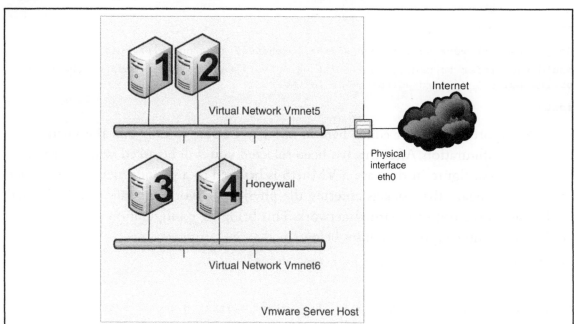

The two virtual networks are called VMnet5 and VMnet6. VMnet5 is connected to an external network through a physical network interface, eth0. In comparison VMnet6 is an internal-only network which exists only within the VMware server; it is not connected to any physical network devices and has no direct external network connectivity. In the diagram virtual hosts 1, 2 and 4 are connected to VMnet5, and therefore have direct external connectivity.

Host 4 is connected to both networks, and, if configured correctly, could be a virtual honey wall bridge between the two networks.

Finally host 3 is only connected to VMnet6 and all other network data must go through host 4, the honey wall. In this way all network activity entering or leaving host 3 can be monitored and captured.

To recreate the above architecture using VMware server, it is necessary to first create the two networks, VMnet5 and VMnet6. On a Linux host you use the VMware config.pl script, which unfortunately also includes the VMware kernel module matching and compilation process. However this can just be skipped through until this part.

```
Would you like to skip networking setup and keep your old settings as they are?
(yes/no) [no]
```

no

```
Do you want networking for your virtual machines? (yes/no/help) [yes]
Would you prefer to modify your existing networking configuration using the wizard
or the editor? (wizard/editor/help) [editor]
```

editor

It is important to enter editor here in order to be able to fully edit the virtual network configuration. After this has been selected you will be asked which virtual network to configure in this case 5. VMnet5 is bridged to a physical network interface, eth1, which means that packets entering the physical network interface will be copied or 'bridged' over onto the virtual network. This bridging configuration can be achieved by entering the responses below.

```
The following virtual networks have been defined:
. vmnet0 is bridged to eth0
Do you wish to make any changes to the current virtual networks settings?
(yes/no) [no]
```

Yes

```
Which virtual network do you wish to configure? (0-99)
5
What type of virtual network do you wish to set vmnet5?
(bridged,hostonly,nat,none) [none]
```

bridged

```
Your computer has multiple ethernet network interfaces available: eth1,
eth2. Which one do you want to bridge to vmnet6? [eth1]
```

eth1

```
The following virtual networks have been defined:
. vmnet1 is bridged to eth0
. vmnet5 is bridged to eth1
```

This completes the configuration of the first virtual network, VMnet5. The second virtual network has to be configured slightly differently because it is a host-only network. This means that the network is not directly connected to a physical network card so any network traffic is internal to the VMware server only or 'host only'. This configuration can be achieved by entering the following responses:

```
Do you wish to make additional changes to the current virtual networks
settings? (yes/no) [yes]
Which virtual network do you wish to configure? (0-99)

6

What type of virtual network do you wish to set vmnet6?
(bridged,hostonly,nat,none) [hostonly]
```

hostonly

```
Configuring a host-only network for vmnet6.

Do you want this program to probe for an unused private subnet? (yes/no/help)
[yes]
```

Yes

```
Probing for an unused private subnet (this can take some time)…
The subnet 192.168.51.0/255.255.255.0 appears to be unused.

The following virtual networks have been defined:
. vmnet1 is bridged to eth0
. vmnet5 is bridged to
. vmnet6 eth1is a host-only network on private subnet 192.168.51.0.

Do you wish to make additional changes to the current virtual networks
settings? (yes/no) [yes]
```

no

This concludes the configuration of the two virtual networks. You are now ready for the addition of your virtual honeypots. Once you have created your virtual honeypots you can take full advantage of these two virtual networks and can place honeypots onto either network or both. It's possible to create up to 99 virtual network segments in this way, so there is plenty of scope available for creating quite complicated honeynets.

You can place a virtual honeypot onto one of the networks you have just created by using the VMware Server Console. This is a Graphical User Interface (GUI) which controls the creation, configuration, and status of all your virtual machines and virtual networks. To place honeypot1 onto VMnet5 Go to **VM | Settings |** and select the virtual network interface you want to use and the custom network connection option. With this option selected you are able to then select the virtual network you want to connect to interface. In Figure 5.5 the first network interface has been selected to connect to VMnet5.

Figure 5.5 Virtual Machine Settings

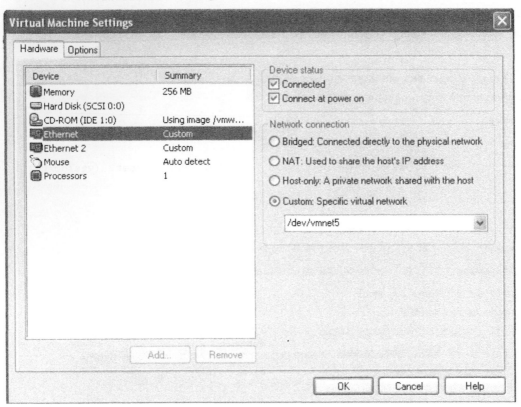

If you are creating a virtual honey wall then you can connect the other virtual network interface to the VMnet6 network so that the honey wall can bridge across the two networks. The configuration of VMnet6 can be seen in Figure 5.6.

Figure 5.6 Configuring a Second Network Interface for Bridging Across
Two Networks

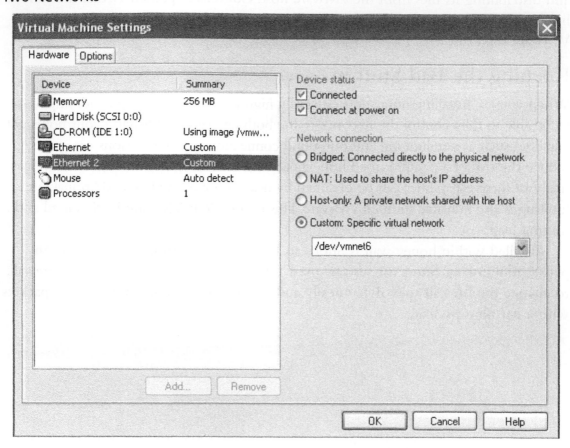

A further reason for utilizing VMware in the deployment of high interaction honeypots (honeynets) is its ability to host more than one full honeypot operating system on one physical server. For example, a single VMware server could host full installations of Solaris 10, Windows 2008, and Fedora Core 9, which can run simultaneously.

Snapshots can be taken of the honeypots in a 'clean' state, and, once a honeypot has been compromised and had all useful data extracted, it can be reverted back to the 'clean' snapshot. This is advantageous as a high interaction honeypot need only be installed once and then reverted back to its initial state as needed rather than the alternative of reinstalling or reimaging each physical machine.

Another aim that can be achieved by using VMware is the ability to distribute compromised honeypots to a colleague or other security professional for further analysis. This can be achieved with VMware server by pausing the virtual honeypot and distributing its files from the VMware host. Conversely paused virtual machine honeypots can be downloaded from the honeynet alliance and imported into the VMware server host.

Keeping the Bad Stuff in

When you are installing honeypots especially high interaction honeypots it's important to be able to fully control the network traffic both entering and leaving your honeypot. Facilities such as rate limiting and outbound connection type restrictions can greatly reduce the risk of a compromised honeypot being used to launch further attacks. Again many of these capabilities can be obtained by using a honey wall, but additional rate limiting is also available through VMware. This is possible if VMware ESX is used as the hosting platform.

Installed within honey wall is Snort, an Intrusion Detection System based on packet monitoring. Snort can also be used 'inline' with iptables, a Linux host firewall, to change the firewall rules dynamically and replace the contents of malicious packets with a harmless payload.

Summary

The objective of honeypots and honeynets is to provide an environment that is attractive to an attacker, thus enabling you to learn how the attacker operates and how the attacks themselves function. In essence it is a surveillance tool that, if implemented properly, provides you with information that you can use to better secure your production resources.

There are many different ways of implementing honeypots, but for any honeypot to be effective it must be appealing to an attacker. It is important to setup realistic environments so that the attacker doesn't realize they are attacking a honeypot but rather they think they are attacking real resources.

A critical element of success for honeypots is the ability to detect and monitor the attack so that you can learn how the attacks work and thus how to protect against them.

Virtualization's flexibility presents a good environment for implementing honeypots since you can set up complex and robust environments with a fraction of the hardware required for a corresponding physical implementation.

Solutions Fast Track

Herding of Sheep

☑ Honeypots are used to attract attackers to a controlled environment where you can learn how the attackers and the attacks function

☑ Honeypots are considered high interaction or low interaction

☑ There are three generations of honeynets: Gen I, Gen II, and Gen III

☑ It is important determine whether you require a local or distributed network of honeypots

Detecting the Attack

☑ You can use both network and host based IDS to detect the attack

☑ You can also capture network traffic to identify an attack

☑ You can use span ports or network taps for monitoring the physical network

☑ You can configure vSwitches to operate in promiscuous mode to capture network traffic on the virtual network

☑ A honey wall or honey wall bridge can be used to provide both packet capture as well as control.

How to Set Up a Realistic Environment

☑ A honeypot should appear to be similar to a legitimate server or resource

☑ Making a honeypot appear to be a development or test system can be an effective way to lure attacks

☑ Nepenthes is a low interaction honeypot that you can use to emulate vulnerabilities

Frequently Asked Questions

Q: Should a honeypot consist of an unpatched or highly vulnerable target?

A: Generally speaking, no. A good honeypot should be very similar to your production resources. While you might reduce the security some (or maybe not apply all patches or apply them as timely as you would to your production resources), if your honeypot is completely unpatched while the rest of your environment is highly secure, it can tip off the attacker that it is a honeypot. They may move on to other systems thus precluding you from gaining the information you require from your honeypot implementation.

Q: Why should I use a honey wall?

A: An important element of a honeypot or honeynet is the ability to rigidly and strictly control the network traffic from an attacker but to be able to do so without the attacker realizing it. Honey walls provide that strict control of network traffic but can do so largely transparently to the attacker.

Note

1.   Cyrus Peikari and Anton Chuvakin, *Security Warrior* (Sebastopol, CA: O'Reilly Media, Inc., 2004).

Chapter 6

Malware Analysis

Solutions in this chapter:

- **How Should Network Access Be Limited?**
- **Looking for Effects**
- **Antivirtualization Techniques**

☑ **Summary**

☑ **Solutions Fast Track**

☑ **Frequently Asked Questions**

Introduction

In the early 1990s viruses were prevalent. Their primary mode of transportation involved being executed by an unsuspecting user. The virus would then infect other similar files on the machine in hopes that one of these files would be copied to another unsuspecting user. The very operating system of the machine might also be altered in an attempt to continue to "infect" every file that the computer might come in contact with.

As computers got more sophisticated, so did the malware problem. Workgroup networks brought about viruses that could infect not only local files, but the files of other users in the workgroup. The Internet gave rise to worms that could move from server to server without the interaction of the user. Eventually some worms were so powerful that they were able to compromise every vulnerable host in a matter of minutes. Even the most innocuous self-replicating code can cause significant amounts of damage to a network running at capacity.

All along the way researchers have been watching this progression in an effort to understand, classify, and with any luck repair the damage done by these malicious programs. Unfortunately the methods of the virus creators have gotten more sophisticated. The true nature of a virus often is disguised in an effort to prevent researchers from discovering its secrets. Researchers need a way to truly see what malware is doing to a server if they have any hope of finding a way to prevent and recover from malware infestations.

This chapter will highlight how virtualization can be used to quarantine malware in an area where it can be studied. You will see how to create an environment in which to test the malware. We will also discuss ways to monitor the environment from afar so that the effects of the malware can be observed.

Setting the Stage

Imagine if you will that you're working for a company, and you get called in to help the CEO with a problem. His computer has started popping up links to pornographic sites, and telling him that he's infected and needs to download a special tool to disinfect his computer. He says he's already tried the tool, but the pop-ups are now coming faster than ever. You immediately realize that he's infected, likely more than once, and that his computer is probably a lost cause. Unfortunately he had sensitive data on the computer, and you need to know what might have been leaked into the wild. This is the point where malware analysis comes in. You need to know what activities the virus performs. Does it send data to the creator? Was the malware specifically targeted in some way to the victim? How does it infect other computers? Can the damage it does be repaired?

There are two primary methods of malware analysis that can be used. One is static analysis, and the second is dynamic analysis. Static analysis involves looking at the code of the malware itself. If you are lucky enough to be able to obtain source code in a high-level language, this can be a fairly straightforward task. Unfortunately for the researchers this almost never happens. Instead the malware is almost exclusively distributed in binary format. In addition, malware writers often use obfuscation tools to cause their binaries to be even more difficult to understand (as if reading assembly code weren't hard enough). They often use encryption techniques to hide portions of their code, and write custom code modification scripts. They may alter their binary structure so that the traditional binary sections are not in place, or worse are corrupted in some fashion to prevent binary analysis tools from working. In many cases the actual binary of the entire malware is never actually in memory at one time. Modules are decoded on demand, and promptly erased when execution is complete.

The other method of analysis is known as dynamic analysis. This analysis involves executing the binary in a controlled environment, and then observing its behavior. These behaviors can be divided into two areas of interest: (1) how does the malware interact with external hosts, and (2) what activities does it perform on the victim machine?

How Should Network Access Be Limited?

During analysis the question of how much network access to grant should be addressed. There are a number of reasons for which you should avoid allowing the malware to contact other servers on the Internet. Indeed, in most circumstances you will want the systems to be on completely isolated networks. This section will attempt to detail how to use a virtualized solution to create an isolated system. Using the proposed implementation will hopefully help you to avoid getting caught in some less desirable situations.

Don't Propagate It Yourself

The biggest and most obvious reason to prevent malware from making contact with live networks (both the Internet and your local networks) is that the malware may be looking for targets to attack. It would be a very bad day for your organization if the malware you were researching were able to escape the sandbox environment in which it was being tested and infect other computers in the corporate network. And even if the malware only has access to the Internet, you could still face liability issues for allowing the malware to propagate from your machine and infect others. More information regarding creating a sandbox environment has been presented in Chapter 3.

The Researcher May Get Discovered

Rumor has it that malware authors have begun collecting lists of "antimalware" researchers and labs. When a malware organization sets up a Web site for malware distribution, they may include the functionality to provide differing content based on which Internet address has created the request. If a network known to be affiliated with malware research makes contact, a different version of malware is served. The goal is to prevent the malware researchers from obtaining the latest versions of the malware.

Create a "Victim" That Is as Close to Real as Possible

In order to research the malware you should have as close to a realistic target as possible. The ideal target would probably be an actual image of someone's computer with any confidential data removed or at least scrubbed. As we will discuss in the following sections, there are a number of advantages to putting such an image into a virtual machine. There are also some disadvantages. Untargeted malware is created to run on standard user-oriented machines. These pieces of software often are designed to discover their environment and capture data (sometimes including information such as the keystrokes of the user). Sometimes they relay that data back to a collection point immediately. In other cases the malware packages things up, and awaits a collector process connection to retrieve the packaged data. In some cases documents will be searched in an effort to collect sensitive information. Often there is a replication function that leverages the credentials of the user to probe other servers on the network.

You Should Have a Variety of Content to Offer

One of the key aspects of current malware is the behavior it exhibits when certain types of files are encountered. Often malware scans files for e-mail addresses to be added to spam lists, as well as to be used as targets for propagation. Some malware searches for financial information in the form of tax preparation software backup files and money management files. Others might be searching for passwords stored in text files. A malware analysis machine that doesn't contain an assortment of content might miss the key behaviors that the researcher may be trying to locate. Worse yet if the machine is too "sterile" the malware may make the determination that it is in a lab, and terminate execution altogether.

Give It That Lived-in Look

The victim should appear to be a live box that actually is used. The idea is that the enemy should find both interesting information and a significant amount of the standard clutter found on a normal machine. Internet history and a cluttered desktop can go along way toward achieving the goal. A handful of spreadsheets with tantalizing names such as "Taxes" and "Passwords" will likely distract them from looking too closely to check if the machine is authentic. Again, some consideration should be given to migrating a real existing machine onto the virtual platform. Nothing looks more "real" than a machine that has actually been used for some period of time.

Making the Local Network More Real

Although limiting network access is important, it is still one of the key areas the researcher will want to observe. One of the ways in which virtualization can be of help is by using two virtual machines. The first machine can be set up to execute the malicious software, and the second can be set up for observation purposes. This is the machine that should contain data for the malware to capture.

In addition to appearing to be a juicy victim on which to observe propagation methods, the secondary server can provide some key services on the network that can greatly aid in analyzing the malware. One key element of the secondary server would be a DNS responder. Malware often uses DNS to in order to locate servers on the Internet. These DNS requests can be redirected by this secondary server to a known location (likely the secondary server itself), which would be of no consequence if it were compromised.

This secondary server should also be able to answer web requests on both port 80 and 443 as though it were an authentic server. In addition to answering the requests, they should be logged so that the researcher will have the ability to discover if other malware is being hosted in these locations. The easiest way to set up a quick web server like this is to create an error handling page that examines the request header, and then responds with content of the appropriate type. You can do this in a number of ways, but the easiest way I've found is to set up a normal web server (Apache or IIS will work fine), and then create a custom error handler for the 404 – File Not Found error.

On Apache you can modify the Web site configuration by adding an ErrorDocument configuration line that directs the web server to run a script every time an unknown resource is requested. An example of the altered configuration is shown in Figure 6.1.

Figure 6.1 Using an Error Document in Apache

```
~/jupiter
<Directory /srv/www/htdocs/test>
  ErrorDocument 404 /cgi-bin/content.pl
  ErrorDocument 403 /cgi-bin/content.pl
</Directory>

"httpd.conf.local" 4L, 128C written                    4,13        All
```

The customhandler.pl script should examine the extension of the file being requested and attempt to return something matching the requested data. Note that the malware may be asking for content of a specific type, and interpreting it as something else. More often than not the content being requested will be indicative of the function of the malware, and will help the researcher to understand what the malware is requesting. I have included a simple example of such a script later.

On IIS similar functionality can be achieved also by setting custom error handlers. You can accomplish this in the Web site configuration dialog under the Custom Error Handlers tab in the IIS configuration wizard. Note that Figure 6.2 shows only one error handler installed, but they could be installed for every type of error message on the server.

Figure 6.2 Using IIS to Catch All Web Requests

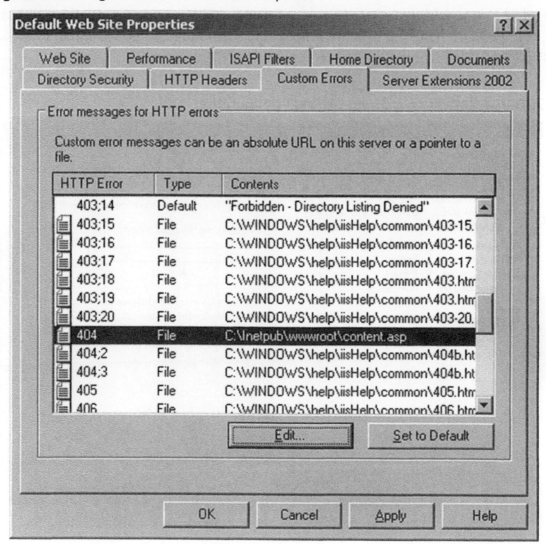

Testing on VMware Workstation

On VMware Workstation the testing scenario just described can be created by making two machines. The first machine is your victim machine, rich in content malware might be interested in, and the second is the "resolver" host, which answers DNS requests, answers web requests, and acts as a possible victim for the original malware to exploit. The networking should be done using a host-only network, with the resolver possibly having two virtual network interfaces to reach the Internet (in the event that it is desirable that some connections be relayed). This "dual homing" should be done with great care however, if the second host is destined to be infected as well while studying the malware propagation methods. Figure 6.3 illustrates how a machine with two network adapters appears on VMware Server.

Figure 6.3 VMware Hardware Setting Configuration

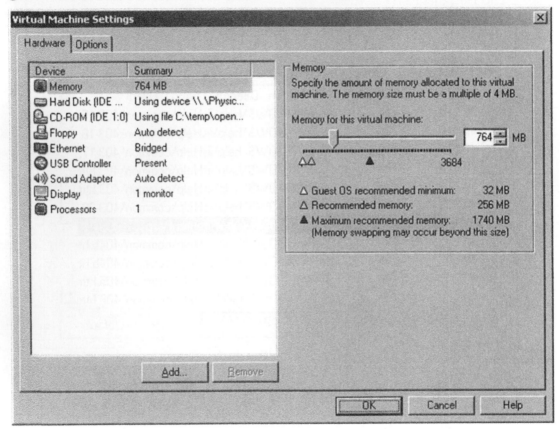

One other thing to be especially careful of is that by default VMware workstation assigns an IP address to the host on host-only networks. This can put the hosting operating system under attack by malware hosted in a virtual server. In order to prevent this issue from affecting your host I would recommend that you get into the virtual network setup, and remove the host adaptor from your infected network. NAT and DHCP should also be disabled on these networks to limit the possible exposure to the host. Figure 6.4 displays the configuration page where this change would be made.

Figure 6.4 Host Virtual Adapter Configuration

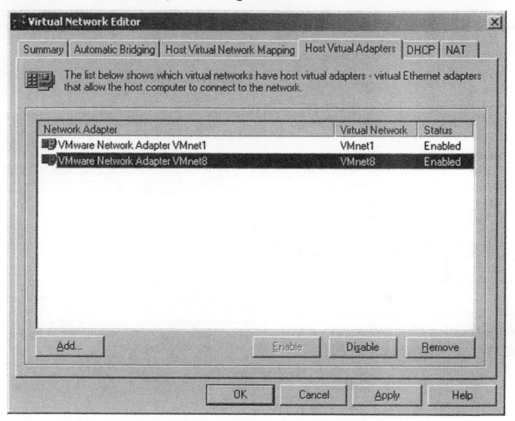

Microsoft Virtual PC

A similar arrangement can be created using Microsoft Virtual PC. Again two machines should be created with local-only network interfaces. Note that Virtual PC does not provide DHCP or natting services for these local-only interfaces, so they will have to be assigned IP addresses manually. This does save the researcher a step in having to deactivate those services. Figure 6.5 provides an example of how host-only network interfaces can be configured in Virtual PC.

Figure 6.5 Hardware Configuration in Virtual PC

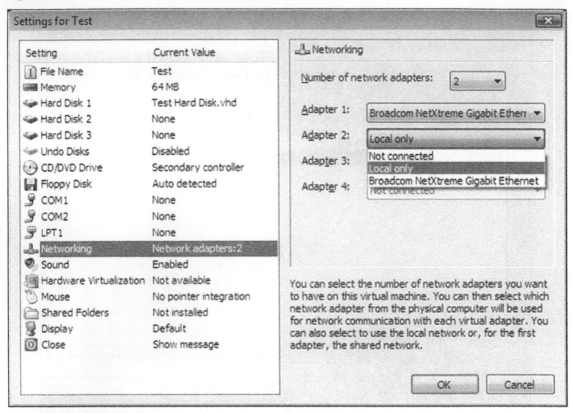

Looking for Effects of Malware

Now that we've discussed some of the issues related with setting up the environment to test in we can move on to the actual work: discovering what the malware actually does, how it does it, and how it communicates with the rest of the network (assuming it interacts with other entities).

What Is the Malware's Purpose?

The malware likely has a primary purpose. This purpose might be to gather information from the victim. The purpose may also be as simple as connecting to a command and control network and awaiting instructions. As we mentioned before, there are two ways to discover this, and in reality a hybrid approach of static analysis (binary disassembly) and dynamic analysis (behavior observation) is likely the best approach to discovering the behavior of the malware in question.

How Does It Propagate?

One of the key areas of focus is the method that the malware uses to infect the host in the first place. Did it use a vulnerability to gain access to the system? What application was exploited? Is there a patch available for this vulnerability? Is the vendor even aware that this vulnerability exists? For the most part malware lurks in the realm of known vulnerabilities. There are a small number that exploit previously unknown vectors, especially in the realm of web browser vulnerabilities, but for the most part they usually are developed with recently disclosed vulnerabilities as the vector of attack. In some cases whole packages of malware are created just waiting for an appropriate vulnerability. Once an appropriate vulnerability is discovered, an exploit can be created, packaged, and deployed with amazing speed. In fact there are some misguided developers who sell malware development kits. These kits lower the skill threshold required to develop these pieces of software significantly.

Does the Malware Phone Home for Updates?

One behavior that the researcher will want to pay close attention to is how the malware gets updated. Often the initial infection vector is nothing but a loader, especially in the case of the malware development kits mentioned earlier. These loaders are designed to gain a toe-hold on the server (often using an exploit), and then retrieve updates to enhance the "functionality" of the malware. Often the updates are served from a compromised web server, but other methods are also used such as FTP, TFTP, and even in some cases, peer-to-peer networks. These updates may be changed to accommodate the current objectives of the malware designer. In some cases new functionality may be added. The updates may even be as simple as downloading a list of commands to be executed on every infected machine.

Another interesting aspect of the "modern malware" scenario is the use of dynamic host lists, and peer-to-peer technologies. In some cases the malware has a long list of dynamic hostnames from which to obtain updates. These hostnames may be generated using an algorithm. The attacker may control a majority of the hosts (and hostnames), or they may control only a small portion of the list. The malware accesses each name in some order, and only when the malware hits a Web site controlled by the attacker does it actually update or perform the actions requested.

Does the Malware Participate in a Bot-Net?

A Bot-net is a collection of drone machines that are directed to act in a cooperative fashion to perform some action on behalf of the Bot-net controller. In many cases these actions consist of flooding the target with packets. It may also emulate a normal user navigating a Web site (and deliberately consuming resources on the target). Even the largest of Web sites can be powerless against an attack by even a moderately sized network of drones.

Does the Malware Send the Spoils Anywhere?

In addition to participating in Denial of Service attacks, infected machines often are employed to search for information that the attacker deems useful. This information could range from personal information such as Social Security numbers or other governmental identification information. Financial information such as bank account numbers and credit card information is also commonly gathered, as are usernames and passwords. Sometimes the victim's computer is even scrubbed for e-mail addresses to be used in carrying out further attacks. An e-mail-based attack has a significantly higher success rate if the person sending the e-mail knows the receiver. These e-mail lists can allow an attacker to discover and leverage these trust relationships.

Gathering all this data would be useless to malware authors unless they have some method of retrieving the files. In some cases the method may be as simple as e-mailing the data to an anonymous mail-drop address. The information may even be encoded or obfuscated and posted on public forums and blogs. The malware may employ a technique known as steganography. Steganography is a method of adding encoded information to a picture while preserving the appearance of the picture. A human looking at the picture would see the original image, but an attacker with the proper tools can extract the information from the picture at a later time. These pictures could be posted on photo distribution sites or even on social networks of various types. In other cases the communication method may be as sophisticated as a complex peer-to-peer network relaying information from infected host to infected host. The author can join the network and lurk, receiving copies of the information in much the same way as the other infected hosts. This allows the author to remain anonymous. It is very difficult to determine which hosts are keeping copies of the data, and which hosts are merely innocent victims of the malware plague.

Regardless of the method, the drop location is likely something that the researcher is attempting to discover. The information gathering step is likely a promising method for locating the person disseminating the malware. In addition it can be a place to tell with some degree of accuracy how much information may already have been "liberated" by other infections.

Does the Malware Behave Differently Depending on the Domain?

Another area of research to be conducted is whether the malware's behavior is different depending on the network on which it is run. There has been some recent research on malware that modifies its behavior depending on the identity of the victim. We can easily imagine malware that performs its standard nefarious actions on most computers, but once a US military computer is detected (possibly discovered by its domain name ending in .mil) it uses more stealthy methods to communicate, and gathers a different set of information.

How Does the Malware Hide and How Can It Be Detected?

One common priority for malware authors is to remain hidden. Once upon a time malware was just another process running on the machine. In some cases it tried to disguise itself using a known process name. It was obvious when you discovered a process running that was vastly different from what it normally was, that something was wrong. At that point you could look in a directory and find all the keystrokes you had typed in the last week. Malware has gotten significantly more sophisticated. Malware is sometimes able to infect the kernel, and prevent files and directories from being displayed at all. In an attempt to evade virus scanners, some can even hide in existing processes and not write anything to disk.

A big challenge for the researcher is finding ways to detect the malware. Does it change any settings that can be detected? Is there a way to detect the malware by creating a specific directory and then checking to see if it exists? Malware that hides directories or files may hide files created by the user as well. The malware may modify certain kernel structures and tables that can be detected. It may also be detectable by looking at memory dumps of the various processes on the system to see if there is anything out of the ordinary. These methods are quite tedious, but may be the only way to discover the malware in action.

One method that can be especially helpful in determining some of these issues is to boot the infected virtual machine under an alternate operating system. This might be a system similar to the original system (same platform), or it might be an entirely different operating system. By examining a disk using an alternate operating system, you can examine the file system and directory structures without being subject to the effects of the infection. By noting any abnormalities you stand a fair chance of discovering the files that are associated with the infection. These abnormalities can be encountered in the existence of files and directories, as well as in the files themselves. To be thorough it is likely a good idea to perform some sort of hash on all the files inside the original operating system, and then to perform the same hash on every file under the alternate operating system. Any differences will certainly be something that should be investigated. It should be noted that files are changing all the time while the system is running, so abnormalities may also be attributable to other sources. Unfortunately each of these inconsistencies would have to be examined and checked to ensure that the changes were not caused by the infection.

How Do You Recover from It?

On our virtualized victim, recovery is likely as simple as restoring from a snapshot. One push of a button, and any sign that the malware was executed is erased. Unfortunately, the researcher likely wants to know how if and how other victims might be able to repair the damage done. The most effective way (and only sure way) to recover from a malware infection is to rebuild the machine, but in some cases where the malware and its activity are fully understood it may be possible to clean out the infection, and continue operating. The files that make up the malware may be located on the system. Disinfection would likely also involve changing system settings back to their original values. It may even be possible to remove a root-kit, although this task can be significantly more difficult.

As we mentioned before, the best and recommended action for malware recovery is to boot the system under an alternate operating system, retrieve as much data as possible, and rebuild the system. Special care should be taken to prevent copying any infected data over to the new system. Infected content are normally executable files such as those ending in EXE, COM, SCR, and so forth. Unfortunately certain other files can contain scripts of various kinds, and can thus be infected by malware. These would include word processing documents and spreadsheet files. In the ideal case these files would be opened only in a safe environment, and then only to print or copy their data over to a safe destination.

Examining a Sample Analysis Report

The result of a malware analysis in CWSandbox is an XML analysis report, which contains information about all participating processes and the actions performed by them. This document type can be read by humans as well as by machines, which makes post-processing easier. For better human-readability XSL templates are used to transform the XML report into HTML or plain text documents. Nevertheless, in the following the contents of the raw XML file are described, but we also give an example of a resulting HTML report at the end of this section. In this section we will use the same sample malware file like seen above.

The <Analysis> Section

Each XML report contains the root element <analysis> and its two child element sections <calltree> and <processes>:

```
<analysis cwsversion="1.97" time="16.12.2006 23:51:28"
file="82f78a89bde09a71ef99b3cedb991bcc.exe"
logpath="c:\analysis\log\82f78a89bde09a71ef99b3cedb991bcc.exe\run_1\">
<calltree>...</calltree>
<processes>...</processes>
</analysis>
```

The attributes of the <analysis> element reveal several information about the particular analysis run, e.g. the used CWSandbox version, the date and time of the analysis, and the name of the analyzed executable. The <calltree> section covers a call tree of all monitored processes, where a father–child-relation shows that the father process has created or injected into the child process. This is the calltree for our malware sample:

```
<calltree>
  <process_call filename="c:\82f78a89bde09a71ef99b3cedb991bcc.exe"
  starttime="00:00.219" startreason="AnalysisTarget">
    <calltree>
     <process_call filename="C:\WINDOWS\system32\arman.exe --install
     c:\82f78a89bde09a71ef99b3cedb991bcc.exe"
      starttime="00:02.031" startreason="CreateProcess"/>
    </calltree>
  </process_call>
</calltree>
```

From that output you can see that the initial malware process, which was created from the binary c:\82f78a89bde09a71ef99b3cedb991bcc.exe, starts a new process using the command line C:\WINDOWS\system32\arman.exe --install c:\82f78a89bde09a71ef9 9b3cedb991bcc.exe. This new file c:\windows\system32\arman.exe most probably was created previously by the initial process. Via the call parameters it may be informed, that it recently has been installed and where the original malware file is stored. We will see in detail later, what is going on inside of this first process. Furthermore, you can see the relative start timepoints of the two processes: the first one is started only a few hundred milliseconds after the analysis has started, and the second one starts roughly after 2 seconds. By the attribute `startreason` we know, that the first process was started by the sandbox itself and that this process has created the second one by calling a Windows API function for creating new processes, e.g. *CreateProcess*. Another possible value for this attributes is `InjectedCode`, which is used for those processes which were not newly created, but which were already running and then injected with malicious code.

Analysis of 82f78a89bde09a71ef99b3cedb991bcc.exe

The `<processes>` section contains one `<process>` subsection with detailed information for each participating process. By the attributes of the `<process>` element we learn some more information about the process itself:

```
<process index="1" pid="1192"
filename="c:\82f78a89bde09a71ef99b3cedb991bcc.exe" filesize="113152"
md5="82f78a89bde09a71ef99b3cedb991bcc" username="Administrator"
parentindex="0" starttime="00:00.219" terminationtime="00:02.328"
startreason="AnalysisTarget" terminationreason="NormalTermination"
executionstatus="OK">
```

- `index`: each process gets its own unique process index for later identification

- `pid`: the process identifier that is assigned by the operating system

- `filename`: the filename from which the process initially was created from

- `filesize`: the size of this process file

- `md5`: the MD5 hash value of this process file

- `username`: the username of the security context the process is running within

- `parentindex`: the index of the parent process which has started this one; the value 0 indicates that the process was started by the sandbox application

- `starttime`: relative time when the process was started or injected like described above in the `<calltree>` section

- `endtime`: relative time when the process was terminated; from the difference between `starttime` and `endtime` you can know the overall execution time of this process

- startreason: the reason why this process was monitored like described above in the <calltree> section

- terminationreason: the reason why the process was terminated; NormalTermination means that the process has terminated by itself; another possible value would be Timeout, which means that the sandbox has terminated this process at the end of the specified maximum analysis duration time

- executionstatus: normally this attribute has the value OK; if for some reason the process could not be started, e.g. because it is no valid Win32 application, the value CouldNotCreateProcess is used

The *<process>* element always contains several sections, which describe all the actions which are performed during the execution of this process. For each of the possible *TNotification*-objects, a separate section is included, if such notifications have been monitored during the execution. In the following, some interesting extracts from these sections are shown and explained. Please notice that sometimes we have skipped several notifications or left out some of their attributes for better readability.

```
<dll_handling_section>
<load_dll dll="c:\82f78a89bde09a71ef99b3cedb991bcc.exe" successful="1"/>
<load_dll dll="C:\WINDOWS\system32\ntdll.dll" successful="1"/>
<load_dll dll="C:\WINDOWS\system32\kernel32.dll" successful="1"/>
<load_dll dll="C:\WINDOWS\system32\msvcrt.dll" successful="1"/>
<load_dll dll="C:\WINDOWS\system32\WS2_32.dll" successful="1"/>
<load_dll dll="C:\WINDOWS\system32\WININET.dll" successful="1"/>
<load_dll dll="C:\WINDOWS\system32\pstorec.dll" successful="1"/>
</dll_handling_section>
```

The upper section gives us information about the loaded modules of the malware process. It starts with the particular malware image file followed by the Windows standard libraries *ntdll.dll* and *kernel32.dll*, which are loaded into each Windows user process. From the information that *msvcrt.dll* is loaded, we can know (or at least assume) that the malware is written in C, as it is the standard runtime library for Microsoft C applications. As the libraries *ws2_32.dll* and *wininet.dll* are loaded, we know that the malware is going to use the Winsock library in order to set up outgoing or incoming TCP/IP connections. As the examined malware file is a bot application, this is not amazing. From the fact that *pstorec.dll* is loaded, we can assume that the malware is going to access the Protected Storage, most probably for stealing some authentication data which is stored within of it. In the next analysis section you can see what we already assumed before: the malware copies itself to the Windows system directory by using the destination filename *arman.exe*:

```
<filesystem_section>
<copy_file srcfile="c:\82f78a89bde09a71ef99b3cedb991bcc.exe"
dstfile="C:\WINDOWS\system32\arman.exe"
creationdistribution="CREATE_ALWAYS"/>
</filesystem_section>
```

The following outputs show us that a new process is started from this created *arman.exe* file. We see that the new process should be created without showing the main window: showwindow="SW_HIDE". Furthermore, we are informed that the API function *CreateProcessA* was used for that purpose. The notification <kill_process> approves the fact that the malware process terminates itself after starting its copy from the Windows system directory.

```
<process_section>
<create_process commandline="C:\WINDOWS\system32\arman.exe --install
c:\82f78a89bde09a71ef99b3cedb991bcc.exe" targetpid="1612"
creationflags="DETACHED_PROCESS" showwindow="SW_HIDE"
apifunction="CreateProcessA" successful="1"/>
<kill_process targetpid="1192" showwindow="SW_HIDE"
apifunction="NtTerminateProcess"/>
</process_section>
```

That is all for the first process and this is exactly what we see for the most of these simple bots: on their first start, they simply copy themselves to the Windows directory, then they execute this new copy and terminate the initial application.

Analysis of arman.exe

Let us know have an intensive look at the actions of the second process, which is promising more interesting results:

```
<process index="2" pid="1612" filename="C:\WINDOWS\system32\arman.exe
--install c:\82f78a89bde09a71ef99b3cedb991bcc.exe" filesize="113152"
md5="82f78a89bde09a71ef99b3cedb991bcc" username="Administrator"
parentindex="1" starttime="00:02.031" terminationtime="02:00.547"
startreason="CreateProcess" terminationreason="Timeout"
executionstatus="OK">
```

We know that this process is created from the same binary, only from a different location. Therefore, the MD5 and the file size have the same values as for the first one. By the values of the attributes parentindex and startreason we know that the execution was initiated by the first process. The terminationreason tells us, that this second process did not terminate itself, but would have continued to execute if the sandbox application has not terminated it at the end of the analysis.

```
<filesystem_section>
<delete_file srcfile="c:\82f78a89bde09a71ef99b3cedb991bcc.exe"
desiredaccess="FILE_ANY_ACCESS" flags="SECURITY_ANONYMOUS"/>
</filesystem_section>
```

Here we can see the probable reason for the second command line parameter of *arman.exe*: it is used to inform the application where the original malware file can be found for deleting it. We do not know the regular distribution mechanism of this bot. Since it was collected by a honeypot we can assume that it is usually copied to a remote host after this host has been exploited. Depending on the exploit used, the malware file would be copied to a temporary or application dependent directory. The existence of an *.exe*-file in such a folder would raise suspicion or it would be deleted automatically due to some system clean up routine. Therefore, in nearly all cases we have seen, malware first copies itself to the Windows folder and then deletes the initial source file.

Many applications use named mutexes to ensure that only one instance of them is running. The funny thing about this is that very often you can learn more information about the malware from the name of their mutexes. Sometimes you can determine the malware name, how the author has intended it. Also very often you can recognize the malware family by that, as the mutex does not change from version to version or simply uses the same value plus a newer version number. The mutex of our sample probably reveals its intended name:

```
<mutex_section>
<create_mutex name="arm4n" owned="1"/>
</mutex_section>
```

The malware opens the registry section `HKLM\SOFTWARE\Microsoft\Windows\CurrentVersion\Run`, whose entries are loaded automatically on system startup. It checks if already an entry for the *arman.exe* file exists. As this is not the case, a new entry is created. After that, the malware checks if the entry could be created successfully. This modifies the system startup sequence, such that *arman.exe* will be started automatically each time the machine boots up:

```
<registry_section>
<open_key key="HKLM"
subkey_or_value="SOFTWARE\Microsoft\Windows\CurrentVersion\Run"/>
<query_value key="HKLM\SOFTWARE\Microsoft\Windows\CurrentVersion\Run"
```

```
subkey_or_value="Arman"/>
<set_value key="HKLM\SOFTWARE\Microsoft\Windows\CurrentVersion\Run"
subkey_or_value="Arman" data="C:\WINDOWS\system32\arman.exe"/>
<open_key key="HKLM"
subkey_or_value="SOFTWARE\Microsoft\CTF\Compatibility\arman.exe"/>
</registry_section>
```

Now for the interesting stuff, namely those operations dealing with network connections. Each analysis report for malware that calls at least one Winsock operation contains a `<winsock_section>`. This has several subsections, one for all UDP connections, one for the incoming TCP connections, one for the allowed outgoing TCP connections, one for the blocked TCP connections and a last one for all operations for which the underlying protocol and direction could not be determined as no indicating function was called. These latter sections normally are used for using the Windows built-in DNS query functions. In our case the Winsock notifications sections starts like this:

```
<winsock_section>
<connections_unknown>
<connection connectionestablished="0" socket="0">
<gethostbyname requested_host="sexccc.serveftp.com"/>
<gethostbyname requested_host="sexccc.ath.cx" result_addr="208.98.19.3"/>
</connection>
</connections_unknown>
```

We can see that the first DNS query did not deliver an IP address. This is because at the moment of the analysis the domain name sexccc.serveftp.com was not connected to a valid IP. In contrast to that, the second request for sexccc.ath.cx delivers the IP 208.98.19.3, which is the address of the botnet C&C server, as we see here:

```
<connections_outgoing>
  <connection transportprotocol="TCP" remoteaddr="208.98.19.3"
    remoteport="6666" protocol="IRC" connectionestablished="1" socket="1396">
    <irc_data username="XP-DEU 0 0 :[XP|DEU|P|00|gcoDZaUz]"
    nick="[XP|DEU|P|00|gcoDZaUz]">
    <channel name="##tibia2##" password="tibiablows"
      topic_deleted=":.scan.stop -s;.scan.start NETAPI 40 -a -s;
      .scan.start NETAPI 40 -b -s"/>
    </irc_data>
  </connection>
</connections_outgoing>
```

The malware initiates an outgoing TCP connection to `208.98.19.3` on port `6666` which can be established successfully. Furthermore, CWSandbox has detected (by inspecting the traffic) that the protocol used in this connection is `IRC`. Because of that it was able to retrieve all the protocol dependent IRC data from the traffic stream:

- the parameter of the user command is `XP-DEU 0 0 :[XP|DEU|P|00|gcoDZaUz]`, which means that the username is `XP-DEU`, the IRC usermode is `0` and the realname is `:[XP|DEU|P|00|gcoDZaUz]`

- the nick name is `[XP|DEU|P|00|gcoDZaUz]`

- the channel `##tibia2##` is joined with using the password `tibiablows`

- the channel topic is `:.scan.stop -s;.scan.start NETAPI 40 -a -s; .scan.start NETAPI 40 -b -s`

- by the name of the attribute `topic_deleted` you can see that the channel topic is received but in fact not let being passed to the malware; the CWSandbox can be configured in multiple ways in order to prevent a further processing of received bot commands

The last entries of the analysis report reveals that the malware opens a backdoor on TCP port 1910, but which is not being connected during the analysis run:

```
<connections_listening>
  <connection transportprotocol="TCP" localport="1910"
  connectionestablished="0" socket="1392"/>
</connections_listening>
```

That is it for the second process of this malware analysis. We have seen the most essential operations of such simple bot applications: after it has copied itself to the Windows directory and started, this new instance deletes the originally malware file, sets up an autostart registry entry, opens a backdoor, resolves the domain name of its C&C server, connects to this server and joins the correct channel. As we did not let the channel topic pass to the malware receiving function, its functionality stops there. An extract of the transformed HTML report of this analysis is given below, showing the analysis only for the second process. Again, some unimportant parts have been removed to reduce its length.

Analysis Number	2
Parent ID	1
Process ID	2028
File Name	C:\WINDOWS\system32\arman.exe --install c:\82f78a89bde09a71ef99b3cedb991bcc.exe
File Size	113152 bytes
MD5	82f78a89bde09a71ef99b3cedb991bcc
Start Reason	CreateProcess
Termination Reason	Timeout
Start Time	00:05.391
Stop Time	02:00.469
DLL-Handling	**Loaded DLLs** C:\WINDOWS\system32\arman.exe C:\WINDOWS\system32\ntdll.dll C:\WINDOWS\system32\kernel32.dll …
File System	**Deleted Files** c:\malware.exe
Mutexes	Creates Mutex: arm4n
Registry	**Changes** HKLM\SOFTWARE\Microsoft\Windows\CurrentVersion\Run "Arman" = C:\WINDOWS\system32\arman.exe **Reads** HKLM\SOFTWARE\Microsoft\Windows\CurrentVersion\Run "Arman" HKLM\Software\Microsoft\Rpc\SecurityService "DefaultAuthLevel"
System Info	Get System Directory
Network Activity	**DNS Lookup**

Host Name	IP Address
sexccc.serveftp.com	
sexccc.ath.cx	208.98.19.3

UDP Connections
Opened listening TCP connection on port: 11666
C&C Server: 208.98.19.3:6666
Username: XP-DEU 0 0 :[XP|DEU|P|00|gcoDZaUz]
Nickname: [XP|DEU|P|00|gcoDZaUz]
Channel: ##tibia2## (Password: tibiablows)

TIP

Based on the raw XML analysis report you are able to create your own customized HTML or plain text transformation. For that you will have to create an XSL template, which contains instructions how to parse an XML document. Having this, there exist several tools for performing the transformation. One easy way to do this is by including a line like this into the XML file (you need to use the correct filename of your XSL with the *href* parameter): **<?xml-stylesheet type="text/xsl" href="templae.xsl"?>**

Interpreting an Analysis Report

The results which can be obtained from the analysis of a malware application can be used mainly for two purposes: protecting and disinfecting the bot-hosting client systems and destroying the functionality of the currently existing botnet. Obviously, the botnet will be left ineffective, if all bots have been disabled, but as it is not possible to deactivate all bots at the same time and as there always is the risk of new infections, it is also very important to shutdown the C&C server respectively servers. Important analysis results that can be used for the purposes of removing and avoiding the infection of a bot application and of shutting down the botnet may be:

- Where does the bot application store its files on the infected system?
- What mechanisms are used to automatically start the bot application at system startup?
- How does the bot protect the infected host from infection by other malware?
- How does the bot protect itself from detection and removal?
- How are new infectable hosts found?
- What exploits/mechanisms are used to infect new hosts?
- How does the bot connect to the C&C server(s) and what servers are used?
- Where does the bot application get updates from?
- What malicious operations are performed locally and remotely?

Evidence for all of this information can be obtained from an analysis report that is created by CWSandbox. In the following sections those items are examined in detail and the proceeding of extracting evidences for them from an analysis report is explained.

How Does the Bot Install?

If we want to check if a given host already is infected with a particular malware or if we want to clean a host from that parasite, we need information about the locations where the malware installs its files and about the mechanisms it uses to automatically execute at system startup. Finding the answer on the latter question normally also solves the first one, as any autostart mechanism needs the information where to find the process to start. Windows offers a lot of different possibilities to instruct the system to execute a specific application automatically on startup. The great tool *autoruns* shows the most of them (For more information about autoruns, go to www. microsoft.com/technet/sysinternals/SystemInformation/Autoruns.mspx). Although there are many ways, nearly all malware either uses one of the \run-sections of the registry or installs a *Windows Service application* or *kernel driver*. However, the malware needs to modify a registry setting to setup any form of autostart mechanism. As CWSandbox reports all accesses to the registry, you easily can filter out those accesses. As already seen, registry accesses are contained in the `<registry_section>` and the relevant entries are `<create_key>` and `<set_value>`. Here are some examples for malware that installs as an autostart process, using different registry sections:

```
<registry_section>
<set_value key="HKLM\Software\Microsoft\Windows\CurrentVersion\Run"
subkey_or_value="mirosoftware" data="C:\WINDOWS\MEDIA\microsoftware.exe"/>
<set_value key="HKCU\Software\Microsoft\Windows\CurrentVersion\Run"
subkey_or_value="MS Domain Name Server Deamon" data="MSDNSD32.exe"/>
<set_value key="HKLM\Software\Microsoft\Windows NT\CurrentVersion\Windows"
subkey_or_value="AppInit_DLLs" data="bampklkf.dll"/>
<set_value key="HKLM\SOFTWARE\Microsoft\Windows NT\CurrentVersion\Winlogon\
Notify\directut" subkey_or_value="DllName" data="directut.dll"/>
```

As mentioned, some bots do not install as normal programs, but as Windows Service applications. In that case, beside the changes to the registry, the analysis report will contain lines like these:

```
<service_section>
<open_scmanager name="SCM"/>
<open_service name="Netlib" desiredaccess="SERVICE_ALL_ACCESS"/>
<create_service name="Netlib" displayname="Net Functions Library"
filename="C:\WINDOWS\system32\Netlib.exe" starttype="SERVICE_AUTO_START"
```

```
servicetype="SERVICE_WIN32_OWN_PROCESS,SERVICE_INTERACTIVE_PROCESS"/>
</service_section>
```

A very powerful technique for infecting a system is to install a *kernel device driver*. Once loaded, this driver executes in kernel mode and underlies no more security restrictions. As it has full control over all running kernel and user mode processes, it could be very hard to detect such a malware. In most cases a kernel driver implements rootkit functions to hide itself and/or to provide system backdoors. CWSandbox can be configured to forbid the installation of kernel drivers completely or to fool the installer by returning a successful error code while suppressing the real installation. In any case, the attempt to load a kernel driver can be detected by the attribute servicetype="SERVICE_KERNEL_DRIVER" of a <create_service> notification. The analysis report section of the installing process would look like this:

```
<service_section>
<open_scmanager servicename="SCM"/>
<create_service servicename="xmsk64" displayname="XMM coprocessor driver"
filename="C:\WINDOWS\system32\xmsk64.sys" starttype="SERVICE_SYSTEM_START"
servicetype="SERVICE_KERNEL_DRIVER" desiredaccess="SERVICE_ALL_ACCESS"/>
<start_service servicename="xmsk64"/>
<create_service servicename="xmsk32" displayname="XMMZ coprocessor driver"
filename="C:\WINDOWS\system32\xmsk64.sys " starttype="SERVICE_AUTO_START"
servicetype="SERVICE_KERNEL_DRIVER" desiredaccess="SERVICE_ALL_ACCESS"/>
</service_section>
```

Ultimately, loading of the driver is performed by the *Service Control Manager (SCM)*. This process is hooked automatically and in its report section an entry like the following will be given. By the attribute behavior="SimulateOK" we can see that CWSandbox was configured to only simulate this call and to suppress the real loading.

```
<service_section>
<load_driver behavior="SimulateOK"
servicename="\Registry\Machine\System\CurrentControlSet\Services\xmsk64"/>
</service_section>
```

Finding Out How New Hosts Are Infected

In order to find new infectable machines, a lot of malware probes remote hosts for known vulnerabilities. For determining which hosts to probe, several strategies exist: some malware generate random IPs, others scan complete (also randomly chosen) IP ranges. There are also applications that use predefined internal or external target lists. Internal lists are contained inside the malware binary, external ones need to be reloaded from one or multiple possible locations from the Internet. After one potential target has been determined it is probed against one or several vulnerabilities. As the possible exploits all work in different ways and use several different target services, it is hard to give a standard procedure of how to detect their usage from an analysis report, but there are some clues which always will be there. In any case, a connection to a remote host needs to be established on one or more of the specific possible ports. For some ports, any attempt to establish a connection is a promising hint of an exploitation attempt. For example: though they are really old, malware still searches for known security leaks in the *LSASS* and the *DCOM RPC Service* is searched. Therefore, often you will see outgoing connections on the TCP ports 135, 139 and 445. As these ports normally are blocked by CWSandbox by default, the connection establishment attempts will be included in the `<connections_outgoing_blocked>`. The analysis report would include some outputs like these:

```
<connections_outgoing_blocked>
<connection transportprotocol="TCP" remoteaddr="192.168.1.0"
remoteport="445" connectionestablished="0" socket="2700"/>
<connection transportprotocol="TCP" remoteaddr="193.126.165.204"
remoteport="445" connectionestablished="0" socket="2700"/>
<connection transportprotocol="TCP" remoteaddr="136.59.147.32"
remoteport="445" connectionestablished="0" socket="2700"/>
<connection transportprotocol="TCP" remoteaddr="183.208.49.198"
remoteport="445" connectionestablished="0" socket="2700"/>
<connection transportprotocol="TCP" remoteaddr="191.255.181.117"
remoteport="445" connectionestablished="0" socket="2700"/>
</connections_outgoing_blocked>
```

To get more information about these attempts, you should not forbid connections to those ports. Furthermore you should configure the CWSandbox such that all communication data is logged. Even if this logging is not enabled, the *.cab*-file will contain the content of all TCP packets that are sent or received. By examining this data, you can learn about what the malware has intended by these connections.

Oftentimes you will also be able to infer the host determination strategy from the reports, especially if you find complete ranges of target IPs that are trying to be connected or pinged, like in this case:

```
<icmp_section>
<ping host="192.168.1.1"/>
<ping host="192.168.1.2"/>
<ping host="192.168.1.3"/>
<ping host="192.168.1.4"/>
<ping host="192.168.1.5"/>
<ping host="192.168.1.6"/>
<ping host="192.168.1.7"/>
...
</icmp_section>
```

How Does the Bot Protect the Local Host and Itself?

A lot of bots try to protect a new infected host against further exploitation by others. Of course, this is not being done for charitable reasons, rather for the selfish reason of trying to ensue that that no one else can take control of the host. This protection is accomplished by fixing known security leaks or by completely disabling Windows Services which can be exploited. Mostly this is done by removing existing Windows shares. In the following you can see how first all existing shares are enumerated (enum_share) and then deleted (delete_share):

```
<network_section>
<enum_share/>
<delete_share networkressource="IPC$"/>
<delete_share networkressource="ADMIN$"/>
<delete_share networkressource="C$"/>
</network_section>
```

To hide and protect its own existence, most malware performs the following actions on a new infected system: it searches for known antivirus and security products and stops them or modifies their configuration. When a malware tries to detect such running security applications, this normally is done by searching for the commonly known names of their corresponding services, processes, or windows. This either can be done by enumerating all of the existing objects and then comparing each found one to the entries of an internal list, or by using functions for opening a handle to a named object by providing the known name as a parameter. In the first case, you will find the actions <enum_services/>, <enum_processes/> or <enum_window/> in your report. In the second case long lists of actions with the known object names as parameter will appear in the analysis. The following example shows how a malware looks for services of antivirus software:

```
<service_section>
<open_service name="AntiVir Service"/>
<open_service name="AVUPDService"/>
<open_service name="BlackICE"/>
...
<open_service name="McAfee Firewall"/>
<open_service name="McAfeeFramework"/>
<open_service name="McShield"/>
<open_service name="NOD32krn"/>
<open_service name="NOD32Service"/>
<open_service name="Norton AntiVirus Server"/>
...
```

```
<open_service name="SharedAccess"/>
<control_service name="SharedAccess" control="SERVICE_CONTROL_STOP"/>
<change_service_config name="SharedAccess" starttype="SERVICE_DISABLED"/>
</service_section>
```

You can see that the bot loops through a long list (the original output has over 50 tests) of hard-wired service names. As most of those applications are not installed on our test-system nothing more is done than just querying for those services. The last actions show us what happens if such a security service could be found: the malware stops and disables the Windows *SharedAccess* service, which implements the *Application Layer Gateway* and is the low level service for controlling network connections. Normally this one is used for the *Windows Firewall* and for *Internet Connection Sharing (ICS)*, but it also runs if neither of them is enabled. By shutting down this service, the Windows Firewall becomes inactive, but also other unforeseen problems may occur.

Some malware does not search for the services. Rather, this type of malware tries to kill the corresponding processes. In our example the Windows XP command taskkill is used, for which the parameter /im imagename specifies the filename of the process and /f forces its termination. Again, we only present a short extract of the real analysis report output:

```
<process_section>
<create_process commandline="taskkill /f /im Mcdetect.exe"/>
<create_process commandline="taskkill /f /im avgupsvc.exe"/>
<create_process commandline="taskkill /f /im avgamsvr.exe"/>
<create_process commandline="taskkill /f /im avgcc.exe"/>
<create_process commandline="taskkill /f /im ccapp.exe"/>
...
<create_process commandline="taskkill /f /im nod32krn.exe"/>
<create_process commandline="taskkill /f /im nod32kui.exe"/>
</process_section>
```

As a further example we present a malware that searches for the main windows of known antivirus scanners. We do not know what would happen if a searched window would be found, but this is not very hard to guess:

```
<window_section>
<find_window classname="NAVAP Wnd Class"/>
<find_window windowname="Norton AntiVirus"/>
<find_window windowname="AVGCC.exe"/>
<find_window windowname="AVG Resident Shield"/>
<find_window windowname="avg"/>
```

```
<find_window windowname="AVGUPSVC.EXE"/>
<find_window windowname="AVG Free Edition - Control Center"/>
...
</window_section>
```

Some malware tries to find running debuggers and other activity-monitoring tools, which can be used for malware code analysis, by trying to open their devices. In our example these are SICE and NTICE (NT version) for the *Softice* debugger and FILEMON and REGMON, the famous tools from *www.sysinternals.com*. Filemon monitors file system activity in real-time (for more information go to www.microsoft.com/technet/sysinternals/FileAndDisk/Filemon.mspx). Regmon monitors registry accesses in real-time (for more information, go to www.microsoft.com/technet/sysinternals/utilities/regmon.mspx). Again, we do not know what would happen if one of the queried devices would exist. Most probably the application would crash the system or simply not perform any of its malicious operations in order to not reveal anything.

```
<file_section>
<open_file filetype="File" srcfile="\\.\SICE"
creationdistribution="OPEN_EXISTING" desiredaccess="FILE_ANY_ACCESS"/>
<open_file filetype="File" srcfile="\\.\NTICE"
creationdistribution="OPEN_EXISTING" desiredaccess="FILE_ANY_ACCESS"/>
<open_file filetype="File" srcfile="\\.\FILEMON"
creationdistribution="OPEN_EXISTING" desiredaccess="FILE_ANY_ACCESS"/>
<open_file filetype="File" srcfile="\\.\REGMON"
creationdistribution="OPEN_EXISTING" desiredaccess="FILE_ANY_ACCESS"/>
</file_section>
```

Sometimes malware does not try to stop found security services, but to modify their configuration, such that the malware is not detected or is enabled to circumvent the security mechanisms. For the Windows Firewall this could be done by using the netsh command or by modifying the corresponding registry key directly:

```
<process_section>
<create_process commandline="netsh firewall set allowedprogram
C:\WINDOWS\sysbinar\bin3.exe enable" showwindow="SW_HIDE"/>
</process_section>

<registry_section>
<set_value key="HKLM\SYSTEM\CurrentControlSet\Services\SharedAccess\
Parameters\FirewallPolicy\StandardProfile\AuthorizedApplications\List"
subkey_or_value="C:\WINDOWS\sysbinar\bin3.exe"
data="C:\WINDOWS\sysbinar\bin3.exe:*:Enabled:enable"/>
</registry_section>
```

NOTE

CWSandbox includes rootkit functionality to hide its existence from the malware. For that purpose all of its objects like processes, windows, modules, or handles are hidden. You can deactivate this feature by the configuration parameter `HIDE_ENVIRONMENT`, but it is enabled per default.

Determing How/Which C&C Servers Are Contacted

Most bots use a central C&C server for communicating with their botherder, and normally they use the standard IRC protocol for that purpose. CWSandbox detects such communication and reacts in two ways on that: first, all the interesting connection information is extracted from the traffic, and second, all received commands are deleted such that they never arrive at the malware's receiving function. Some bots use slight modifications of the IRC protocol and some modified IRC servers also do not answer with RFC conform messages or do not answer at all until the IRC client has authenticated completely. CWSandbox tries to recognize these custom protocols as well, but it is obvious that this is only possible within a certain range of modifications. Often the communications of these modified IRC servers can be read manually if the traffic logging option is used. If an IRC communication could be detected successfully, an output like the following will be contained in the analysis report:

```
<connection transportprotocol="TCP" remoteaddr="203.115.204.58"
 remoteport="7000" protocol="IRC" connectionestablished="1"
 socket="476">
  <irc_data username="SIS-21920206516" nick="SIS-21920206516">
   <channel name="#n" password=".n."
    topic_deleted=":.asc asn1smbnt 200 5 0 -b -r"/>
  </irc_data>
</connection>
```

We see that a TCP connection was established to the host 203.115.204.58 on port 7000. Although port 7000 is not the most well known port associated with IRC (that would be port 6667), it is a common choice along with 6665 and 6666. After authenticating itself with the username SIS-21920206516 and nickname SIS-21920206516, the client joins the channel #n by using the password .n.. Some IRC servers are additionally secured with a server password and in that case also the value used for that would be included in the report. Normally, after joining an IRC channel the channel topic is transmitted automatically to the client. In case of bots this topic is mostly used to send an initial command to the client, in this case this is .asc asn1s-mbnt 200 5 0 -b -r (see Chapter 4 for further description of commonly used bot commands). The last section of this chapter contains detailed information about the results on IRC connections which we were able to retrieve by the analysis of over 1,800 found bot samples.

How Does the Bot Get Binary Updates?

Often the first thing a malware does is to retrieve new files or instructions from its operator. This is done to get code updates or actualized configuration data, as the running malware may be an outdated version or may contain the addresses of already shut down machines. In the case of bots, this configuration data is most often received via their C&C channel, but there are also variants that try to get this from hardwired URLs. In any case, you will see an outgoing TCP connection and/or DNS requests as evidences for such an update request. If you are lucky, the reloading of code or data is done via HTTP or FTP. In that case the report would contain outputs like this:

```
<connections_outgoing>
<connection transportprotocol="TCP" remoteaddr="194.187.45.55"
remoteport="80" protocol="HTTP" connectionestablished="1" socket="2004">
<http_data>
 <http_cmd method="GET" url="/RDFX4.exe" http_version="HTTP/1.1"/>
</http_data>
</connection>
<connection transportprotocol="TCP" remoteaddr="194.187.45.55"
remoteport="80" protocol="HTTP" connectionestablished="1" socket="2004">
<http_data>
 <http_cmd method="GET" url="/MTE3NDI6ODoxN.exe"> <http_version="HTTP/1.1"/>
</http_data>
</connection>
<connection transportprotocol="TCP" remoteaddr="194.187.45.55"
emoteport="80" protocol="HTTP" connectionestablished="1" socket="2040">
<http_data>
 <http_cmd method="GET" url="/DXC9.exe" http_version="HTTP/1.1"/>
</http_data>
</connection>
</connections_outgoing>
```

As you can see, there are several .*exe*-files downloaded from the same host 194.187.45.55. In fact for this particular malware (*NOD32* calls it *Win32/ TrojanDownloader.Adload.NAN Trojaner*) altogether 10 (!) different .*exe*-files are reloaded. After the malware has downloaded them to the local disk, they are executed:

```
<process_section>
<create_process commandline="c:\RDFX4.exe /NCRC" targetpid="1272"
showwindow="SW_MAXIMIZE" apifunction="CreateProcessW" successful="1"/>
<create_process commandline="c:\MTE3NDI6ODoxN.exe" targetpid="620"
showwindow="SW_MAXIMIZE" apifunction="CreateProcessW" successful="1"/>
<create_process commandline="c:\DXC9.exe /S /NCRC" targetpid="1308"
showwindow="SW_MAXIMIZE" apifunction="CreateProcessW" successful="1"/>
</process_section>
```

Sometimes the malware does not use one of the standard web protocols to reload data. Then it is harder to determine the fact, that something executable or configuration data is retrieved. Again, the CWSandbox feature to log all communication data will help in this case. In any case you should use the option *STORE_CREATED_FILES*. By doing that you will get a copy of each created file, no matter if this is an executable or data file and if it was downloaded, copied or created completely new. All these created files can be found in the corresponding *created_files*-subfolder inside the *.cab*-archive. Another helpful option is *FAIL_ON_ALL_DNS_REQUESTS*. By enabling this one, each DNS request will fail and the malware will disclose all of its internally stored remote host contact addresses.

What Malicious Operations Are Performed?

The possible malicious operations a bot could perform on the infected host and to remote hosts are only limited by the imagination of its developer. It is obvious that the operations mentioned in the sections above are malicious as well. However, the operations above are only intended to infect and secure a system. They are not intended to do harm. Once the infection process with all its side actions is finished, the bot is free to pursue its real purpose: using the hosting system to perform illegal and criminal operations, directed by its operator. Some examples for these are:

- Sending spam or notification mails
- Performing DDoS attacks
- Installing a backdoor
- Stealing sensitive data
- Harvesting e-mail addresses from the local host

In the following, we will present hints for those operations which can be found in the analysis reports. We start with the detection of mail delivery. In general an SMTP mail delivery looks like this in the report:

```
<connection transportprotocol="TCP" remoteaddr="68.142.229.41"
remoteport="25" protocol="SMTP" connectionestablished="1" socket="1560">
<smtp_data username="kalonline@sbcglobal.net" password="vi3tridaz">
 <send_mail rcpts="<kalonline@sbcglobal.net>" behavior="Simulate_And_Log">
 From: kalonline@sbcglobal.net
 To: kalonline@sbcglobal.net
 Subject: Perfect Keylogger was installed successfully: 11.11.2006, 06:47
 Date: Sat, 11 Nov 2006 06:47:04 +0100
 Content-Type: text/plain;

 Perfect Keylogger was installed on the computer FOO2,
 with IP address 192.168.1.1, user victim at 11.11.2006, 06:47.
</send_mail>
</smtp_data>
</connection>
```

From this output we can learn the SMTP server (68.142.229.41), the used authentication data (username: *kalonline@sbcglobal.net*, password: vi3tridaz), and the recipient's mail address (<kalonline@sbcglobal.net>). Furthermore, we can read the mail body in plaintext. Without doubt this is a notification mail that is used to inform the malware operator about a new infected host. As we have seen CWSandbox recognizes SMTP traffic and extracts all the relevant data from it. Furthermore, it can be configured to trick the malware by exchanging informational data with the SMTP Server, but only pretending to send the e-mail. The attribute behavior="Simulate_And_Log" enables this feature during the malware's execution. There is another feature that constricts the number of allowed SMTP send operations in order to limit the report size for mass mailing malware.

Huge botnets often are used to perform DDoS attacks. Commonly known attacks are *TCP Syn floods*, *UDP floods* and *ICMP floods*. If you find a lot of notifications for such connections in your report, which all use the same target IP address, this is an assured evidence for such an attack (or sometimes only for the foolishness of the malware's developer). The relevant entries could look like the following ones and have to occur in a high amount:

```
<connection transportprotocol="TCP" remoteaddr="192.168.1.4"
remoteport="80" protocol="Unknown" connectionestablished="1"
socket="122"/>
<connection transportprotocol="TCP" remoteaddr="192.168.1.4"
remoteport="80" protocol="Unknown" connectionestablished="1" socket="124"/>
<connection transportprotocol="TCP" remoteaddr="192.168.1.4"
remoteport="80" protocol="Unknown" connectionestablished="1" socket="123"/>
<connection transportprotocol="UDP" remoteaddr="192.168.1.4"
remoteport="123" connectionestablished="0" socket="3496"/>
```

```
<connection transportprotocol="UDP" remoteaddr="192.168.1.4"
remoteport="123" connectionestablished="0" socket="3488"/>
<connection transportprotocol="UDP" remoteaddr="192.168.1.4"
remoteport="123" connectionestablished="0" socket="3444"/>
```

An analysis report normally contains only one output line for each type of received notification, no matter how often this one was received. Usually a DOS attack is performed by using a lot of parallel threads using a lot of different sockets, so one notification will be reported for each different socket. If due to bad implementation always the same socket would used, only one notification would be reported for that. Therefore, it may be necessary to use the parameter SHOW_QUANTITIES_IN_REPORT. If this attribute is enabled, the quantities for each contained notification are included into the analysis report additionally. In that case a (badly implemented) DOS attack would look like one of these:

```
<connection transportprotocol="TCP" remoteaddr="192.168.1.4"
remoteport="80" protocol="Unknown" connectionestablished="1"
socket="1228" quantity="324"/>
<connection transportprotocol="UDP" remoteaddr="192.168.1.4"
remoteport="123" connectionestablished="0" socket="3444"
quantity="432"/>
<ping host="192.168.1.4" quantity="433"/>
```

A lot of malware programs install backdoors on the infected host, such that its operator (or whoever) is able to connect to this host remotely. The power of such backdoors ranges from simply enabling remote access to the local file system, giving a simple command shell to the attacker, to offering a complete graphical interface. Remote access to the file system can be set up easily by creating a new share:

```
<network_section>
 <add_share networkressource="C$" filename="C:\"/>
</network_section>
```

Malware could also try to escalate the security privileges of existing users, such that a regular login can be used for much more powerful operations than it was intended to:

```
<process_section>
<create_process filename="C:\WINDOWS\system32\net.exe"
 commandline="net localgroup administrators ftpuser /add"/>
<create_process filename="C:\WINDOWS\system32\net.exe"
 commandline="net localgroup administratoren ftpuser /add"/>
<create_process filename="C:\WINDOWS\system32\net.exe"
 commandline="net localgroup administradores ftpuser /add"/>
<create_process filename="C:\WINDOWS\system32\net.exe"
```

```
commandline="net localgroup administrateures ftpuser /add"/>
</process_section>
```

Real backdoors bind themselves to a network port and implement complete servers. Evidences for such activity can be found in the section of *<connection_listening>*:

```
<connections_listening>
 <connection transportprotocol="TCP" localport="6918"
connectionestablished="0" socket="652"/>
</connections_listening>
```

Some malware programs use the integrated *Terminalserver* of Windows to allow remote access. They modify the relevant registry settings to allow remote connections in general. In that case you will find some lines in report that look like these:

```
<registry_section>
<set_value key="HKLM\SYSTEM\CurrentControlSet\Control\Terminal Server"
 subkey_or_value="TSEnabled" data="[REG_DWORD, value: 00000001]"/>
<set_value key="HKLM\SYSTEM\CurrentControlSet\Services\TermService"
 subkey_or_value="Start" data="[REG_DWORD, value: 00000002]"/>
<set_value key="HKLM\SYSTEM\CurrentControlSet\Control\Terminal Server"
 subkey_or_value="fDenyTSConnections" data="[REG_DWORD, value: 00000000]"/>
</registry_section>
```

Changing the network routes or hijacking the DNS resolving process is also part of the performed evil operations. By that, the malware either completely blocks accesses to hosts which provide updates for security software or the operating system or it routes all of those requests to infected hosts. This can be be performed by modifying the *hosts*-file that resides in the *system32\drivers\etc\log*-directory in the Windows folder. An attempt to do so can be detected by locating an <open_file> action that refers to that file and requests WRITE access. Some malware completely reroutes all DNS requests to a special host, which by that is enabled to return different IP addresses dynamically. Such a modification normally takes place in two steps: first the network configuration for the network adapter is modified by changing the relevant registry settings and then the network interface is advised to refresh its configuration. Of course, the second step is only optional. If it is not performed, the modified network configuration is activated on next system startup. The tracks of these actions will look like this:

```
<registry_section>
<set_value key="HKLM\SYSTEM\CurrentControlSet\Services\Tcpip\Parameters\
 Interfaces\{9E4D711D-1234-5678-9ABC-9E6F3F301B84}"
 subkey_or_value="NameServer" data="85.255.114.68,85.255.112.150"/>
<set_value key="HKLM\System\CurrentControlSet\Services\Tcpip\Parameters"
```

```
subkey_or_value="NameServer" data="85.255.114.68 85.255.112.150"/>
</registry_section>

<process_section>
<create_process filename="ipconfig.exe" commandline=" /flushdns"/>
<create_process filename="ipconfig.exe" commandline=" /registerdns"/>
<create_process filename="ipconfig.exe" commandline=" /dnsflush"/>
<create_process filename="ipconfig.exe" commandline=" /renew"/>
<create_process filename="ipconfig.exe" commandline=" /renew_all"/>
</process_section>
```

Finally, a lot of malware tries to steal sensitive data from the local host. This can be done by installing a keylogger or by directly accessing the places, where such data is stored. The explicit process of keylogging is not detected by current version of CWSandbox and will be added as a new feature in coming releases. Nevertheless, as some file needs to be installed as an autostart application or as a service or driver for that purpose, this will become obvious by examining the report. If the malware tries to read the data directly from their storage location, this could happen in several ways, depending on that location. Examples for retrieving dialup network configuration data and contents of address books for several mail clients are these (please notice that some malware uses <open_file> and other <find_file> or even <get_file_attributes> to check for the existence of such files):

```
<file_section>
<find_file filetype="File" srcfile="C:\WINDOWS\system32\Ras\*.pbk"/>
<find_file filetype="File" srcfile="C:\Dokumente und Einstellungen\victim\
 Anwendungsdaten\Microsoft\Network\Connections\Pbk\*.pbk"/>
<find_file filetype="File" srcfile="C:\Documents and Settings\Application Data\
 Qualcomm\Eudora\NNdbase.txt" creationdistribution="OPEN_EXISTING"/>
<find_file filetype="File" srcfile="C:\Documents and Settings\Application Data\
 The Bat!\TheBat.ABD" creationdistribution="OPEN_EXISTING"/>
</file_section>
```

In Windows 2000 the *Protected Storage Service* was introduced, which is a service for storing sensitive data like passwords or private keys in a protected and encrypted way. It is used to save the passwords that have been entered in the *Internet Explorer* or *Microsoft Outlook* and *Outlook Express*, but also can be used by any other user application to protect its sensitive data. By that it is an open treasure chest for each malicious application. CWSandbox detects all accesses to this Protected Storage and reports them in a <pstorage_section>. An example for such a report follows:

```
<pstorage_section>
<enum_subtypes key="PST_KEY_CURRENT_USER" typename="InfoDelivery"/>
<enum_items key="PST_KEY_CURRENT_USER" typename="InfoDelivery"
 subtypename="Subscriptions"/>
```

```
<enum_items key="PST_KEY_CURRENT_USER" typename="Identification"
 subtypename="INETCOMM Server Passwords"/>
<read_item key="PST_KEY_CURRENT_USER" typename="Identification"
 subtypename="INETCOMM Server Passwords"
 itemname="mail.microsoft.com5E3655B0"/>
<enum_subtypes key="PST_KEY_CURRENT_USER" typename="IdentityMgr"/>
<enum_items key="PST_KEY_CURRENT_USER" typename="IdentityMgr"
 subtypename="Identities"/>
<read_item key="PST_KEY_CURRENT_USER" typename="IdentityMgr"
 subtypename="Identities" itemname="IdentitiesPass"/>
<enum_subtypes key="PST_KEY_CURRENT_USER" typename="Internet Explorer"/>
<enum_items key="PST_KEY_CURRENT_USER" typename="Internet Explorer"
 subtypename="Internet Explorer"/>
<read_item key="PST_KEY_CURRENT_USER" typename="Internet Explorer"
 subtypename="Internet Explorer"
 itemname="http://www.gmx.net/de/:StringData"/>
</pstorage_section>
```

Bot-Related Findings of Our Live Sandbox

We have running a live sandbox system at the *University of Mannheim* in Germany, which consists of four *CWSandbox Hosts* and uses a *MySQL* database as repository. New samples can be submitted via the web-interface at *www.cwsandbox.org*, but a lot of persons use scripts to transmit files automatically. In the last few months we have successfully analyzed altogether 11,965 unique malware samples. Inside this set CWSandbox has detected 1283 programs that have successfully established an IRC connection to a remote host. From those 108 did not follow an RFC conform protocol, but a slightly modified variant instead. Furthermore, of the others 40 did send a TCP packet with data like NICK (null)abcdef without having a connection established. Those probably are bad designed applications or some other unforeseen error occurred during their execution. (We have checked some examples and could see that these applications do not even create a socket after WSAStartup and use -1 as a socket handle when calling the send operation.) Anyway, we can assume that these also are applications that implement some form of IRC communication. Finally, 492 of the rest tried to connect to a TCP server on port 6665, 6666 or 6667, which lets us assume that they are also going to initiate an IRC session. So, from the 11965 samples 1815 tried to or succeeded in establishing an IRC connection and, therefore, can be seen as bots or, at least, as malware that contains bot-like behavior.

Tools & Traps...

Using the Live CWSandbox

A live version of CWSandbox can be accessed at the project homepage www.cwsandbox.org and at the *Sunbelt ResearchCenter* at http://research.sunbeltsoftware.com/Submit.aspx. After submitting a suspicious file, your email address and an optional comment you simply have to wait until the analysis report is sent to you. Depending on the current file queue length and on the fact if the submitted malware file has already been analyzed before this can happen immediately or take some minutes.

Those programs, that successfully have used an IRC connection have connected to IRC servers at 317 different IP addresses and have used 120 different TCP ports. As the IRC servers only could be identified by their IP addresses, it is possible (and probable) that due to using dynamic DNS services not all of these hosts are unique. We could presume that two different bot applications which connect to the same channel on the same host and use the same channel password for that are only two variants of one and the same malware and, therefore, belong to the same botnet. As we have found 590 unique host-channel-password combinations, this would mean that we have found 590 different botnets. We can presume that two connections to the same channel using the same channel password but connecting to different IRC servers also belong to the same botnet. This is probable but may not hold in every case, the amount of unique botnets found decreases to the number of 497. Figure 6.6 shows a diagram of the dispersion for the 50 top most seen channels-password combinations. The x-axis holds the different channels and the y-axis shows the number of found malware samples that connect to each channel. The top position was the channel *#dd* in combination with the password *dpass*, which we have seen for 95 times, followed by *#hotgirls* (no password) with 44 and *#i#* (*@d00k@*) with 38 instances.

Figure 6.6 Dispersion of Found Channel-Password Combinations

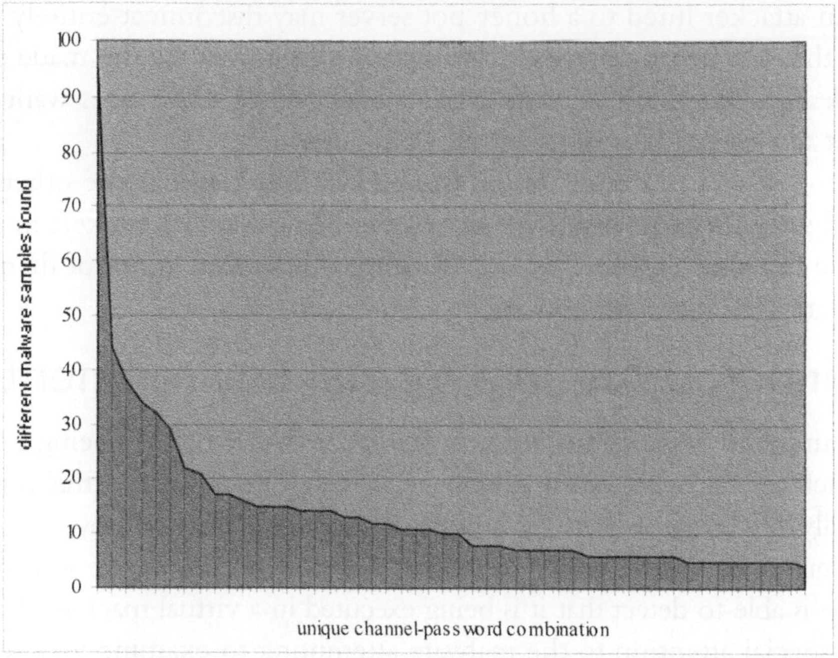

As mentioned, we have found 120 different TCP ports. Most of them only appeared once or a few times, which leads to the suspicion that these were used in malware that is only rarely spread or is a test- or betaversion. Of course, the most often used port is 6667 (375 times), as this is the IRC default port. At the second position comes port 8585 (89 times), followed by 7000 (86 times). But also the ports 1863, 6556, 19555 and 11640 have been seen more than 30 times each.

Please keep in mind, that this analysis may not be representative of what you will find. It should only give you an impression of a real live example of a running CWSandbox system.

Antivirtualization Techniques

Some of the topics we've discussed have been dependent on users within the virtual environment not being aware that they are in a virtual environment. Some of our uses of virtualization such as malware analysis and honey pot deployment could be significantly compromised if the malicious object of interest detects that the compromised host is not genuine.

Malware may have alternate behavior if it detects that it's running on a virtual platform. An attacker lured to a honey pot server may disconnect entirely if they detect that they are being observed (although the argument can be made that this is actually a desired behavior). Security professionals will in some cases want to disguise the fact that the virtual environments are being used.

What kind of security book would this be if it didn't discuss the other side of the fence? I feel some need to cover the techniques being used by hackers in an attempt to detect the fact that they are not on a legitimate platform. Some of them are well known, others are a bit more obscure.

Detecting You Are in a Virtual Environment

There are numerous ways for malware to attempt to detect that it's being executed on a virtual machine. There are active debates on whether being in a virtual machine is fundamentally detectable or not. Each method that is implemented by one side seems to be counterable by the other side in a tiny arms race. Following are some of the ways that malware is able to detect that it is being executed in a virtual machine. The researcher should pay special attention to the malware attempting to examine various system parameters. There are two possible ways this can be addressed. First the underlying system parameters can be changed. Second the malware can be "patched" so that it doesn't ask, asks in the wrong way, or gets an erroneous answer so that the virtual machine is not detected. Both methods have merit, and each has its own disadvantages.

Virtualization Utilities

Both VMware and Virtual PC include a number of utilities to be run in the guest operating system. They often consist of special drivers, and tools used to join clipboards. They may also be used to assist in transferring files between the guest and host systems. Unfortunately for the malware researchers the presence of these processes is a dead giveaway that the process is running in a virtualized environment. Luckily these helper tools are not required, and should likely not be installed in the malware testing environment.

VMware I/O Port

In the case of VMware there is an interesting device that is used to provide some functionality to VMware guest systems. This function comes in the form of an additional I/O port. This port acts in much the same way as other hardware I/O ports on the system. Values can be written to the port, and values can be read. Depending on the parameters passed in control registers during these reads and writes different information such as the version of VMware can be obtained. I would suggest that anyone looking for further information on this port visit the following URLs:

> http://open-vm-tools.sourceforge.net/
>
> http://chitchat.at.infoseek.co.jp/VMware/

I have not yet found a method to deactivate or disguise this port so that it can't be detected. It may be possible to edit the VMware binary, and cause the port to use a different number, but I have no information on how difficult that might be, and what other effects might be caused by this modification.

Emulated Hardware Detection

The most common method for a process to detect that it's in a virtual environment is for it to look at the hardware on which the machine is running. Virtual machine monitors (such as VMware and Virtual PC) emulate a specific set of hardware (with very little variation). When the process detects that it's on the VMware set of hardware then it can make the assumption that it's running in VMware. The same methods can be used in Virtual PC.

Hardware Identifiers

We'll now discuss three types of hardware identifiers: MAC addresses, hard drives, and PCI identifiers.

MAC Addresses

MAC addresses are used on Ethernet interfaces in much the same way that IP addresses are used on the Internet. If an IP address is considered to be a phone number, then the MAC address might be the extension number. It's a number that is used only on the local subnet. MAC addresses need to be unique on the subnet. In order to prevent manufacturers from choosing the same MAC address, the idea of manufacturer codes was introduced. The first six hex digits in a MAC address are known as the manufacturer code. Both VMware and Virtual PC have been assigned their own MAC manufacturer codes. VMware's manufacturer code is: 00:0C:29. Virtual PC interfaces begin with 00:03:FF. Note that the MAC address of the interface can be changed in the .vmx file of the virtual machine on VMware.

Hard Drives

Hard drives also identify themselves in unique ways that are quite easily determined to be parts of a virtual environment. Both the volume name, as well as the driver associated with the disks, are obviously parts of a virtual environment. This label can be changed using the built-in operating system utilities such as e2label, and Disk Manager. Figure 6.7 shows how the virtualized hardware can reveal itself on the guest in the form of manufacturer codes and labels.

Figure 6.7 Virtualized Hardware in a Windows Guest Environment

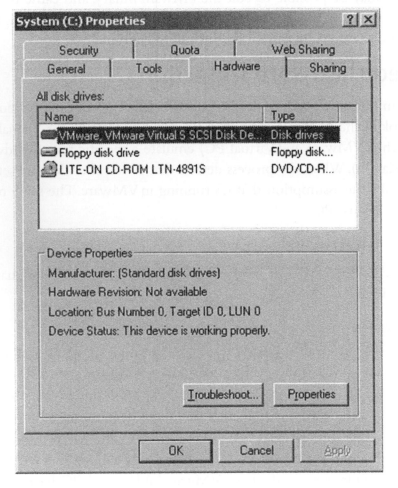

PCI Identifiers

In addition the very hardware itself will report that it is running in a virtual machine. PCI devices again have a manufacturer code, as well as a text label so that operating systems will know which drivers to install. These identifiers (both the numeric and textual) can be used to determine if the hardware is virtual or not. Figure 6.8 again shows how the hardware can be detected, this time using Linux as the guest operating system.

Figure 6.8 Virtualized Hardware in a Linux Guest Environment

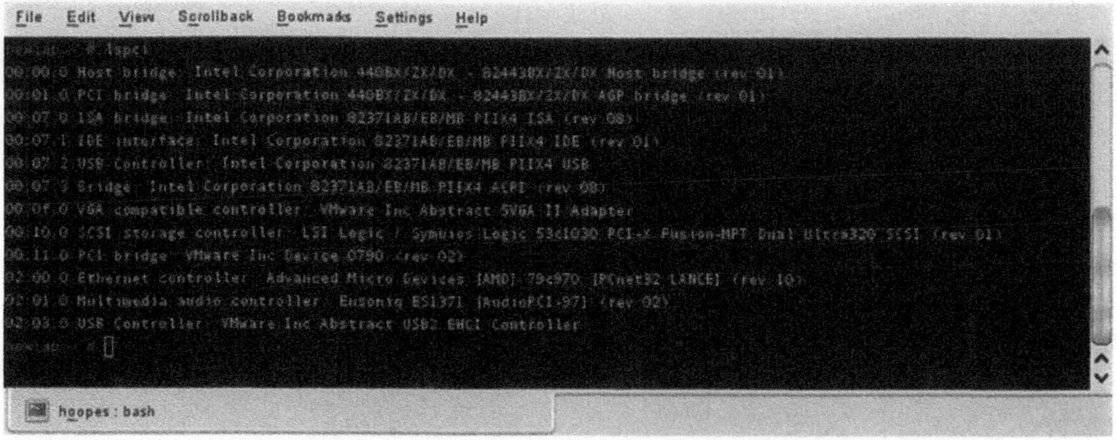

Detecting You Are in a Hypervisor Environment

Another interesting form of virtualization for malware analysis is the hypervisor environment. These environments are created using features of recent processors from Intel and AMD. These processors support going into a privileged mode known as hyper-visor mode. The hypervisor process has control of the virtualized machine. It gains control on certain operations performed by the guest machine such as memory paging operations. When the guest operating system makes a page request to access a segment of memory that has not been accessed recently, the hypervisor process can intercede. While the guest is paused, the hypervisor can inspect and modify the state of the guest machine. Methods have been created that allow the researcher to catch system library calls, and to manipulate the results of those calls.

The hardware of the guest is the actual hardware of the machine so the methods discussed earlier regarding detecting virtualization in general don't apply. It is very difficult (and some argue impossible) to detect a virtualized environment from the guest machine. In an interesting twist there has also been research on malware that puts the victim into a virtual environment. The malware then becomes the entity attempting to prevent the host from discovering that it's been "virtualized." It's really a race to be the first to "initialize" the virtualization. If a second attempt at entering hypervisor mode is attempted, the hypervisor process can "convince" the victim that it has attained hypervisor mode when in actuality the victim is not in control.

Summary

Malware research has benefited significantly from being able to virtualize the victim machine. The ability to test malware against a wide variety of software architectures without requiring the resources of an extensive test lab cannot be understated. Infected machines can be studied, and observed with much greater accuracy without disturbing the environment of the malware.

Although not perfect, virtualization has raised the bar on malware developers. They can still detect many forms of virtualization, but it is getting harder for them. This is a good thing for the virus researchers because the malware developers are constantly devising better and better methods for obfuscating their creations.

Solutions Fast Track

How Should Network Access Be Limited?

- ☑ Add content that might be found on a real system.
- ☑ Make it look like the box is really used.
- ☑ Limited network access.

Looking for Effects of Malware

- ☑ What is its purpose?
- ☑ How does it propagate?
- ☑ How does it update?
- ☑ Is it part of a Bot-net?
- ☑ Does it transmit any data?
- ☑ How does it attempt to hide itself?
- ☑ Can it be effectively removed?

Antivirtualization Techniques

- ☑ Virtualization Tools
- ☑ Guest / Host communication Facilities
- ☑ Emulated Hardware Identifiers

Frequently Asked Questions

Q: Where can I get Malware to practice with?

A: One of the best sites on the Internet for this topic is http://www.offensive computing.net/.

Q: I've been infected. Can I use these methods to disinfect my machine?

A: I wouldn't recommend it. Though performing research can be highly educational, the risks of performing a "partial" removal are significant. Removing only part of the malware can cause the malware to trigger even worse behavior. Unless you are positive you know every step that the malware performs, and that no one has "visited" your machine while you were infected, the safest course of action is always to rebuild the machine. You should also be very careful when transferring files from an infected machine that you do not carry the malware to the new machine as well.

Chapter 7

Application Testing

Solutions in this chapter:

- Getting Up to Speed Quickly
- Debugging

- ☑ Summary
- ☑ Solutions Fast Track
- ☑ Frequently Asked Questions

Introduction

Application testing involves deploying an application in a configured environment that simulates a real-world scenario. The application is then tested in such a manner as to reveal divergence between the intended use of the application and its actual behavior. In simpler terms, the testers install the application, and then they try to break it in as many ways as possible. While they are exercising the application they monitor it to detect subtle breakage. Using the data collected from monitoring, an experienced application tester can often determine if an application failure has security implications, or if it's just a lowly bug.

The time of an application tester is often consumed with the creation of an environment suitable for testing. Merely installing the base operating system on a handful of physical servers can be an all-day task, and this is assuming that there are enough physical servers on hand to deploy a functioning environment. Although this task has been simplified by unattended installation utilities, it can still require a significant investment of time and resources.

A testing environment can be easily deployed using virtualization. Fully configured servers are mere keystrokes away from being ready to go. They can even be stored in a "suspended" state, so the tester doesn't have to wait for the machine to complete a boot cycle.

This chapter will discuss how virtualization can significantly reduce the resources required to create a working test environment. It will also discuss some of the pitfalls that testers might encounter, and give recommendations for creating a test environment with testing tools already in place.

Getting Up to Speed Quickly

I was once one of the people in charge of application testing for a large organization. My role was to examine an application and determine if the application was "secure" enough to host the data for multiple customers. There were two main goals. The first was to ensure that no customer could compromise the data of the other customers. The second was to ensure that no customer could compromise the resources of my employer. Such an undertaking usually required significant planning in order to get resources properly allocated and configured. Setting up even a modest environment of a Web server, database server, and two client machines could take a week or more. I often felt as though I lived in the lab, installing operating systems that were to be used for a single two-week test and then discarded. We would go through the exercise again in the event that an application had to be retested.

Happily, those days came to an end when we discovered VMware's GSX platform (now released as VMware Server). We could create an image of an installed operating system. We could have it fully updated, hardened, and patched. We could install our debugging tools and any sort of monitoring tools we felt we'd be using. We could even have the image booted up to a login prompt so we wouldn't have to wait for it to boot.

NOTE

You should be aware that making a copy of a machine may have licensing implications for the operating system, as well as any software you have chosen to install on the image. While this issue may be resolved by running only one virtual machine at a time (for any license you possess), you should review any licensing agreements to ensure that you are compliant. Some agreements may allow for testing or use in lab environments, and others may prohibit installation in a virtual machine all together.

Default Platform

At this point we could take one of two approaches. We could take a snapshot of the image before we customized it for any applications and then work from the snapshot, with a "revert" to the previous snapshot after the testing had completed, or we could copy the image and register it with the server. We chose the latter for the simple reason that we could save entire virtual machines by saving copy of a directory, and we wouldn't have to worry abut managing a complicated snapshot tree in the event that we needed to go back to a previous version. The environment could be compressed, and then saved offline (in full working order), to be restored if the application were ever tested again.

Copying a Machine in VMware Server

The first step in copying a working machine is to copy the entire directory. At this point it would be a good idea to edit the .vmx file, and change the line:

    displayName = "Windows Server 2003 Template"

It should be changed to another name that describes the function of this machine, or perhaps how the new machine will be different from the original machine. For example:

displayName = "IIS .Net Test"

Registering a machine with VMware Server is done using the vmware-cmd command. Figure 7.1 shows the command which should be run where the config file path is the full path to the .vmx file of the machine you are registering.

Figure 7.1 Registering a Machine with VMware Server

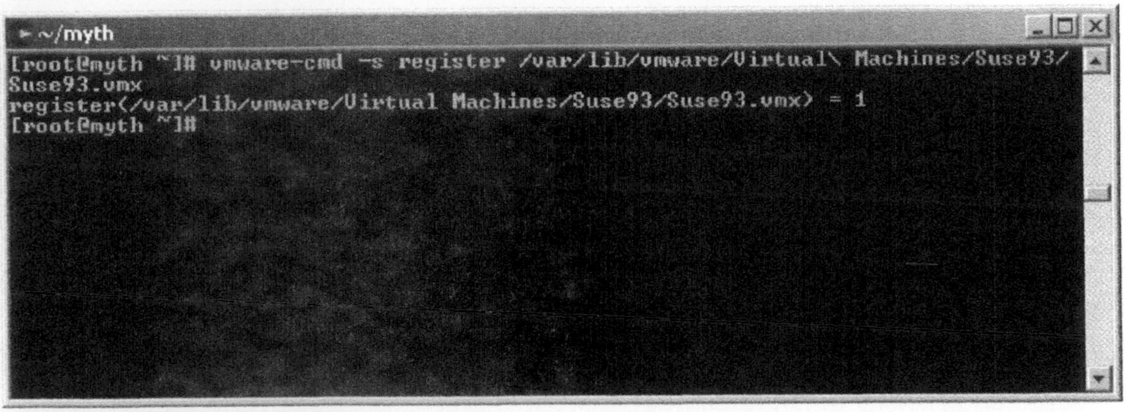

Notice the number "1" at the end of the response line. This is an indication that the machine was successfully registered. In case it can't be registered (such as when the machine has already been registered), the command would respond with an error message indicating the nature of the error.

Upon starting the machine you may be presented with an error message indicating that the machine may have been copied. Figure 7.2 shows the message dialog asking how you would like to respond to this condition.

Figure 7.2 Dialog Box When Registering a Copied Virtual Machine

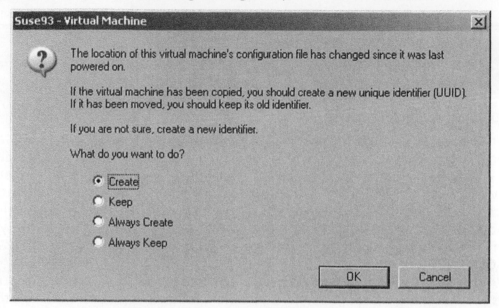

We would also recommend creating a new unique identifier to avoid any conflicts with other machines. At this point you should be able to power up the machine and begin testing.

Registering a Machine in Microsoft Virtual Server

Registering a copy of a virtual machine in Microsoft Virtual Server is almost as easy. The following VB script will register an existing machine which is located at C:\Virtual Machines.

```
On Error Resume Next
Set objVS = CreateObject("VirtualServer.Application")
errReturn = objVS.RegisterVirtualMachine("Windows 2000 Server", _
"C:\Virtual Machines")
```

Tools & Traps…

Update Your Machine

Depending on the age of your image, I'd recommend checking for software updates for all of the software on your virtual machine. I was once the victim of a very old worm because I brought an older image online in a hostile environment. You might also consider setting the machine's network interfaces to use NAT so that external traffic can't reach it. This will give you time to retrieve updates without having to worry about something attacking you before they're installed. Configuring the network interface for NAT is discussed in Chapter 4.

It is also a good idea to keep your virtual images updated on a regular basis. These images should be managed with similar levels of care as any other machine on your network. Regular patching, hardening, and maintenance should not be neglected just because the server isn't online very often.

Known Good Starting Point

One of the best features of using virtualization to quickly enable testing environments is that you are using clean servers that are known to be stable, and have reliable hardware. The ideal testing lab will have virtual machine "templates" at the ready. If a Windows 2003 server is needed, it can be copied, registered to the virtualization platform, and started in less than five minutes. Compare this to the rough hour that would be needed to install from scratch. In addition the templates can be kept updated so that nothing needs to be downloaded in order to get a test started.

Beyond the base operating system, testing tools can already be in place. Supporting software such as network sniffers, debuggers, and even application disassembly tools can be in place and ready for use. There is little need for testing personnel to install any software that is not directly related to the test application.

Using standard hardware is also a convenient bonus. Working hardware drivers should be installed on the template. This is a great change from the days when a spare server was pieced together for a test, and drivers had to be sought out (often legacy drivers which may or may not have been readily available). On top of that you never knew if the drivers were entirely compatible with the operating system.

Downloading Preconfigured Appliances

Another application testing advance that has come about as a result of virtualization is the ability to download fully working appliances. We expect this trend to continue and become a more popular way to distribute customer demonstration environments. I can imagine that a number of product demonstrations did not result in a sale because of the installation and configuration hurdles related to getting to know a new product. Virtualization allows vendors to ship fully installed, fully configured appliances to prospective customers. Sample data can be preloaded into the environment, and this allows customers to be able to see the value of the application in its most useful state (instead of seeing a "bare-bones" environment with a handful of data). This is a much easier sell for salesmen who may or may not be able to actually configure the product in question.

As a side benefit this can also be a boon for application testing personnel. A major hurdle when performing application tests is trying to get a valid environment to test in. In a number of previous instances, I have performed tests on environments which were not entirely functional. In some cases this was a result of someone not knowing how to configure an application correctly, or I might not have been familiar with an option and made the wrong choice during the setup. Our standard process was to request that the application be configured in the same manner in which it would be deployed. Demonstration appliances are normally configured by internal engineers who understand how the application should be set up. It should be noted that testing the "difficulty" of the installation process to reveal areas that could become common pitfalls and configuration errors might also be valuable.

I was also sometimes limited as a result of not having enough data to fully utilize an application. Testing scenarios such as "Can customer A access the data of customer B?" cannot be conducted without having both customers set up within an application. How can I know that customer A can't transfer money on behalf of customer B if customer B doesn't exist within the application? Demonstration appliances are often configured with a working dataset that is able to exercise the majority of the functions of the application.

VMware's Appliance Program

VMware is sponsoring a program where user-submitted virtual machines are available to the public. These applications are developed mostly on various open source operating systems (likely due to distribution restrictions associated with their proprietary counterparts). There are significant advantages to delivering an appliance instead of a software package, the first being that the application can be delivered with the common options already set. The hardware and underlying configuration of the operating system would be known and stable; this can greatly simplify how an application is delivered. It will be interesting to see if the appliance model of application delivery makes an impact on traditional application delivery models.

At the time of this writing there were over 900 different appliances available on the VMware site. More information can be found at the following URL:

www.vmware.com/appliances/

In some cases proprietary applications are available for evaluation, and in other cases the appliances are designed to be used on a permanent basis. This is also a great place to go to obtain applications for educational purposes. I have personally used a number of database appliances while developing tools for SQL injection.

Microsoft's Test Drive Program

Microsoft has recently introduced a program called the VHD Test Drive Program, which allows you to download fully configured versions of its software. It is meant to be a way for companies to evaluate a product and determine whether it would be appropriate for their environments. The virtual machines expire after a period of time and cease functioning. These demonstration machines are absolutely ideal for software testing, because the vendor has provided you with an environment configured the way it is supposed to be configured. In a number of cases the test environment even includes data within the application. The software testing team can concentrate on the productive portion of their test without having to install and configure (and gather subcomponents). A list of test drive environments available at the time this book was written is shown in Figure 7.3. Further information can be found at:

http://technet.microsoft.com/en-us/bb738372.aspx

Figure 7.3 Virtual Test Drive Environments Available from Microsoft

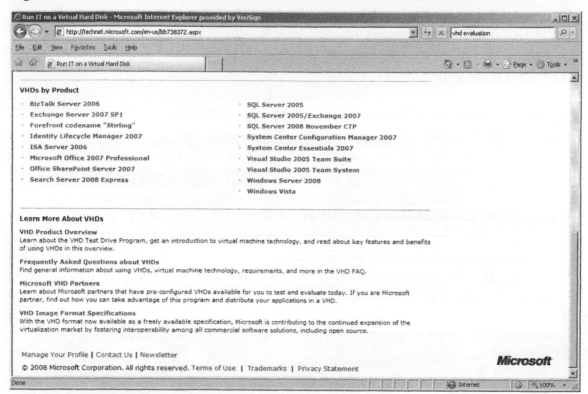

Debugging

Recent versions of Microsoft Windows have introduced a new method of remote debugging. Traditionally, this task involved using two machines connected via a serial cable. One machine would be the debugger, and the other the debuggee. Fortunately, you can use virtual machines to accomplish this task using only one machine. In addition, you can debug using a named pipe instead of a serial connection, which enables significantly faster communications between the machines.

Kernel Level Debugging

The first step involves reconfiguring the debuggee so that it has the debugging features of the kernel are enabled, and that the port is configured correctly. To enable the debugging features in the kernel, one must first change the boot.ini file, which is normally found in the root directory of the C drive. You need to copy the line corresponding to the operating system you are debugging (by default there is only one line in the operating systems section). The section in quotes is the label that the boot entry will be given. We recommend that you use something like "Microsoft Windows XP Professional – Debugging Enabled." Following the label you will need to add two options: /debugport = com1 and /baudrate = 115200. Make sure that the options are all on the same line. Your boot.ini file should look similar to the one shown in Figure 7.4.

Figure 7.4 Boot.ini file Showing Kernel Debugging Options

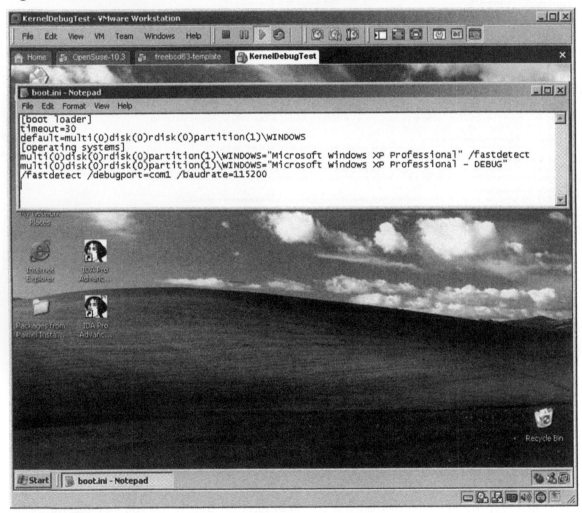

At this point you need to install the com port in your virtual machine, and configure it to point to a named pipe. The machine should be powered off at this point. Open the virtual machine settings menu by clicking on the VM menu, followed by the settings option as shown in Figure 7.5.

Figure 7.5 VMware Hardware Configuration Settings

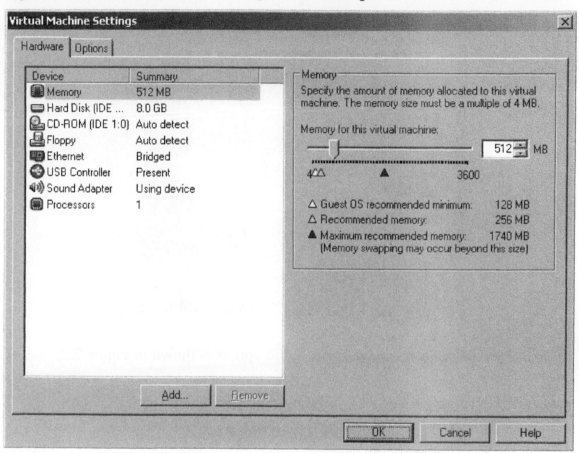

Click **Add** to add new hardware. Clicking the **Serial Port** option should bring up the dialog shown in Figure 7.6.

Figure 7.6 Adding a Serial Port for Debugging Purposes

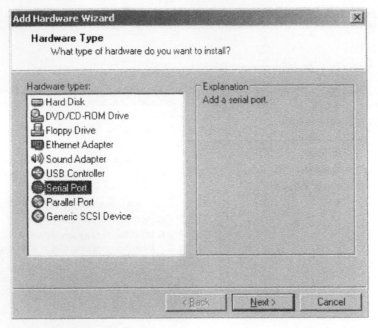

Select the **Output to named pipe** radio option as shown in Figure 7.7.

Figure 7.7 Choosing the Option of Using a Named Pipe

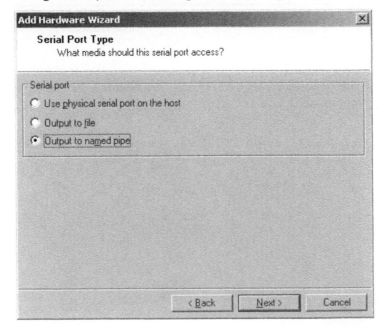

This will bring up the screen (shown in Figure 7.8) in which you can configure the named pipe. For a Windows host, the pipe should be named in the following fashion: \\.\pipe\name_of_your_choice. You should select **This end is the server** if you plan to start the guest and then connect to it (the most common scenario). The option **The other end is an application** should then be selected. When this is done, the options should look something like this:

Figure 7.8 Configuring Options for the Named Pipe

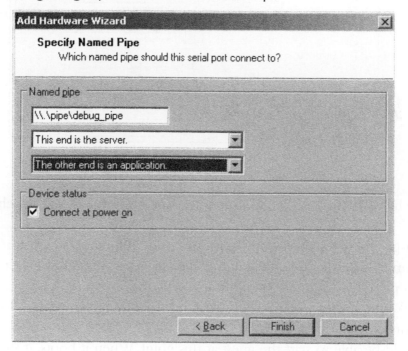

Click **Finish**. There is one final area to configure. On the settings screen shown in Figure 7.9, the settings for the serial port has an advanced option called "Yield CPU on poll" that needs to be enabled.

Figure 7.9 Enabling the "Yield CPU on Poll" Option

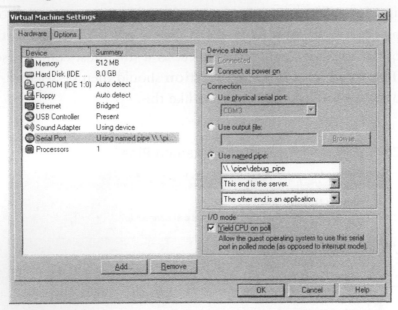

Finally, click **OK** to save the configuration and close the virtual machine settings dialog.

You can get the debugger from Microsoft at the following site: http://www. microsoft.com/whdc/devtools/debugging/default.mspx. In addition to the debugger, this site also provides a number of additions such as the symbols packages for various versions of Windows. You should seriously consider downloading these symbols for the platform(s) you are debugging.

You should be able to start the guest at this point. When it boots, it should pause at a screen similar to the screen shown in Figure 7.10. You should select the debugging version and hit enter.

Figure 7.10 Choosing the Kernel Debugging Boot Option

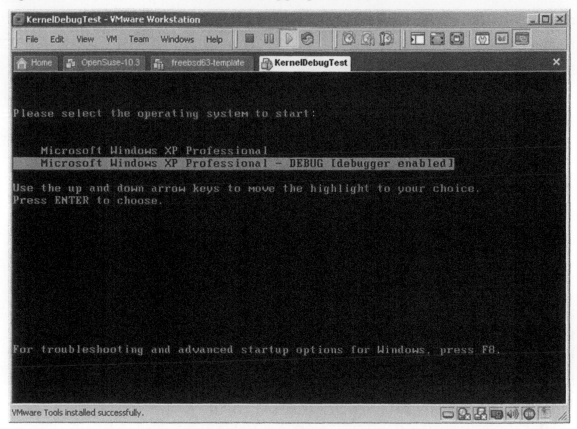

At this point you can connect the debugger to the debuggee machine. To do this the debugger should be started using the options shown in Figure 7.11. The options shown enable debugging over a specific named pipe (which you created using the VMware guest configuration screens). Note that if you find yourself running this command often, then this command can be added to a batch file for the sake of convenience.

Figure 7.11 Windbg Command Line Options for Using a Named Pipe

The debugger should attach to the virtual machine via the named pipe, and you should be able to debug in a fashion very similar to that used in application mode debugging. If you hit CTRL-BREAK in the debugger you should be presented with a screen similar to Figure 7.12.

Figure 7.12 Debugger Attached to a Guest Machine

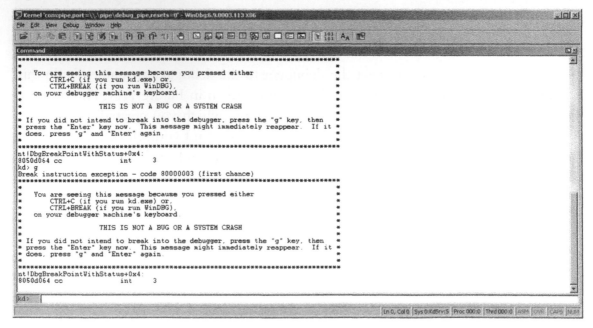

The Advantage of Open Source Virtualization

One of the most intriguing features of open source virtualization tools is the ability to modify the behavior of the underlying hardware. Some very unique situations can be created, which under normal circumstances might almost never happen. The best example of this would probably be classified as a hardware race condition. This type of situation might only occur one in a million times in the real world. These types of issues are very difficult to detect, let alone debug. However, they are much easier to re-create if you are able to control the hardware and the order in which certain events happen. No simulator can exactly replicate hardware inconsistencies (such as shorts, induced interference, and intermittent connections), but their effects can be simulated in an attempt to investigate how drivers and other applications will be affected. Interrupts which normally occur in a serial fashion can be triggered out of order, to replicate a heavily loaded system that is unable to process events in a normal fashion.

Summary

Application testing is a complex process that can be greatly simplified by using virtual environments. We have only scratched the surface of some of the capabilities introduced through the use of virtual hardware. The ability to copy and run a template virtual machine, and be up and running in minutes saves countless hours. Virtual appliances can save even more time by providing a preconfigured environment ready to be "broken."

Solutions Fast Track

Getting Up to Speed Quickly

- ☑ Copy the machine to its own directory.
- ☑ Edit the server file so that the machine has its own name.
- ☑ Register the server using: vmware-cmd –s <path to your .vmx file>.
- ☑ Copy the machine to its own directory.
- ☑ Register the server using the RegisterVirtualMachine method in the VirtualServer.Application control.

Debugging

- ☑ Modify the boot.ini file in the virtual machine to allow kernel debugging.
- ☑ Add a serial port to the guest and connect it to a named pipe.
- ☑ Boot the guest.
- ☑ Connect to the named pipe on the host using a debugger.

Frequently Asked Questions

Q: How can a test environment be quickly created to allow for testing of an application?

A: You can use templates to quickly deploy a virtual machine that is already configured with most, if not all, of the applications and settings necessary to facilitate the test.

Q: Can I debug a virtual machine without needing additional hardware for running the debugger?

A: Yes, you can configure the virtual machine to boot into a debug mode after configuring the virtual hardware to output a com port to a named pipe. Simply power on the virtual machine, then run your debugger while configuring it to listen to the named pipe.

Chapter 8

Fuzzing

Solutions in this chapter:

- **What Is Fuzzing?**
- **Virtualization and Fuzzing**
- **Choosing an Effective Starting Point**
- **Preparing for External Interaction**
- **Executing the Test**

☑ **Summary**

☑ **Solutions Fast Track**

☑ **Frequently Asked Questions**

Introduction

Fuzzing involves providing semi-random data to an application and recording how it behaves. The term can be thought of as starting with something clear such as a valid application file, and "fuzzing" or "blurring" pieces of it. It's a specialized form of application testing that can involve significant automation. It also goes by other names such as fault injection, or error condition evaluation.

Virtualization has proven ideal for resetting the environment to an initial state before any malformed data had been sent. Without using virtualization this can involve restarting the application, or even worse, initiating a reboot just to get to a state where the next test can be performed. In addition, monitoring the application without interfering with the application itself can be a challenge. Some applications attempt to prevent debuggers from observing their behavior. While these attempts can be overcome (defeated, bypassed), it can be an involved process of application modification and research.

This chapter will cover how virtualized environments can significantly increase the efficiency of fuzzing. Using scripted snapshots, the reset of an environment can be done in a matter of seconds instead of minutes. Using the debugging features of a virtualized environment to monitor the application can provide an ideal environment for the hard-to-monitor applications. In addition, it is possible to run multiple instances of the same application in parallel using multiple hardware platforms to increase the speed with which an application can be tested in an automated fashion.

What Is Fuzzing?

The term fuzzing has only recently become popular, but people have been fuzzing to some degree for quite a long time. One documented project conducted in 1990 was designed to send semi-random data to UNIX commands. The team conducting the study issued commands with arguments of various lengths. These tests resulted in abnormal crashes of around 30% of the tested applications. The original study can by found at ftp://ftp.cs.wisc.edu/paradyn/technical_papers/fuzz.ps. Subsequent studies examining X Windows utilities and Windows commands can be found at ftp://ftp.cs.wisc.edu/paradyn/technical_papers/fuzz-revisted.ps and http://pages.cs.wisc.edu/~bart/fuzz/fuzz-nt.html.

The idea of fuzzing is based on two fundamental assumptions. First, that a piece of software has vulnerabilities. Second, that these vulnerabilities can be found by permuting input. It should be noted that fuzzing cannot be used to prove that a program is correct, or even secure. It can only be used as an aid in finding vulnerabilities. It should also be obvious that certain types of data do not lend themselves to fuzzing directly. Included in this category would be encrypted data, as well as data that includes checksums. Both of these situations can be fuzzed to some degree using advanced fuzzing techniques (such as using a debugger to provide input directly into the memory of an application, instead of traditional input methods). These advanced methods are beyond the scope of this book.

There have been a number of frameworks developed to aid in fuzzing, and we'll cover just a handful of them. One of the earlier fuzzing frameworks was put forth by Dave Aitel who released a paper in 2002 entitled "The Advantages of Block-Based Protocol Analysis for Security Testing." (This paper is available on his Web site at www.immunitysec.com/resources-papers.shtml). His framework was called Spike. The idea behind it was that instead of random data, the fuzzing should consist of data of a form similar to valid data. For example, if a valid command consists of a verb followed by two arguments, then the fuzzing data should concentrate on the known verbs and two random arguments. Some exploration of other verbs and tests with one argument or more than two arguments could be done, but they shouldn't be the focus. If an argument appears to take an integer, then the fuzzing library should concentrate on sending integers which often cause problems (such as −1, −0, 0, 32767, etc., instead of random strings). The spike framework simplifies creating blocks of data. These blocks could then be combined to make packets or files. A block might be a string capable of generating tests with strings at that point. The fuzzing would only permute one block at a time in the hopes of generating an exception. Spike can be obtained at www.immunitysec.com.

The Peach framework was created by Michael Eddington. It is a tool written in Python, similar to Spike. To use Peach, the tester creates a Peach Pit file containing information related to the test. The format of the test is specified using XML. Different tags are used to specify various data types such as strings and integers. In addition, these tags have attributes which assist the fuzzer in creating valid tests. The tester then defines the sequence of the test (again using XML for each step). The steps for file fuzzing might include writing the file, running the application, gathering debug data, and storing the file along with the debug data for later analysis. Note that Peach also includes some basic support for parallelization. This can be used with virtualization to great effect. The homepage for the Peach tool is www.peachfuzzer.com.

Virtualization and Fuzzing

We will be using the snapshot features of VMware and Virtual PC to create slave servers that run the application itself. We will also use a master server to control the testing, provide the entropy, and to store and record the results. The Master server need not be on the same platform type as the slave, as long as the master is able to control starting and stopping of the virtual machine slaves. Normally the master runs on the virtual machine host but this is not a requirement. Both VMware and Microsoft Virtual Server can be controlled remotely using programmatic interfaces (details below).

Choosing an Effective Starting Point

By using virtualization features such as snapshots we are able to force the application into a known starting point before each test. This allows us to make sure that testing is consistent and repeatable. There will always be some entropy in our tests such as when external sites are contacted and random numbers are generated, but these sources of entropy should be controlled and defined as much as possible during the test. They should also be considered possible targets for fuzzing. For example, if an application uses DNS to authenticate someone (a very bad idea), what would happen if the DNS server sends a corrupted response?

Using a Clean Slate

A clean slate is key to getting proper results from the testing. By "clean slate," I mean a system which has just been rebooted, the application immediately started, and nothing unrelated to the application (except the actual testing tools) is started. The environment in which the application is executed should be as pristine as possible, although this environment is certainly a possible area for fuzzing.

One area that people often neglect to clean out is environment variables. An environment variable is used to pass information to a program that it might need. Often the environment variables store information related to the local environment. For example Unix/Linux uses environment variables to locate the paths of critical files, as well as information related to the current display. These environment variables can vary on individual systems. Changing environment variables can sometimes modify the behavior of the application. This is yet another area that should be kept as consistent as possible.

Reducing Startup Time

Application fuzzing can take a significant amount of time. The key to success is having a large test bucket. The more tests attempted, the more likely it will be that something will crash. Testing should begin with the point at which the application might take malicious input. This will likely be after some amount of startup processing has occurred. Configuration files have to be read, objects instantiated, and threads created and initialized. Using virtualization we can take a snapshot of the system with the application already running and awaiting our input.

Setting Up the Debugging Tools

Although an extensive coverage of fuzzing is beyond the scope of this book, we will cover the topic to some extent. One of the key factors in fuzzing is monitoring the system to determine when the processing path is altered based on the fuzzing tests. One method is to use the built-in debugging tools provided by the system. You could rely on Windows to let you know when an exception has occurred (similar to the recovery shown in Figure 8.1) or you could install more sophisticated tools to catch the exceptions.

Figure 8.1 An Example of Windows Recovering from an Exception

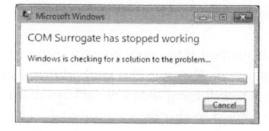

Probably the most powerful tool that I've encountered in this area is called Pai Mei. The tool was written by Pedram Amini. One of the tools in his suite is called "Process Stalker" (shown in Figure 8.2). The tool is available at www.openrce.org. The basic function of the Process Stalker is to connect to an application as a debugger, and then put breakpoints in many locations throughout the code. As the application triggers the breakpoints, the state of the application is recorded in a database, and the application is allowed to continue. Recording is then stopped and each of the breakpoints that were reached is recorded. The application is then restarted, but this time any breakpoint that was reached previously is ignored. The new breakpoints indicate events which occur as a result of the test data.

Figure 8.2 Process Stalker (Part of the Pai Mei Toolset by Pedram Amini)

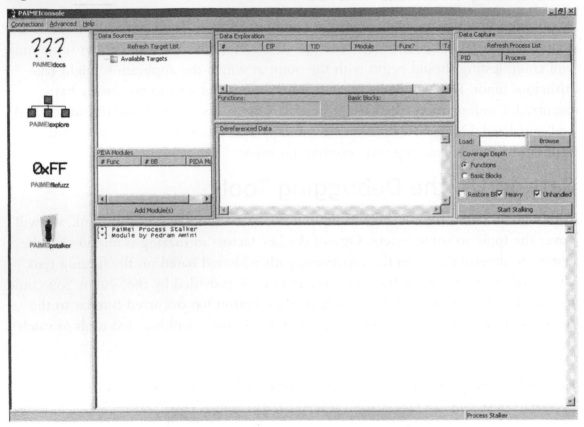

The idea behind this method is to correlate what events trigger each executable block of code in an application. By using this method in conjunction with a fuzzer, a tester can hone in on which fuzzing tests were able to reach various areas of code. These tests can then be refined so that the new areas of code are given greater testing coverage. For example, a specific application may read a file as part of its normal functioning. Depending on the first three characters of the file, different functions may be used to parse the incoming file. Process Stalker could be used to determine each of the valid file types, and then a second round of testing could be started on each individual type. Resources could be focused on testing valid file types, and the invalid file type handler. Research has also been done on ways of increasing code coverage by automatically modifying the input data. By changing the input data, and detecting changes in process flow, valid data can be "organically" grown. A paper was presented at the Blackhat conference in 2006 which discussed these methods entitled "Sidewinder: An Evolutionary Guidance System for Malicious Input Crafting."

Preparing to Take Input

In the simplest case, the application being tested is listening to a network port. The input can then be sent by the fuzzing control machine in a series of packets structured to mimic the protocols being tested. For example, if the server had implemented the file transfer protocol (FTP) then the fuzzing control machine might send packets which established the session, logged in, and then started sending specially structured gibberish in an attempt to cause the application to enter an unknown state.

Unfortunately, the simple case does not always apply. In many cases the application being tested might only initiate network traffic. Or it may not use the network at all. The fuzzing scenarios may all be file based. In these cases the fuzzing controller needs to be able to create the structured data in some other fashion.

Test files can be generated on the server. This can be a very fruitful approach. Unfortunately, using a virtual machine can cause some undesired effects. Each test should be repeatable using parameters which are stored along with the testing results. The fuzzing controller needs to have some method of "injecting" the parameters into the application from somewhere that won't be destroyed when the virtual machine snapshot is restored. The parameters need to be communicated in a way which allows the application to be exercised in the desired fashion, and that allows for maximum flexibility of structured data.

One method that we developed to facilitate this was a client/server approach. A daemon was created which listened on a network port. The fuzzing controller used a client library to send data to the daemon running on the virtual machine. The daemon then translated that data into something that the application could use. In some cases this involved mouse clicks exercising various features. It could also involve key strokes simulating a user providing input. In the most common scenario, files were transmitted onto the virtual machine. Then the application was "told" to open the files using either direct library calls, or mouse/keystroke combinations.

At one point we upgraded this fuzzing framework to use a base file on the server, and only perform particular changes. This method, also known as bit flipping, can be used to observe which areas of a file affect an application in various ways. By observing the behavior of the application, and noting differences when various portions of the file are modified, the tests can be tuned to increase code coverage and testing efficiency.

An even more complex daemon was used to test running applications. By attaching to a process, the internal memory structures of an application can be modified. This method is useful if a program uses a check summing process to detect files that have been modified. In some cases application developers have implemented these checksums as a means to prevent their applications from being fuzzed. This is a dangerous and likely ineffective way to prevent malicious data from being submitted to an application. If an attacker is able to generate the checksum for their malicious data, they will be able to bypass these checks. While it may be possible for the fuzzing framework to generate these checksums, it is unlikely that it will be an efficient use of resources. Instead the checksum routines can be bypassed or modified so that they always confirm the validity of data.

Preparing for External Interaction

We'll now discuss steps to take for preparing for an external interaction.

Taking the Snapshot

Taking the snapshot is a simple task with VMware Workstation. To take a snapshot on VMware Workstation, get the machine in a state to begin fuzzing. Then click on the "Take a snapshot of the virtual machine" button highlighted in Figure 8.3.

Figure 8.3 Create a Snapshot Button

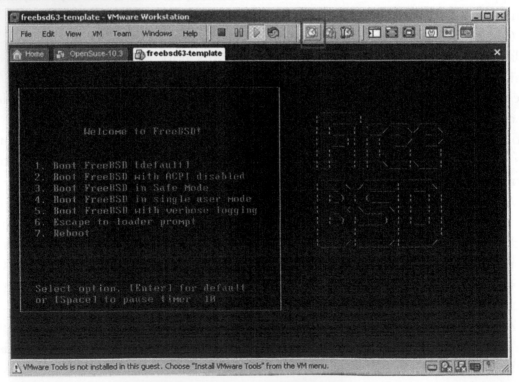

When you are creating virtual machines, especially for the scenario where an application test is to be done, the options made during setup may be critical. It is key that the environment is understood and the options documented. Tests may take place on platforms which were generated a significant time after the creation of the image. Document as much as possible, and maintain that documentation in parallel with the creation and maintenance of each image. Changing an image to be updated to current operating system patch levels should result in the documentation noting at a minimum that the machine was updated and the date and time the updates were completed. Ideally the updates performed would be updated so that each individual package version was known.

Executing the Test

We'll now discuss steps to take for executing the test.

Scripting Snapshot Startup

Snapshot control can also be done from the command line in the host environment. On the VMware Server this can be done with the vmrun command. The command shown in Figure 8.4 will list all of the virtual machines on a server. In each of the figures shown below, the root password has been covered by a white box.

Figure 8.4 Listing the Registered Virtual Machines

Then the command shown in Figure 8.5 can be issued to create a snapshot from the command line.

Figure 8.5 Taking a Snapshot of a Virtual Machine

```
~/myth                                                              _|□|x|
myth:~ # vmrun -T server -h https://localhost:8333/sdk -u root -p ▓▓▓▓ snapshot "[] /s
tore/disk5/vmware/Virtual Machines/WindowsXP/Windows XP Professional.vmx"
myth:~ #
```

And finally when you want to revert to a snapshot, issue the command shown in Figure 8.6.

Figure 8.6 Reverting the Machine Back to a Snapshot

```
~/myth                                                              _|□|x|
myth:~ # vmrun -T server -h https://localhost:8333/sdk -u root -p ▓▓▓▓ revertToSnapsho
t "[] /store/disk5/vmware/Virtual Machines/WindowsXP/Windows XP Professional.vmx"
myth:~ #
```

Note that the application will come up in a suspended state. To resume from the suspended state issue the command shown in Figure 8.7.

Figure 8.7 Resuming Execution on a Suspended Machine

```
~/myth                                                              _|□|x|
myth:~ # vmrun -T server -h https://localhost:8333/sdk -u root -p ▓▓▓▓ start "[] /stor
e/disk5/vmware/Virtual Machines/WindowsXP/Windows XP Professional.vmx"
myth:~ #
```

Interacting with the Application

At this point the daemon we created comes into play. The fuzzing framework needs to create test data and communicate that data to the virtual machine. In the case of network applications this might mean only connecting to the network port and sending a series of packets. As mentioned above, the testing may also consist of modifying files to be opened by the application. In this case the fuzzing framework would submit either the test file itself or the changes which are to be performed on a base file. In each case the test data should be saved on the fuzzing control machine so that the testing can be replicated in the event that the data somehow triggers an "interesting" condition.

Selecting Test Data

Entire books have been written on the theory of fuzzing and how to choose data. We refer to fuzzing data as "structured" gibberish. There is always some chance that random data might cause issues with an application. Given enough time the proverbial million monkeys might just be able to type out a Shakespearean play. Unfortunately, application tests rarely have such generous testing schedules (and even if they did, the human resources wouldn't appreciate it). Instead, a more efficient method of creating data that is mostly correct should be used.

One great source when attempting to create interesting test data is to base it on valid data which is captured while exercising the application in a standard manner. This valid data is then used as a base from which tests can be generated. Once the valid data is captured, and a method for injecting data of the fuzzer's choosing is created, the testing can begin.

Strings within the data should be changed. They can be made longer or shorter, they can be zero padded, or the file might be truncated. Various malicious strings might be inserted in an attempt to cause the application to perform in a new manner. Integers contained within the data should be changed. Perhaps adding a "1" to the number will cause unique code to be executed. In other cases the application may not be expecting negative or very large numbers. Bit fields should be tested to determine the functionality of each bit. Structures within the data may be modified, or reordered in an attempt to create unique scenarios.

In some cases entirely different file types may be tested. Some applications have internal logic which is executed depending on the type of the file. In some cases the file type might be determined by the extension of the file. In other cases the file type might be determined by the presence of certain strings at the beginning of the file. Alternate file types should be tested in order to achieve maximum code coverage.

Similar procedures should also be performed on network protocols. In addition the out-of-order arrival (both at the packet and application levels) should be investigated. How is the application affected if a packet performing function two is sent before the packet calling function one which normally arrives first?

It is probably becoming obvious that creating useful test data often requires investigation into the inner workings of the program. Luckily, tools have been created which can greatly aid in this process.

Checking for Exceptions

The next important function of a fuzzing framework is to detect whether interesting behavior has occurred. In its simplest form, this interesting behavior might only be that the application terminates. This may or may not generate debugging information such as memory dumps, stack traces, and log files In other cases the application may execute non standard code paths. It may have error recovery logic, or it may terminate the processing of the offending data. Each of these cases can possibly be interesting to the fuzzer, and in many instances these error states can be used to create more useful test data.

Debuggers can be used to observe whether an application has generated an exception. Ideally these exceptions will be detected before any exception handling routines are called. This gives the fuzzer the best chance to know what data was invalid. This information can be used to create test data uniquely formed to exercise the entire breadth of the exception handling routines. It can also be used to create data which doesn't trigger the exception routines.

One of the most powerful tools I've seen for observing code execution paths is a tool called Pai Mei. One of the components of Pai Mei is called Process stalker. The main idea behind Pai Mei is to attach to a process as a debugger. Using procedure information generated from the disassembly of a process, a breakpoint is set on every function. A breakpoint is an instruction which when executed by the processor an exception is generated. This exception will suspend the applications execution and allow the debugger to investigate. The debugger has access to the state of the processor. It can see and change things like what each register is set to and which flags are set. The debugger can also examine and possibly modify the contents of memory.

When Pai Mei gains control because a breakpoint is hit, it records which function was accessed in a database. It also saves the parameters of the function when it is called. It then returns control of the running process. The result is a list of functions that were called during that run. The power of Process Stalker arises when one begins to use sets of functions as filters. The tester will determine which functions are called during set up and then data is submitted. Any functions related to the setup of the machine are removed, and the remaining functions are related to processing the test data. In addition, any functions resulting in exceptions are noted.

Saving the Results

A special consideration when using virtual machines for fuzzing is for any data generated during the test to be preserved. Ideally the only data required to replicate the results of the test would be the test data submitted via the fuzzing framework. In the real world, sometimes other uncontrolled factors may play a part in the abnormal condition. For the sake of convenience, memory dumps, and stack traces should be preserved for further analysis as well. There are two ways to do this. First of all a script can be written which gathers pertinent logs, dumps and data. It should then package them up, and submit them (possibly via the fuzzing framework) for archival purposes. This script should be triggerable by the fuzzing framework.

The second method which could be implemented (and likely the simplest), is to save the results in the form of a virtual machine snapshot. This snapshot should be backed up and saved along with the test data which created the abnormal scenario.

Running Concurrent Tests

All of this automation can be extended one step further. One of the greatest efficiencies that can be realized by using virtualization is parallelization. Multiple machines can each run scenarios at once. This allows the fuzzing framework to control multiple servers at once. The efficiency gains are obvious.

To set up a concurrent test the base machine is created as above. There are some additional issues that need to be addressed. The first problem is the sheer factor of putting two identical machines into the same environment. There are certain parameters of a machine that need to be unique in order for the machine to exist in an environment with other machines. One example that many people are familiar with would be the IP address. One of the benefits of DHCP is that machines can request an IP address that isn't being used on the network. DHCP uses an identifier that is supposed to be unique to the machine (namely the mac address). When you make a copy of a virtual machine these unique identifiers are sometimes left unchanged.

Two strategies can be used to make this manageable. First of all, some of the parameters can be modified in the configuration of the virtual machine. Other parameters only become a factor when the machine is used in a domain environment which may not be a requirement for your testing.

The other strategy that can be employed is to have separate environments for each machine being tested in much the same way the sandbox scenarios of previous chapters were implemented. This would likely include separate virtual networks.

Virtual machine hosting server would have to either host the fuzzing platform or provide routing services into the various testing networks.

One factor that should be noted is that the fact that you're working from a snapshot can be a great asset. It should only be necessary to save the differential disk files after a test. Further these differential disks can likely be compressed significantly. It is key to remember not to modify the original virtual disk files, or the snapshots being used will become useless.

Summary

By using virtualization the efficiency of a fuzzing test can be vastly increased and by using snapshots every test can begin in the same place making repeatable tests much more likely. Testing initialization is a matter of restoring a snapshot, instead of rebooting the server, restarting an application, and waiting for it all to settle. It is also much easier to gather the data for fuzzing tests which have resulted in interesting behaviors Finally, the value of parallelization cannot be understated. An efficient way to have multiple tests running concurrently with identical environments can dramatically cut the time required for testing.

Solutions Fast Track

What Is Fuzzing?

☑ Fuzzing is sending causing an application to process semi-random data in order to test the application's behavior.

Virtualization and Fuzzing

☑ Virtualization can assist in fuzzing by isolating the test machine from the test management server.

☑ Snapshots can be used to increase testing efficiency by reducing startup and cleanup time.

☑ Virtual machines can be used to perform multiple tests in parallel.

Choosing an Effective Starting Point

☑ By choosing an effective starting point, all tests can be started from a consistent point.

☑ Debugging tools should already be in place and running.

☑ The application should have already completed its initialization routines, and be ready for our test input.

Preparing for External Interaction

☑ A snapshot can be taken either manually—using the virtual machine console—or scripted using a command line interface or API.

Executing the Test

☑ Revert to the starting point snapshot.

☑ Send the test input.

☑ Monitor for exceptions.

☑ Record the results.

Frequently Asked Questions

Q: Why does fuzzing work?

A: Ideally fuzzing will have little to no effect on an application. The idea that random data that is so unstructured can damage an application is sad, but unfortunately true in many cases. Fuzzing has proven to be effective at finding issues with applications which developers missed, and testing scenarios were unable to catch.

Q: How do you know when you've got a good starting point?

A: If you find yourself having to execute the same steps before you can get to the point of running your test (such as starting a debugging tool, etc.), you should consider running that step by hand and then taking the snapshot.

Chapter 9

Forensic Analysis

Solutions in this chapter:

- Preparing Your Forensic Environment

- Capturing the Machine

- Preparing the Captured Machine to Boot on New Hardware

- What Can Be Gained by Booting the Captured Machine?

☑ Summary

☑ Solutions Fast Track

☑ Frequently Asked Questions

Introduction

According to Bologna and Lindquist (*Fraud Auditing and Forensic Accounting: New Tools and Technique,* John Wiley & Sons Inc., 1995), the term *forensic* means "belonging to, used in, or suitable to courts of judicature or to public discussion and debate." The College of American Pathologists, in *Handbook of Forensic Pathology,* 1990, defines forensics as "the application of the principles of the physical sciences in the search for truth in civil, criminal, and social behavioral matters to the end that injustices shall not be done to any member of society." Kruse and Heiser, authors of *Computer Forensics. Incident Response Essentials,* Addison–Wesley, Boston 2001, defined computer forensics as the "coherent application of methodical investigatory techniques to solve crime cases." For the purposes of this chapter, I choose to expand the definition by Kruse and Heiser to include the use of methodical investigatory techniques to gather intelligence as well as evidence and to include the use of these techniques for civil cases as well as in investigating policy violations and intrusions. This approach speaks to the "search for truth in civil, criminal, and social behavioral matters to the end that injustices shall not be done to any member of society" portion of the pathologists' definition of forensics. As will be shown, criminal cases will benefit from the availability and use of techniques made possible by virtualization as long as the rigors required by the courts are observed when collecting the evidence to be presented.

Investigating computer crime can be a very involved process. The first rule of forensics work is that the evidence must be preserved. Common forensics practice is to make an image of all media from a computer. All disks are copied using great care not to modify the data contained on the disks. All work pertaining to the investigation is then performed using these forensically sound copies of the data. It is equally important that the results of forensic examination be reproducible. Steve Mancini, a security professional with extensive forensic experience for Intel, says the investigator should be able to hand another investigator a copy of the image and a copy of his notes. The second investigation should lead to the same empirical results and (hopefully) the same assertions that were originally made about that image.

Virtualization is well suited to working on a copy of a hard drive without modifying it. In the days prior to virtualization, this process required the investigator to clone the hard drive, put the clone into new hardware, and boot. From the time of that first boot, the investigator couldn't be sure that his "cloned image" was still good. Anytime the investigator had any suspicion that the clone was tainted, it meant that the clone had to be recopied from a known good copy. This was a time-consuming process and one the defense attorney might challenge. The defense attorney would not have to prove that the integrity of the clone was lost, only that the potential for it to be lost was possible.

This chapter will illustrate the process of turning a copy of a drive into something that an investigator can use with confidence, knowing that he can get back to the original state with the push of a button. By using a virtual machine, the contents of the machine can be viewed in the same ways that the suspect viewed them. The chapter will also discuss the concept of "best evidence," the acceptability of evidence obtained from virtual instances of a suspect's computer, and will describe a method proposed by Derek Bem and Ewa Huebner, University of Western Sydney, Australia, that combines traditional methods with virtual technology to gain the benefits of virtualization and still meet the rigors expected by the courts.

Preparing Your Forensic Environment

Before capturing the suspect's machine and creating images, you should prepare a computer for use as your forensic system. The computer should be the fastest computer you can find, with USB 2.0 ports, firewire, or the ability to connect IDE, SATA, or PATA drives without opening the case; a large, fast internal hard drive; and a large enough external hard drive to house several of the biggest hard drives found in your environment. If you are working in a forensic lab where you can segregate your networks, the hard drives could be networked drives or SANS. These hard drives should be single-purpose and should not be used for any other storage. When cases are removed from the hard drive, you will want to use a secure delete utility such as sdelete for Windows; Shred (RHEL), gshred (Solaris), or scrub (erase partition) for Unix; or the Secure Empty Trash option on a Mac, to ensure that no vestigial data remains. In some cases (for example, cases involving government-classified "above secret" or cases where you attempt to recover previously overwritten data) you should use new hard drives for each case. Some have argued that every case requires new hard drives.

The computer and your VM environment should be secured against external and internal attacks, and particularly attacks from within the virtual system. For VMware you can find guidance for this process in the VMware security guide or in the *ESX Server Security Technical Implementation Guide* produced by the Defense Information Systems Agency in April 2008. Once you have secured the system, it will be useful to create a Live-CD of the system similar to the one created by Ernie Baca.

Baca developed the Penguin Sleuth Kit and later made a VMware version and placed the VM appliance and documentation on the VMware site, www.vmware.com/vmtn/appliances/directory/249/. Once the system is assembled, you should create an inventory of all systems, applications, and hardware used. This inventory should be placed under configuration control so that as you make changes you will simultaneously update the documentation. Each case file should include a copy of the inventory document as it existed during the investigation (for reproduceability).

To be effective and to limit challenges you must be able to build and update the Live-CD as patches are made available for the software you use.

Capturing the Machine

You can convert physical media to virtual media using tools like the VMware Converter and Virtual Machine Manager (VMM). When going from physical media to virtual, these products require the source system to be running and thus cannot create a forensically sound image. When creating a forensically sound image, you must be able to prove that the image is an exact duplicate or that you can explain any and all differences and how they occurred. You can create a forensically sound image and then convert the image to a virtual system. This becomes an issue when you have very large cases with many hard drives. Simson Garfinkel describes this in a 2006 presentation to Black Hat entitled "New Directions in Disk Forensics." In the presentation he describes the difficulties he faced processing hundreds of hard drives using traditional forensic methods and the solution he designed. Garfinkel developed a new image format called Advanced Forensic Format (AFF). A benefit of the format is that it is designed to help the investigator to handle very large hard drives and is able to handle cases with many hard drives. It does this by keeping metadata about a drive with the drive data and by segmenting the drive into manageable chunks. Traditional forensics requires us to image an entire drive, making it nearly impossible to perform forensics on Terabyte and above hard drives. Harlan Carvey and Dave Kleiman in *Windows Forensic Analysis* (Syngress, 2008) provide an excellent example. "Imagine a RAID system with five or eight such hard drives, topping out at 6 terabytes (TB) of storage. How long would it take you to image those hard drives? With certain configurations, it can take investigators four or more hours to acquire and verify a single 80-GB hard drive. And would you need to image the entire system if you were interested in only the activities of a single process and not in the thousands of files resident on the system?" To address this type of situation, Kleiman and Carvey propose the use of two techniques, Live Response and Live Acquisition. In Live Response, the investigator accesses a live, running system and collects volatile and nonvolatile information. Live Acquisition creates an image of a hard drive while the system is still running. These two techniques challenge the present-day "best practices" in order to solve problems that can't be solved using traditional forensic techniques.

In order to reduce the potential for "junk science" challenges to forensic tools (see "Junk Science Legal Challenge Explained," by Mike Anderson, founder of New Technologies, Inc., www.forensics-intl.com/def14.html), NIST produced a set of test specifications (Digital Imaging Tool Specifications) that were intended to be used to validate the tools used to produce disk images for use in courts. The specifications ensure that disk imaging tools that produce images in the traditional method actually deliver a forensically sound image, but in doing so, they preclude any newer technology from consideration. Make no mistake, the specification and the testing is very valuable for the forensic community. The test reports for disk imaging systems that have been tested so far can be found here (www.cftt.nist. gov/disk_imaging.htm).

This means, unless you take on the challenge of explaining to the court how and why your tools and procedures preserve the integrity of the original drive, at least for now, traditional means (preferably one of the systems tested by NIST above) should be used to created the forensically sound image. If you are faced with a situation that can only be met using nontraditional forensic techniques, Kleiman and Carvey prescribe an application of Locard's exchange principle. In essence, you would research the changes that occur to a system because of the chosen technique so that these changes can be explained and defended. If your find yourself in this position, I recommend you read "The Tools 'Proven In Court' Question" (www.csisite.net/tpicq.htm), a treatise by Steve Hailey, President/CEO of CyberSecurity Institute.

Icove, Seger, and VonStorch in 1995 described three rules for maintaining the reliability of electronic evidence: "It must be produced, maintained, and used in a normal environment; be professionally authenticated (i.e. the report from the forensic experts is reliable); and also meet the 'best evidence rule.' This means that what is produced must be the best evidence available and not a substitute for the evidence offered." In a simple example, when an original photo exists, you cannot use a copy of the photo as evidence.

Notes from the Good Guys...

RFC 3227 Guidance on Good Evidence

RFC 3227 describes legal considerations related to gathering evidence. "Computer evidence needs to be

- **Admissible:** It must conform to certain legal rules before it can be put before a court.
- **Authentic:** It must be possible to positively tie evidentiary material to the incident.
- **Complete:** It must tell the whole story and not just a particular perspective.
- **Reliable:** There must be nothing about how the evidence was collected and subsequently handled that casts doubt about its authenticity and veracity.
- **Believable:** It must be readily believable and understandable by a court."

If virtual images do not represent "best evidence," can they still be useful in a civil or criminal case? In some civil cases, the attorneys will accept copies of relevant files without requiring forensically sound images, but as an investigator you can't expect that will happen. It is likely that the use of virtual instances, surrounded by best practices to ensure that integrity is maintained throughout the virtualization and forensic processes, will eventually be accepted by the courts. In the process of getting images of the suspect's computer to run in a virtual environment, changes are made to system files to reflect the differences between the virtual environment and the real hardware. A case can be made that the content portions of the image are unchanged, a fact that can be verified by comparing hashes (MD5 or SHA-2) made from files on the original hard drive. Once forensic professionals have a good understanding of the changes that occur when virtualizing a suspect's computer and we have developed an easy to understand means of explaining these changes to a judge, jury, and opposing expert witnesses, we should be able to use results from forensic examinations in court. In the meantime, Bem and Huebner suggest using the virtual environment to locate data of interest and the forensically sound copy of the suspect's drive to extract the evidence for the court.

The suspect's computer can be captured and converted to a virtual image either directly from the suspect's computer (or a clone of that drive), or from an image file taken from the suspect's computer (or a clone). The Hillsboro (Oregon) Police Department Computer Forensic lab is run by Police Reserve Specialists (PRS). The PRS are information security professionals with a background in computer forensics who volunteer their time to run the forensic lab and perform other duties. They've been exploring procedures for creating VM files using full images or just relevant partitions. They begin by creating a new VM, selecting the same operating system as the suspect's drive, and on the Specify Disk Capacity page, instructing VMware to "allocate all space now" rather than later. This creates a set of files that can be modified for the specific image you intend to virtualize.

The HPD Computer forensics lab uses an Ultrablock disk write blocker when creating images. Prior to making the image of the suspect's drive they will verify that the write blocker blocks writes and that the imager makes good images. Then they either image the suspect's entire drive or they image the Master Boot Record (MBR) and any relevant partitions to individual files. The byte space value should be set to 512 to produce records in the form needed by VMware.

In VMware Workstation, they edit the text file ending in ".vmdk" and the ". vmx" file related to your VM. In the ".vmdk" file, under the "# Extent description" heading, in the first line highlighted below, replace the string in quotes with the name of your MBR image file. In the second line, replace the string in quotes with the name of your partition image file. Both of these filenames and the filename and display name parameters in the "./vmx" file should be named using a standard that helps you manage the cases. HPD includes the Serial Number of the original hard drive in every filename. You should add the second line if it doesn't already exist. For both lines, replace the number at the end with the number of records that were copied with "dd".

In "The Disk Data Base" section, replace the ddb.geometry.cylinder value with the actual number of cylinders from the original physical hard disk.

```
Sample .vmdk file

# Disk DescriptorFile
version = 1
CID = 2734fd20
parentCID = ffffffff
createType = "monolithicFlat"
```

```
# Extent description
RW 4194304 FLAT "Windows XP Professional-flat.vmdk" 0

# The Disk Data Base
#DDB

ddb.virtualHWVersion = "4"
ddb.geometry.cylinders = "4161"
ddb.geometry.heads = "16"
ddb.geometry.sectors = "63"
ddb.adapterType = "ide"
```

Edit the ".vmx" file, to modify or add the entry labeled Ide0.0.mode.
Ide0:0.mode = "independent-nonpersistent"

This setting prevents changes in the VM from affecting the raw disk image.

```
Sample .vmx file

config.version = "8"
virtualHW.version = "4"
scsi0.present = "TRUE"
memsize = "256"
ide0:0.present = "TRUE"
ide0:0.fileName = "Windows XP Professional.vmdk"
        ide0:0.deviceType = "disk"
        ide0:0.mode = "persistent"
ide1:0.present = "TRUE"
ide1:0.fileName = "auto detect"
ide1:0.deviceType = "cdrom-raw"
floppy0.present = "FALSE"
displayName = "Windows XP Professional"
guestOS = "winxppro"
priority.grabbed = "normal"
priority.ungrabbed = "normal"
```

If the ide0.0.mode entry is not present, add both of the following entries after the
ide0.0.fileName entry.

> ide0:0.deviceType = "disk"
>
> ide0:0.mode = "independent-nonpersistent"

An easier alternative is to use Live View (http://liveview.sourceforge.net/),
see Figure 9.1, to create the above files. Live View is a utility developed by Brian
Kaplan of the CERT (Computer Emergency Response Team) for converting raw
disks and images into VMs for VMware. With Live View you can connect a cloned
drive or an image file created with dd, FTK, Encase, etc. Live View supports *.img,
*.dd, *.raw and {split} images. Live View will use the source to create the necessary
VMware files.

Figure 9.1 Live View P2V

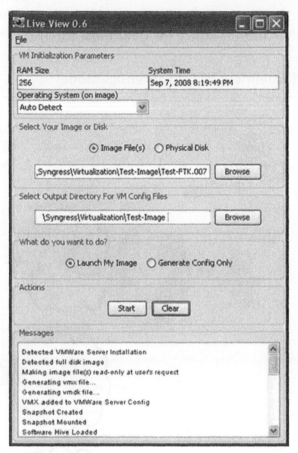

After creating the files, Live View will start up VMware and boot the Suspect's virtual computer. Because this is a virtual environment, Windows will make some changes to the system files reflecting the differences in peripherals that were attached to the suspect's computer. The content should be provably unchanged, as observed above. In the days before virtualization, the investigator would need to make a new forensically sound copy every time there was any danger that the copy they were working with had been modified. With virtualization you can refresh the copy you are working with any time with the press of a button. Using the method described by Derek Bem and Ewa Huebner, University of Western Sydney, Australia, in "Computer Forensic Analysis in a Virtual Environment" (see Figure 9.2), the investigator would make two clones of the original drive. The diagram includes the four phases of computer forensics (Access, Acquire, Analyze, and Report) as described by Kruse and Heiser in Computer Forensics: Incident Response Essentials. The access phase is not relevant to the chapter and is mostly a concern of law enforcement (warrant preparation, etc.). In the Acquire phase, you would produce two images, one to be used to create a VM and the other for traditional forensics.

Figure 9.2 Bem and Huebner's Hybrid Forensics Model

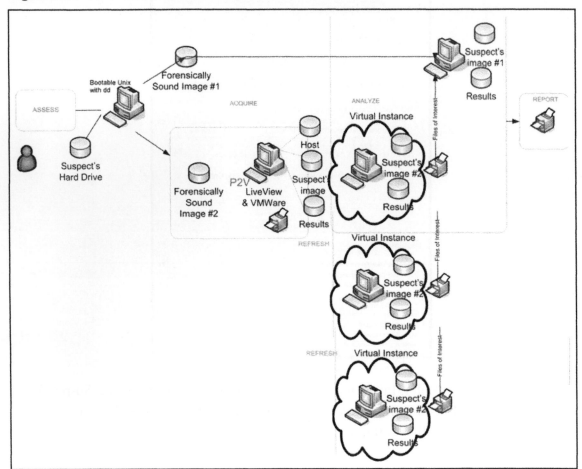

Preparing the Captured Machine to Boot on New Hardware

Once you have created an image, you should generate an MD5 or SHA-2 checksum for the image. Compare this checksum to the one you generated using the original drive. Place all of these files, images, and the original drive under chain of custody rigors. One of the images would be stored safely until after the virtualization analysis was complete. The other would be placed into the virtual environment using one of the P2V tools like Live View. If you don't have the password to the suspect's computer, you can reboot the Virtual Machine (VM) and change the BIOS settings to boot using a CD. Then put NTPasswd (http://home.eunet.no/~pnordahl/ntpasswd/), or whatever Crack utility you use, in the CD drive and reboot. Use NTPasswd to set the Administrator password to blank or another password. Then remove the CD and reboot into the suspect's VM. Once VMware has configured the monitor and peripherals you will want to save a snapshot so that you can refresh back to this point.

What Can Be Gained by Booting the Captured Machine?

In Bem and Huebner's model, the Analyze phase is split into two parts. Initial analysis is performed in the virtual environment. Traditional methods of gathering most evidence involve extracting data from static image files. Gathering dynamic or time dependent evidence required the investigator to create forensically sound work images, which had to be re-created many times to ensure the image you were working had not been modified by any previous procedures. Today's large-capacity hard drives have made this approach problematic. However, with virtual machines, the investigator can restore the image to its original state by saving the original image when it is first booted. A touch of the refresh button is all it takes to get a clean image. In addition, in some virtual systems, restore points can be set at critical times so that a sequence can begin at any point in a process and can be repeated as many times as necessary to document every aspect of the behavior of interest. Using the same tools as the suspect, interesting information can be identified and then retrieved from the image that was created for the traditional forensic approach. Using the VM, we can use tools that are normally used by first responders to incidents. Many of our virus infection or bot client cases start as potential computer crime cases until we can determine the potential damage or intent. At Portland State University, we use the RAPIER tool developed by Steve Mancini and Joe Schwendt from Intel. The RAPIER tool is adapted from a tool called Rapier that is used internally in Intel to collect a consistent set of data from a machine that is involved in an incident no matter where in the world the incident occurs and regardless of the skill of the first responder. In our case, we are able to have the Desktop Support

Techs (DST) gather this information as part of normal response to suspected bot clients or virus-infected systems. Using this information we are able to determine the identity of other infected machines by examining security event and firewall logs. We also learn about the ports that are opened on the system by the malicious code. Sometimes the anti-virus logs will identify files associated with a bot client or dates and times that it found malicious or suspicious files. This information can then be used by the information security team to search for other files that may be related to or affected by the malicious code. The results of the RAPIER run are examined by the Information security team. The logs may indicate a need for deeper forensics.

In many cases the investigator might want to use some Unix tools and also some Windows tools. Because of the traditional forensics requirement to ensure that no changes are introduced to the image, every time you switch between operating systems you would have to ensure you still had a clean image. With a VM, you can refresh your image with the touch of a button and then restart the VM. To boot into Unix, you can load a Helix (www.e-fense.com/helix/) or your favorite bootable CD in the CD drive, change the bios settings for the VM to boot by CD, and then use your favorite Unix forensics tools. When you are done you can refresh the image, then reboot the VM back into windows. The Helix CD also contains powerful Windows-based forensics tools to make Windows-centric forensic analysis easier and more effective. In addition some System Internals tools (http://technet.microsoft.com/en-us/sysinternals/) provide more information in the GUI than what is captured in the command line version. For example, process explorer highlights packed images in purple. The presence of a packed image executing on a system is a red flag that should be investigated. Unfortunately, pslist, the command line version of process explorer, does not record this kind of information. In fact, pslist does not record the detail that can be collected in the property tabs of process explorer. Thanks to the virtual environment, investigators can use the GUI tools without fear of contaminating the image.

Tools & Traps...

RAPIER: Rapid Assessment and Potential Incident Examination Report

Originally designed by Steve Mancini and Joe Schwendt of Intel® to be used by remote first responders (or by Unix administrators investigating a Windows machine) to gather and forward a consistent set of information about suspected incidents to trained investigators. RAPIER can be found on Google Code (http://code.google.com/p/rapier/). RAPIER is highly configurable. It provides an interactive interface, a set of command line parameters, and .conf files that can be used to specify which tests to run, email addresses for investigators, and ip addresses of a central RAPIER server. In a 2006 presentation to FIRST (Forum for Incident Response and Security Teams), the developers claimed, "RAPIER is not a forensics tool. It does not honor most industry guidelines for a proper forensics examination with regard to not affecting the image or files upon the system." However, in a virtual environment, RAPIER becomes a powerful tool for forensics, for two reasons. If the investigator has established a clean snapshot, then investigators need only refresh the image to the clean snapshot following a RAPIER run. In addition, one of the reports that RAPIER provides is a report of the system prior to the run and all changes that were made during the run.

The reports produced in the virtual environment are used to develop the list of information that is to be harvested from the traditional forensic process's image. The final report phase is drawn from the evidence that is retrieved from the traditional forensic image. In this way we gain the benefit of using the suspect's machine, programs, and data to find and interpret information but are still able to present "best evidence" to the courts.

The following are examples of ways that virtualization can add value to investigations.

Virtualization May Permit You to Observe Behavior That Is Only Visible While Live

When Windows starts, there are a myriad of places that can contain instructions to be executed upon startup. Looking in each location that can contain startup instructions and trying to interpret what those text and binary instructions might do is next to impossible. However, if you could boot the system in a virtual instance, you might be able to tell easily that the malicious code you were investigating had replaced the background with a fake security alert. In addition, you run the system and collect network information from the network about open ports and network connections that are initiated or accepted. You can add tools that can look for and interpret information on VM running the suspect's image.

Using the System to Demonstrate the Meaning of the Evidence

Sometimes the data that is collected in the traditional forensic manner, while accurate and the best evidence, is not easily understood by jurors or the courts. Using a VM, the investigator or attorney can demonstrate the interpretation of the data using the programs on the suspect's image. Seeing the movie is much more meaningful for jurors than looking at printed copies of the associated binary. While the binary printout may be the actual evidence, using a demonstration can give the evidence meaning. The same is true of programs that use proprietary formats for data storage. Without the programs to interpret the data, the actual file content isn't very useful for convincing a judge or jury.

The System May Have Proprietary/ Old Files That Require Special Software

You can look at files using the suspect's programs (MS Word, Excel, etc) that can interpret them. If the suspect is using a program that is no longer available, you can and should use the copy of the program that is on the suspect's image. The program you need may even be a program developed by the suspect that can't be obtained anywhere else.

Analyzing Time Bombs and Booby Traps

If an application is booby-trapped you will be able to examine and analyze (without suffering) the effects of the trap, then refresh the image. In 2006, Frederic T. Chong of the University of California Santa Barbara (UCSB) and a team of researchers from the University of California at Davis (UCSD), Jedidiah Crandall, Gary Wassermann, Daniela de Oliveira. Zhendon Su, and S. Felix Wu, authored material about using VMs to detect malware time bombs. The paper, entitled "Temporal Search: Detecting Hidden Malware Timebombs with Virtual Machines," describes a technique to find malicious code that is set to trigger at a specific time or a specified relative time, by manipulating time for a VM. Just changing the time wouldn't find malware like the Kama Sutra worm that deletes the victims files on the 3rd day of every month; it only checks the day of the month after the initial infection or a reboot. Instead, their approach (in a greatly simplified explanation) changes the rate of time and watches for correlations with rate of updates to each physical memory location. They analyze these physical memory locations to determine which ones are legitimate timers and which are suspect. It is hoped that analysis of these timers will yield the target time in advance of the trigger date/time.

Easier to Get in the Mind-Set of the Suspect

Even the investigator can benefit from seeing the data in the same context as the suspect would have viewed it. Without proper context, we may interpret files as sinister that are in fact innocent when viewed in context. In gathering potential evidence regarding a case where it was suspected that an employee was using company systems to distribute hardcore pornography internationally, an investigator searched through the image for keywords that might reveal files related to the case. One of the sets of files that turned up in the keyword search had the phrase "sexchange" in the directory and several filenames, which was duly reported to superiors. Imagine the investigators' embarrassment when they later examined the files and discovered they were msexchange files, that's right, Microsoft Exchange. While Exchange may be a dirty word to some, it is hardly pornographic.

Sometimes we gain additional insights just by seeing the data as it is displayed by the program used by the suspect. The data displayed in the context of explanatory headings, the look and feel of the application, help you to see what the suspect saw when using the system. There are tools available that operate in a Windows environment that will interpret the contents of index.dat files to reveal Internet access history and cookies even if the user has deleted the history and cache.

Collecting Intelligence about Botnets or Virus-Infected Systems

Using virtualization to execute the code on a suspected bot client or virus-infected system permits the investigator to gather valuable insights about the workings of malicious code. From the security event log you can see any attempts to guess passwords using brute force. You also find the identity of other bot clients that are involved in the brute force attacks. Using the firewall logs you see any inbound-opens that have been attempted. You can learn the identity of websites that delivered malicious code by looking at the firewall logs around the time of the malware detection. Watching network traffic from the suspect computer, you can identify ports opened by malicious code and the ip addresses of other parts of the botnet. These other parts of the botnet may be providing malicious code, such as retroviruses, to kill off your anti-virus protection, or lists of email addresses and spam templates. If the bot client uses Internet Relay Chat (IRC) you may find the Command and Control server, nick, userid, and password. You can then use this information to detect other infected computers in your organization and prevent future communications with the mother ship.

Locating the actual malware is a primary goal of a forensic examination of a bot client or virus-infected computer. Chapter 6, "Malware Analysis," describes the process of running code samples in a sandbox to perform malware analysis.

Collecting Intelligence about a Case

When investigators gather evidence, they must ensure that no unexplained changes occur to the suspect's computer. If the goal of the examination is to gather intelligence rather than evidence, the VM can be used without restraint. The investigator must take pains to ensure that information gathered during an intelligence gathering run does not mix with information gathered as evidence. In these circumstances the investigator can use institution and even hearsay to suggest keywords for searches or other settings in the suspect's computer, using the VM to check out "what if?" scenarios. The intelligence may then suggest a set of information that can be gathered in a traditional manner that may be used as evidence.

Capturing Processes and Data in Memory

Today's malware is frequently delivered in packaged (compressed and encrypted) form. In order to run it needs to decrypt itself. To make interception more difficult, malware performs the decryption and execution in memory. However, in a VM you can force the VM to write all of its memory space to a file by pausing the VM. The contents of a .vmss file will contain the contents of physical memory when the pause button is pushed.

When paused, the VM will create a file whose extension will be ".vmss" (Virtual Machine Suspended State). This file will contain the contents of memory at the time the VM execution was suspended. The investigator can then use tools like strings to search through memory for key words. The tool process explorer, part of the System Internals suite of tools, provides a limited but useful means of peeking at memory. For each process running in your VM, process explorer can display associated properties. One tab permits the investigator to examine the strings in the file, both in the file and in memory. Running process explorer from a utility drive in your VM permits you to examine process specific strings without affecting the forensic copy. Once you have found something of interest, you can use the pause feature of VMware to capture all of memory. Then you can show that the information you found with process explorer exists in the memory space.

Performing Forensics of a Virtual Machine

More and more organizations are using virtualization in the data center. It is inevitable that a virtual system will be involved in a case requiring forensic analysis. How would you go about acquiring a forensically sound image of a VM? You could extract an image of the full physical hard drive of the host VM server. That could be a tremendous waste of time and storage space. These systems tend to be very large with multiple multi-Terabyte hard drives or SANs. They have to be large enough to provide storage for several machines or there is no point in using the technology.

Edward Haletky, a columnist for *IT World* magazine, recommends copying (not imaging) the VM files related to the suspect VM and associated image files to media that can be secured for chain of custody. This approach should work for all cases except for those where the virtualization server is being used to corrupt or influence its VMs. The image file used by the VM contains all of the slack space and unallocated space from the original computer, so if the suspect activity is in the original computer, then copies of the image file and the associated VM files should be sufficient.

However, if there is any possibility of the specter of corruption or influence from outside the VM affecting the files, then the files should be imaged instead of copied. Is it sufficient to image just the files related to the VM or is it necessary to image the entire Virtual server? If the VM was bigger at one time and has shrunk, you may want more than just the existing VM file system (VMFS). These topics are still being debated by forensic professionals, but it is likely that the answer will be driven by the specifics of each case.

When copying the VM from VMware, Mr. Haletky recommends grabbing the .vm* files in same directory as the target VM's vmdk file. You should also copy the file that is listed in the .vmx configuration file as "ide0:0.fileName =" If listed, this file is the original image file used to create the VM.

The .vmdk files (Virtual Machine DisK) are the primary VM files. They document the virtual environment and how it is stored. The *-delta.vmdk is produced when you take a snapshot. When the snapshot is taken, VM stops writing to *-flat.vmdk and begins writing to the differential file *-delta.vmdk. This file would be helpful in determining the changes that occurred on the VM following a snapshot, if one had tools to interpret the information. The VM also creates a .vmsn (Virtual Memory SNapshot file), which contains the contents of memory when the snapshot was taken. As described earlier, the VM produces a .vmss (Virtual Machine Suspended State file) when the VM is paused.

Acquiring the files is just the beginning, as Mr. Haletky reminds us in "Virtual Server Investigations: VM Forensic Tools Remain MIA," an online article in the July 28, 2008 *CIO* magazine. Once the files are acquired, the investigator faces the problem of the lack of accepted VM forensic tools, processes and procedures.

Unless and until these tools, processes, and procedures are created, it will be up to each of us to solve the problems we encounter when working cases involving VMs, and in the process, to develop the very tools we are seeking.

We have only begun to scratch the surface of the complexity and potential benefits which virtualization will bring us. Take, for example, the challenges to forensics represented by the VMware product called VMotion. Here's a quote from a VMware overview of the product "VMware VMotion technology, unique to VMware, leverages the complete virtualization of servers, storage and networking to move an entire running virtual machine instantaneously from one server to another." VMotion allows you to perform live transparent (invisible to the user) migrations without downtime, continuous automatic optimization of VMs in a resource pool, and to proactively move VMs away from a failing server or one with performance issues.

The use of virtualization will only grow from this point on, bringing more challenges for forensics and security in general.

Tools & Traps...

Tools Referenced

Here are the tools referenced in this chapter:

Edward Baca's Virtual Penguin Sleuth Kit	www.vmware.com/vmtn/appliances/directory/249/
e-fense's Helix Forensics CD	www.e-fense.com/helix/
Mark Russinovich's System Internals tools	http://technet.microsoft.com/en-us/sysinternals
Intel®'s Steve Mancini and Joe Schwendt RAPIER	http://RAPIER.sourceforge.net
Brian Kaplan's (CERT) Live View	http://liveview.sourceforge.net/
Digital Intelligence's Ultrablock write blocker	www.digitalintelligence.com/products/ultrablock/
Peter Nordal–Hagen's NTPasswd	http://home.eunet.no/~pnordahl/ntpasswd/
Accessdata's FTK Imager	www.accessdata.com/downloads.html
Guidance Software's EnCase	www.guidancesoftware.com/products/ef_index.aspx
VMware's VMotion	www.vmware.com/products/vi/vc/vmotion.html

Caution: VM-Aware Malware Ahead

Investigators need to be aware that some malware is VM-aware and that they behave differently in a VM environment than they would normally. If you are lucky, then the malware will fool either your malware analysis tools or the investigator but not both. In some cases, the measures taken to fool the malware analysis code do so in a way that a trained observer would spot. In a case like this, static forensics might reveal the subterfuge. In any event, investigators should watch for signs that the system might be VM-aware and not just for malware analysis. It is inevitable that the bad guys will develop a capability to hide evidence when their software detects a VM.

We are still in the early days of applying this virtualization technology. We must look for any instances where we lose something by placing the suspect's image in a VM. Look at the copy protection technique from the early 1990s where the vendor has made a portion of a floppy unwritable and then check by writing to that location. If the hard drive could write something there, then the program executed different code that would not give the user access to its application. We need to discover situations like this that may exist in a virtual environment before we encounter them in a real case.

Summary

Virtualization technology offers many benefits in the field of digital forensics. With virtualization, investigators have the ability to produce higher quality forensics in less time. The choice to refresh the image to ensure integrity is no longer painful; it is a simple touch of the "refresh" button. Moving from your Windows tools to your Unix tools is just a reboot away. Virtualization permits us to observe the suspect's computer operating on the suspect's data without fear of contamination. This alone would make the use of virtualization desirable, but there is much more. Virtualization gives us the ability to analyze booby-traps and time bombs left by the suspect without putting the evidence in jeopardy. If the case you are investigating affects your entire enterprise, virtualization permits you to observe and instrument the suspect computer to gather intelligence about external components of the incident and to identify internal participants.

Let us not forget the value obtained by using virtualization to demonstrate complex evidence in a way the judge and jury can readily understand. Even though the demonstration is not in and of itself evidence, the power of demonstration cannot be understated.

In short, virtualization is a powerful tool in the forensic investigator's toolkit.

Solutions Fast Track

Preparing Your Forensic Environment

- ☑ Set aside dedicated workstations for Forensics:
    a. Size the hard drives to handle the largest drives in your organization.
    b. Be able to attach drives by any means (USB, firewire, IDE, SATA, PATA, etc) that exist in your organization.

- ☑ Image drives should be single purpose. Nothing else but images should be stored there.

- ☑ Securely delete images or replace the image drive when cases are removed from the forensic system.

- ☑ Secure the VM environment host against external and internal attack, particularly from attacks from within the virtual systems.

☑ Document and configuration control the deployed Forensic workstation. Place a copy of this inventory in each case file (for reproducibility).

☑ Create a Live-CD of this system to use when performing digital forensics in the field.

Capturing the Machine

☑ Court expectations and traditional forensic methods face several challenges today:

   a. Very large hard drives.

   b. Complex cases involving many hard drives.

   c. Cases where volatile but important information will be lost if the suspect's computer is shut down.

   d. Critical systems that can't be shut down in order to take an image.

☑ Ensure that the tools that you use and the way that you use them will produce a forensically sound image.

☑ Using two forensically sound images, set up parallel forensic environments. One will be used for traditional forensic techniques. The other will use a virtual instance of the suspect's computer, made from one of the two forensically sound images.

☑ Use a tool like Live View to make a virtual instance from a forensically sound image.

Preparing the Captured
Machine to Boot on New Hardware

☑ Create an MD5 or SHA-2 checksum for the forensically sound images. Note-SHA-1 is no longer accepted for this purpose.

☑ Once the VM is able to boot, all peripherals have been configured, and the password has been cracked. If necessary, save a VM snapshot so that the image of the VM in this state can be restored using Refresh.

☑ Save a copy of the configuration files of this snapshot to document the changes from the basic image which are necessary for the VM to run inside the VM environment instead of on the suspect's hardware.

What Can Be Gained by Booting the Captured Machine?

☑ Virtualization may permit you to observe behavior which is only visible while the system is live.

☑ Attorneys can use a VM of the suspect's computer in the courtroom to demonstrate the meaning of mountains of printed data.

☑ A VM of the suspect's machine will permit investigator's to view old files or files which require special or proprietary software.

☑ Investigators can discover and analyze time bombs and booby traps left by the defendant with impunity.

☑ Using the suspect's programs and data, it is easier to get in the mindset of the suspect

☑ Using the suspect's programs and data will reveal some relations between data more easily.

☑ You can examine any malicious code found during the investigation and collect intelligence information about botnets or virus infected systems used, operated, or distributed by the suspect.

☑ By examining malicious code in an instrumented, virtual environment, you can collect intelligence information about other participants in the crime being investigated.

☑ Pausing the VM will cause VMware to capture processes and data in memory in *.vmss files, which can be examined. This can reveal decrypted versions of packaged, malicious code.

☑ This section also discussed the unique concepts involved when the suspect's computer is a VM. Performing forensics on an instance of a virtual machine is different than performing forensics using a VM.

☑ Investigators should understand that VM aware malware exists. They should look for signs that the suspect's computer may include software that detects the presence of a VM environment and alters its behavior accordingly.

☑ We are in the early days of using virtualization in the forensics arena. We should be on the lookout for any instance where investigators might lose information by examining the image in a virtual environment instead of in a physical environment.

Frequently Asked Questions

Q: What is different about imaging a VM (e.g., a production virtual server) from imaging a physical drive?

A: We image a physical drive to ensure that information that may reside in slack space and unallocated space is available for forensic examination. The information in slack space and unallocated space may represent information from previous activity on the suspect's computer. It may contain information related to a case in which a suspect or malicious code may have attempted to delete. For a VM, the slack space and unallocated space investigators may be interested in is located in the image file and its representation associated with the VM. Copying the image file and associated VM files is sufficient to recreate the VM, with the exception being the case where tampering via the host computer is suspected. In that case the host becomes suspect and the slack and unallocated space of the physical drives of the host become the target of the investigation and would need to be acquired.

Q: What is Locard's Exchange principle and how is it related to forensics?

A: Edmund Locard (1877–1966) was the director of the first (according to some) crime lab, in Lyon, France. Locard's Exchange principle is a fundamental concept of forensic science. In its simplest form it says that every contact leaves a trace. Professor Locard, in "Manuel de Technique Policière," Paris: Payot, 1923" and his other works, explains the principle in this way. "Wherever he steps, whatever he touches, whatever he leaves, even unconsciously, will serve as a silent witness against him. Not only his fingerprints or his footprints, but his hair, the fibers from his clothes, the glass he breaks, the tool mark he leaves, the paint he scratches, the blood or semen he deposits or collects. All of these and more bear mute witness against him. This is evidence that does not forget. It is not confused by the excitement of the moment. It is not absent because human witnesses are. It is factual evidence. Physical evidence cannot be wrong, it cannot perjure itself, it cannot be wholly absent. Only human failure to find it, study and understand it can diminish its value."

Q: Can you repeat the steps involved in using virtualization for forensics without all the explanation?

A: Sure.

1. First, you gain access to the suspect's drive through your normal means (e.g., warrant).
2. Next, you acquire two images and associated cryptographic checksums using dd, FTK Imager, or another tool.
3. Both are placed in a chain of custody process.
4. One image is used to create a VM using Live View or another means.
5. The VM is started and password is cracked (Ntpasswd) if needed.
6. The VM is restarted, and a snapshot is taken of the cracked VM.
7. The investigator does the investigation using windows or UNIX tools as desired.
8. The investigator prepares a report with the findings and recommends the information that needs to be extracted using traditional forensics methods from the second image.
9. Using traditional forensic methods the evidence is extracted from the second image.
10. The investigator prepares the evidence report with the information extracted using traditional methods.
11. Optionally, demonstrations are prepared using the VM for use in the trial to explain the meaning of the evidence.

Chapter 10

Disaster Recovery

Solutions in this chapter:

- **Disaster Recovery in a Virtual Environment**
- **Simplifying Backup and Recovery**
- **Allowing Greater Variation in Hardware Restoration**
- **Recovering from Hardware Failures**
- **Redistributing the Data Center**

- ☑ **Summary**
- ☑ **Solutions Fast Track**
- ☑ **Frequently Asked Questions**

Introduction

I was once in a class talking to a guy who was using a virtualization tool to run Windows inside of Windows. The idea of doing this intrigued me. I asked him about it and he explained that he did it for a couple reasons. The first was that he could back all of his important data up by dragging a handful of files to a removable drive. The second was that whenever he got a new computer, migrating to the new computer was as simple as installing his virtualization tool, and copying his virtual machine onto the new computer. He didn't have to reinstall anything. He didn't have to go through every directory looking for things that he might want. He didn't have to set up directories marked _OLD just in case he forgot something.

Disaster recovery poses very similar issues to the ones he solved on a minor scale. It can be prohibitively expensive to maintain hardware of the proper configuration for each critical server in a data center. Just trying to keep backups current without having to shutdown services for the copy can be cumbersome.

Happily by having machines virtualized, a number of benefits can be realized. This chapter will illustrate some of those benefits. Hopefully the reader will see the flexibility which comes from having servers that can be moved from hardware platform to hardware platform with minimal reconfiguration.

Disaster Recovery in a Virtual Environment

The nuances of disaster recovery can mean many things to many people. Fundamentally however, disaster recovery implies the ability to recover and restore an organization's IT infrastructure, reducing (or eliminating) the amount of time the organization experiences a business outage. Disaster recovery includes not only recovering from things like natural disasters that impact the entire datacenter, but also recovering from incidents that may impact a single system such as hardware failure, a security compromise, etc. In a virtual environment, the definition of disaster recovery is no different than in a traditional/physical environment. You still need to determine:

- What is the maximum downtime that can be tolerated?

- What is the maximum amount of data loss that can be tolerated?

- What is the classification of resources (critical, urgent, normal, nonessential, etc.) for restoration?

- What kind of recovery plan is required for various types of disasters?

What is unique to a virtual environment is the number of options for disaster recovery that are available and how disaster recovery can be implemented. Unlike traditional physical infrastructure, because the virtualized environment typically exists as discrete sets of files, disaster recovery of virtualized assets typically enjoy a much more simplified backup and recovery process, greater portability of resources, and a decreased recovery time.

Simplifying Backup and Recovery

A fundamental tenet of most disaster recovery plans is the ability to back up critical data and then restore the data as part of the recovery process. In traditional environments this typically entails running a backup agent on the system and backing up the relevant files to tape, disk, or other offline storage media. In the event of a disaster, you can restore the data to a system with the only data loss typically being the data after the time of the last backup. Additionally, some backup applications support backing up and restoring the entire system. The benefit of this approach is that you don't need to have a system running and operational to restore the data to; rather, you simply restore the entire system to a new server.

The basics of backup and recovery in a virtual environment aren't any different; however, the options available are. In addition to treating a virtual machine like a physical machine and backing up and restoring the system at the file level—because virtual machines are typically discrete files themselves—some additional backup and restore options become available.

File Level Backup and Restore

The first backup and restore option is to simply treat the virtual machine like a physical machine and back it up in the exact same manner as you would the physical machines in your environment. The biggest benefit to this approach is that it provides a consistent backup and restore methodology throughout the entire organization. Regardless of whether the system is a virtual machine or not, the backup and restore procedures will likely be consistent for all systems. This consistency can reduce both training and complexity in your environment since there is nothing fundamentally unique or different with regard to managing the virtual machines.

There are some significant drawbacks to this methodology however. First, because virtual machines are designed to share the hardware resources of the host that is running the hypervisor, performing file-level backups within the same backup window can potentially result in resource contention and performance degradation as all virtual machines try to use the same CPU cycles for their backups at the same time. Second, because virtual machines are typically discrete files, the backup system can't take advantage of the encapsulation of the VMs into these files, which in turn allows for a robust system-level backup and restore.

System-Level Backup and Restore

Because virtual machines are typically nothing more than a set of files that exist on the virtualization server (for example, .vmdk files on VMware ESX), it is possible to back up and restore the entire system by simply backing up and restoring the files that make up the virtual machine.

This approach provides for a tremendous degree of both flexibility and portability in the back up and restore process. Since the entire system is backed up, during the restoration the entire system can be restored which typically makes the system available as soon as the restoration is completed. This can reduce the downtime required to recover from a disaster. Additionally, since the entire system is contained in the backed up files, the system can potentially be restored to any hardware platform capable of reading the virtual machine files. For example, if you have VMware ESX servers running at both the primary location as well as the disaster recovery location, the restoration can be as simple as restoring the files to the new ESX servers and powering the virtual machines on. As more vendors begin using Open Virtual Machine Format (OVF), this portability of restoration allows for the restoration of a virtual machine between any virtualization vendor's systems. So, for example, you could backup the virtual machine on VMware ESX server and restore it to Microsoft Hyper-V or Citrix XenSource and vice-versa.

For most vendors, the ability to backup and restore at the system level leverages some mechanism of snapshot technology. Snapshots are simply a means for locking the state of the virtual machine at a point in time. This allows the virtual machine to then be potentially restored to the point at which the snapshot is made. Snapshots can typically be made of both running and powered-down systems. Because the snapshot process is typically handled by the virtualization software, the snapshot of a live system can be taken without any downtime, and frequently with little or no performance impact to the virtual machine as well as without needing to do anything special (such as shutting down services) with the software running within the virtual machine. This snapshot, or read only copy of the machine state at the time of the snapshot, can then be backed up using traditional backup mechanisms.

While the portability and ease of recovery are compelling advantages to system-level backup and restore, there are some disadvantages to be aware of. First, a system-level backup and restore is an "all or nothing" exercise. System-level backups lack the ability to back up or restore individual files. If you need to restore, you have to restore the entire VM, which could cause changes you want to be rolled back as well as the failures you may be attempting to recover from. Consequently they are not effective as a means of recovering from the loss of only certain files, such as when a user accidentally deletes something. Additionally, since a virtual machine may consist of tens of gigabytes of data, the space required to back up and store the virtual machine, as well as the time required for the restore (and potentially the backup if an offline backup mechanism isn't utilized) can be significant, and must be planned for accordingly.

Notes from the Underground…

Using Snapshots to Test Patches and Updates

While snapshots are a good mechanism to support system-level backup and restore, they can also be used for saving a virtual machine in a "known good" state in the event that you need to make changes and updates, but want a quick and easy recovery path in the event of a failure. For example, you can take a snapshot of a VM before applying a significant patch/update or before making a major change, and if you run into problems you can potentially rollback the changes by simply reverting to the saved snapshot.

Shared Storage Backup and Restore

In many virtualization implementations, the virtual machine files themselves will actually be stored on some form of shared storage such as SAN, NAS or iSCSI device. As a result, backup mechanisms such as Network Data Management Protocol (NDMP), which can back up the shared storage, can be used to back up the virtual machine files in the same manner that any other files on the shared storage system can be backed up. Similarly, the restoration process is fundamentally no different than restoring any other file on the shared storage.

A good hybrid option available for backing up and restoring files is to take advantage of both the system-level backups and your SAN vendor shared storage replication. If your SAN has been designed to provide for replication to a DR site, storing the snapshots of the system level backup on the SAN and then utilizing the SAN replication functionality will enable you to quickly and reliably bring the virtual machines online at the DR site as shown in Figure 10.1. If a server in the primary location fails, because SAN replication has replicated the virtual machine files to the DR site, the virtual machines on the server that failed can be powered on at the DR site since all the files required for the virtual machine to operate have been replicated to the DR site already.

Figure 10.1 A Shared Storage Replication Example

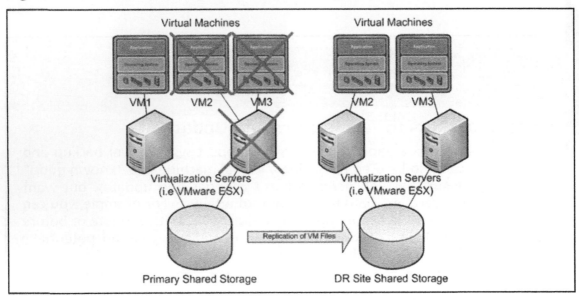

The drawbacks to SAN storage and backup are similar to a system backup and restore. Because the virtual machine files themselves are what is being backed up, it is not possible to perform file-level restoration within the virtual machine. You must back up and restore the entire virtual machine.

Allowing Greater Variation in Hardware Restoration

Because virtual machines tend to be hardware agnostic (that is, the virtual machine tends not to care too much about the physical server hardware) disaster recovery of a virtualized environment typically allows for a much greater variation in the hardware that is required to recover the environment. This level of hardware independence helps to reduce many of the complexities involved in attempting to perform bare-metal restoration operations. Because the hardware that the virtual machine is presented with by the virtualization platform tends to be the same regardless of the physical machine involved, the virtual machine can typically be restored and run on any hardware available. For example, as long as the hardware is capable of running VMware ESX a virtual machine that ran on one physical server can typically be run on any other physical server that is capable of running VMware ESX with little to no configuration required to make the virtual machine work.

Most DR sites use one of two types of methodologies for defining the hardware used at the DR site. For environments with a budget, the DR site will typically consist of the exact same hardware used in the production datacenter. This helps ensure that applications and systems in the production datacenter can run as effectively at the DR site as at the production site, since at the hardware level everything is the same. Obviously the major drawback of this is cost. The DR site will typically double the cost involved in any production server in order to provide for the server functionality in the DR site. If a server cost $50,000 for the production site, you will need to spend an additional $50,000 for the same server to be located at the DR site.

The other DR site methodology consists of lower end (frequently previous generation) hardware that exists solely for the purposes of DR. IT organizations often have a hard time with budgetary justifications for the same hardware that is used in the production environment, since the DR site might be viewed as something that is not used 99% of the time and doesn't need to perform at the same level as the production environment (the classic "we just need enough capacity to get through the disaster, not to run our entire organization" syndrome). While this may save money over the initial investment in standing up and maintaining the DR site, it has the significant drawback that the servers that are being used may not be capable of effectively running the systems and applications required. Additionally, the physical hardware is different and you may have more costs over the long run associated with maintenance and configuration of so many different types of systems.

With virtualization, as long as you have servers that are capable of running the virtualization software, the virtual machines become highly portable and easy to move and bring online at the disaster recovery location. As previously mentioned, from the perspective of the virtual machine, the hardware it "sees" is whatever the hypervisor presents to it. The bare metal is completely transparent to the virtual machine in most cases (32-bit and 64-bit CPUs are a notable exception). So, as long as you are running the same virtualization software (for example Microsoft Hyper-V or VMware ESX), the virtual machine doesn't care what the underlying hardware is and can be moved between hardware types with little or no configuration required. By simply relocating the virtual machine files to servers running at the DR site and powering them on, all critical assets can be quickly and easily recovered, independent of the need for the same hardware running at the DR site as in the production environment.

Additionally, because of the hardware independence there are a number of options for recovery that become available that not only reduce the number of servers required for disaster recovery, but also provide for a means to better manage the required capacity.

Different Number of Servers

Perhaps the most compelling justification for virtualization in a disaster recovery scenario is the potential to significantly reduce the number, and thus the cost, of the servers required to recover functionality for the organization. This exhibits itself particularly in two scenarios:

- Using virtualization for recovery of physical systems
- Using virtualization for recovery of virtual systems

Using Virtualization for Recovery of Physical Systems

A viable use of virtualization in a disaster recovery scenario is to use virtualization at the DR site in order to provide for capacity of physical systems running in the production datacenter. In classic DR methodology, every server running in production requires a corresponding server at the DR site in order maintain the same functionality and capacity that is required by the production computing resources. If you run Microsoft SQL in production, but don't have Microsoft SQL running at the DR site, you can't bring your Microsoft SQL resources online in the event of a disaster. Because of the 1:1 nature of traditional DR sites, the costs required to maintain and operate the DR site can easily double the costs of the production systems. Even if smaller or less powerful hardware is used, it may still require the same amount of hardware, software, and maintenance as well as similar (if not the same) power and cooling requirements.

Virtualization can help reduce the costs associated with maintaining the DR facilities by providing the ability to replicate the functionality of multiple physical systems on a single system running multiple virtual machines—each virtual machine representing a corresponding physical system. In this way, you can maintain the traditional separation of roles that each server may have in your environment, while leveraging the resource sharing aspects of virtualization to provide the same functionality on a smaller quantity of physical resources. Even if you are only able to run 2 virtual machines on each physical server, you can still reduce the number of servers required to maintain DR site operations by half.

A drawback to this methodology is that it typically requires some form of file-level backup in order to restore data between the physical and virtual machine. Additionally, some applications may benefit from application-level replication strategies, such as SQL replication, to maintain data consistency between the physical and virtual machines. The initial setup of the systems, however, can benefit from vendor Physical-to-Virtual (P2V) virtualization tools such as VMware Converter which allow a physical machine to be easily virtualized.

Using Virtualization for Recovery of Virtual Systems

Similar to physical systems, virtualization can also be used for disaster recovery of other virtual systems. The benefits are similar to those of physical systems. In most cases the implementation of the production virtualized assets places a high degree of importance on performance of the virtual machines. Additionally the capacity of the product virtualization implementation is typically designed for 100% of the virtualized resources to be running at any given time.

In a disaster recovery scenario however, it is common that not all production assets are required to be operational at the DR site. As a result, the virtualization resources required at the DR site are frequently smaller than the corresponding production datacenter. For example, if in a DR scenario you only need 75% of the resources to be operational, you can reduce the number of servers running at the DR site by 25%.

A DR scenario also typically does not require the same level of performance that might be expected in the normal production operations environment. This may allow you to be able to further reduce the total number of servers required by running more virtual machines per server than you do in the production environment. For example, you may run six virtual machines per server in production, but you might be able to get by with 10 virtual machines per server in a DR scenario. When used in conjunction with potentially being able to reduce the servers required to be operational in a DR scenario, you may be able to operate the DR site using a much smaller footprint of physical servers than the production environment used. This is a delicate proposition however, and must be extensively tested to ensure that the performance remains at acceptable levels.

Because of the portable nature of virtual machines, there are relatively few drawbacks to this scenario. In addition to supporting file-level backup and restore, just like a physical environment, using virtualization for both the production and DR environments can also take advantage of system-level backup and restore and snapshots for a quick, efficient, and effective disaster recovery.

Damage & Defense...

Portability of Virtual Machines: A Blessing and a Curse

Perhaps the biggest benefit that virtualization provides the DR process is the fact that virtual machines are easily portable. It's easy to make a copy and move it in the event of a disaster. This same portability cuts in other ways however. Remember that those virtual machine files are functionally equivalent to having a physical server. Be very careful to track and secure access to the files, because if a malicious user obtains access, it would be the same as boxing a physical server up and mailing it to them. When old snapshots or backups are no longer needed, they should be destroyed—the same way that you would wipe a physical server before disposing of it.

Recovering from Hardware Failures

While disaster recovery is frequently considered in the context of addressing a natural disaster, or a disaster on a scale of magnitude that impacts the entire datacenter, a far more frequent disaster is a failure that impacts a single server. This can range from something as simple as a basic hardware component failure to a catastrophic failure of the entire system. Much like with the large scale disaster, virtualization can be a very effective method of recovering from the failure.

As we mentioned, the virtual machine is separated from the physical hardware by the virtualization technology, such as Citrix XenSource, Microsoft Hyper-V, or VMware ESX. This allows the virtual machine to be completely independent of the underlying hardware. As a result, the virtual machine has the ability to tolerate being moved to a different piece of hardware (with some restrictions, such as CPU type) in the event of a hardware failure. There are a number of ways that recovering from hardware is facilitated by virtualization.

The most efficient recovery is if the virtual machine files reside on shared storage. In the event that the server has a failure, it can be as easy as connecting the new server to the shared storage, importing the virtual machine files to the new server and powering the virtual machine back up. In this circumstance the virtual machine typically recovers as if it were a physical server and someone had accidentally hit the power button.

If you are actively backing up the virtual machine as a system-level backup, an additional recovery method is to simply restore the virtual machine files to a new server, importing the virtual machine as required.

To further automate the recovery from hardware-related failures and disasters, many virtualization vendors provide the means for automated hardware failure recovery via high-availability solutions. We will explore this more in Chapter 11.

Redistributing the Data Center

The portable nature of virtual machines also lends itself to the ability to forego the traditional concept of a dedicated DR site, in particular if your environment already has multiple production datacenters. Many companies have regional datacenters; for example, one on the west coast and one on the east coast. If virtualization is utilized at both locations, rather than needing a dedicated DR site, you can facilitate the DR functionality by ensuring that there are enough resources available at both locations to allow virtual machines from one location to be run at the other location. For example, if you have two datacenters and you require 10 physical servers to provide the resources and capacity to run 50 virtual machines at either location and in the event of a disaster you need the ability to run 25 of those virtual machines at the other location, you can build out both datacenters with 15 physical servers. This will provide not only the resources to run the local production resources, but provide for spare capacity that can be used in the event of a disaster to bring the virtual machines required online and operational.

Summary

Disaster recovery is one of the most critical elements of successful IT operations. Depending on the sources cited, anywhere from 60 to 90% of companies that experience disaster without a proactive disaster plan will be out of business within two years of the disaster. Virtualization technologies can be a significant enabling technology in building a proactive disaster plan.

Virtualization can simplify backup and recovery by providing an easy way to perform system-level backup and restoration because the virtual machine is encapsulated in a discrete set of files that are easy to back up and restore independently of the application or services residing in the virtual machine.

Virtualization also provides for a greater degree of hardware independence since the virtual machines are separated from the physical hardware by the virtualization technology that is being used. Consequently it is easy to move a virtual machine between different physical server hardware with little or no configuration or changes required on the virtual machine.

In addition to facilitating and simplifying broad scale disaster recovery, virtualization can simplify the recovery of hardware failures—again largely due to the fact that the virtual machine is independent of the actual hardware in use. As long as another server is available to process the virtual machine files, the virtual machine can be quickly and easily brought back into operation.

Finally, virtualization enables the ability to quickly and easily redistribute resources between datacenters providing the same degree of recovery that a dedicated DR site does, without the additional expenses and costs of a dedicated DR site.

Regardless of how you implement your disaster recovery, something that must never be overlooked is the need to test, verify, and validate the disaster recovery process. Any disaster recovery process can look solid on paper, but you want to make sure to regularly and routinely test and validate that you are able to successfully execute the disaster recovery plan so that if you are ever in a situation where you must implement it, you have a high degree of confidence in its success.

Solutions Fast Track

Disaster Recovery in a Virtual Environment

☑ Disaster recovery implies the ability to recover and restore an organization's IT infrastructure, reducing (or eliminating) the amount of time the organization experiences a business outage.

☑ In a virtual environment, the definition of disaster recovery is no different than in a traditional/physical environment.

☑ What is unique to a virtual environment is the number of options for disaster recovery that are available and how disaster recovery can be implemented.

Simplifying Backup and Recovery

☑ Supports File Level, System Level and Shared Storage backup and restore.

☑ File level backup and restore provides for consistency of function throughout the organization.

☑ System level backup and restore leverages snapshots and the portability of the virtual machine for quick backup and restoration to other virtualization servers.

☑ Shared storage level backup and restore takes advantage of storage vendor tools to back up the entire virtual machine.

Allowing Greater Variation in Hardware restoration

☑ Virtual machines are independent of underlying hardware

☑ This independence makes it easy to restore virtual machines regardless of the physical hardware that is being used.

Recovering from Hardware Failures

☑ Because of the portability of virtual machines, it is relatively easy to move a virtual machine from failed hardware to functional hardware.

☑ Many vendors provide automated mechanisms for hardware recovery in the form of high availability configurations and options.

Redistributing the Data Center

☑ Virtualization can be used to provide for disaster recovery without the need for a dedicated DR site by allowing resources to be quickly and easily redistributed between datacenters.

Frequently Asked Questions

Q: What backup and recovery options are available to virtualized resources?

A: Virtualized resources such as virtual machines can typically be backed up and restored using one of three methodologies: file-level backup and restore, system-level backup and restore, and shared storage-level backup and restore.

Q: How often should the DR plan be tested?

A: At the very minimum the DR plan should be tested on an annual basis. This should include validating that all of the resources required to be operational in the event of a disaster are able to be successfully restored both to the DR site as well as back into production. In areas that experience known disaster times (for example hurricane season) the DR plan should be validated more frequently.

Chapter 11

High Availability: Reset to Good

Solutions in this chapter:

- **Understanding High Availability**
- **Reset to Good**
- **Configuring High Availability**
- **Maintaining High Availability**

☑ **Summary**

☑ **Solutions Fast Track**

☑ **Frequently Asked Questions**

Introduction

One of the most frequent causes of downtime is a failure of the underlying server hardware. One of the early promises of virtualization is the ability to keep virtualized systems online and operational regardless of problems with the underlying hardware by allowing the virtual machine to run on any host in the virtual environment. If an individual host fails, it's no problem because the virtual machine can be run on another host with little to no downtime.

High availability is a design methodology used to ensure the uptime and availability of virtual machines. Generally speaking, there are two types of downtime that are mitigated by high availability provided by virtualization technologies:

- Planned downtime
- Unplanned downtime

The chapter will discuss different methods of providing high availability in a virtual environment as well as how to maintain and operate the virtualization hosts. It will also cover some of the pitfalls of building a high availability infrastructure.

Understanding High Availability

Before any discussion of how to provide for high availability can occur, you must first understand what high availability is and distinguish between planned and unplanned downtime. Planned downtime is downtime that has been scheduled and is expected in the environment. It is typically caused by system maintenance that, while disruptive to the overall system, usually can't be avoided. Reasons for planned downtime range from applying patches or configuration changes that may require a reboot to upgrading or replacing hardware. One benefit of planned downtime is that it can be more easily managed in order to minimize disruption. In many cases, as we will examine, virtualization can actually provide for zero downtime.

On the other hand, unplanned downtime is just the opposite of planned downtime. Unplanned downtime typically results from things like power outages, hardware failures, software crashes, network connectivity failures, security breaches, and operating system failures. While unplanned downtime cannot be easily predicted, it can be more easily recovered from in a virtual environment than in a physical environment.

Providing High Availability for Planned Downtime

While virtualization cannot provide for zero downtime high availability in all circumstances, it can provide for zero downtime in many circumstances. If you recall from previous chapters, the virtual machine is isolated from the underlying hardware and operating system by the hypervisor. This isolation allows the virtual machine to operate completely independently of the underlying hardware. Consequently, the actual host is effectively irrelevant. As long as there is a host available with the capacity necessary for the virtual machine to operate, the virtual machine can be run there.

This capability creates the first scenario for providing high availability in a virtual environment. Ultimately what matters is that the applications running in the virtual machine remain available. If you can do that, you have achieved zero downtime. So in circumstances where the downtime is planned and does not require the virtual machine itself to be rebooted or taken offline in any manner, providing high availability is as simple as relocating the virtual machine to another host, performing whatever maintenance is required, then bringing the host back online. This is depicted in Figure 11.1.

Figure 11.1 How High Availability Works

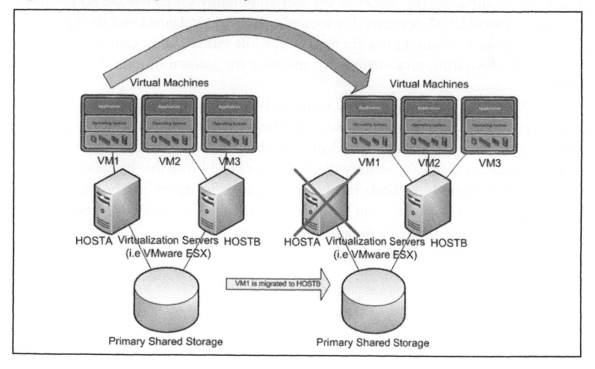

Virtual machines are running on both HOSTA and HOSTB. If HOSTA needs to be taken down for maintenance, VM1 can be moved to HOSTB while the relevant maintenance is performed on HOSTA. HOSTA can then be brought back online returning the overall virtualization environment to its original capacity. In many cases the migration of the virtual machine between hosts can be done with no downtime using "live migration" technologies such as VMware VMotion. VMotion requires shared storage to be configured for all of the hosts, which in turn allows the virtual machine to be migrated between hosts while it remains online and operational. In many cases the migration occurs without any indication that the virtual machine has been moved.

Obviously if the virtual machine itself requires maintenance, for example applying patches to the virtual machine, which requires a reboot, you cannot have zero downtime. However if you need to replace or upgrade hardware on the host, apply patches to the host, or reconfigure the network on the host, virtualization can truly provide for zero downtime maintenance.

Providing High Availability for Unplanned Downtime

In a perfect world we would anticipate potential downtime and plan accordingly to minimize or eliminate the impact to the user community. Of course we do not live in a perfect world, which means that sooner or later an unplanned and unexpected outage is going to occur. In this circumstance, while virtualization cannot typically prevent the downtime, it can frequently minimize the amount of time the systems are down.

Similar to the planned downtime scenario, because the virtual machines are independent of the underlying hardware, if a failure occurs on a given host most virtualization vendors provide a mechanism such as VMware High Availability Clustering to automatically identify the host failure and bring the virtual machines online on a different host. While this will not prevent the downtime, because of the automation that virtualization provides the amount of downtime is typically a fraction of what it would be on a physical system.

**Common Misconceptions
of High Availability and Virtualization**

A common misconception of high availability in a virtual environment is that it operates similarly to traditional high availability cluster technologies such as Microsoft Cluster Server (MSCS) or Veritas Cluster Server (VCS). Unfortunately this is not typically the case. MSCS and VCS are designed to provide zero application downtime for both planned and unplanned downtime. In a virtual environment while you can typically provide zero application downtime for planned downtime, most virtualization vendors allow the virtual machines to be inaccessible and started up on a new host in the event of unplanned downtime. If you require zero downtime in all circumstances, you will probably need to invest in traditional high availability cluster solutions. The good news is that many of them can actually be installed in a virtual environment giving you the best of both worlds: the portability of the virtual environment with the zero downtime capabilities of the high availability cluster software.

Reset to Good

The fundamental objective of any high availability implementation is to be able to reset the environment to a good, functional state as quickly as possible. There are a number of methods by which this can be provided, but they typically fall into two broad categories:

- Utilizing vendor tools to reset to good
- Utilizing scripting or other mechanisms to reset to good

Utilizing Vendor Tools to Reset to Good

Because of how easy it is to provide high availability in a virtual environment, many vendors have begun providing everything required for configuring high availability native to the virtualization management consoles and tools. This is typically the easiest way to not only configure but maintain and support high availability in an environment. Frequently, however, this functionality is more expensive than basic virtualization and requires the purchase of additional licenses or enterprise versions of a vendor product.

For environments that utilize VMware ESX and VMware VirtualCenter, high availability is provided as a component of the VI3 Standard and Enterprise editions. VMware HA is capable of providing for high availability of virtual machines in the event of either virtual machine or host failures. For example, VMware HA can monitor the virtual machine for a "guest OS" failure and if detected can automatically restart the virtual machine. Similarly, VMware HA can monitor the ESX host and if a failure is detected, restart the virtual machines that were running on that ESX host on a functional host. It's important to understand the VMware HA relies on the detection of a failure to function. In other words, VMware HA doesn't prevent a system from being down or inaccessible, but it can automatically bring the system back online in the event that a failure is detected. This is shown in Figure 11.2.

Figure 11.2 VMware HA

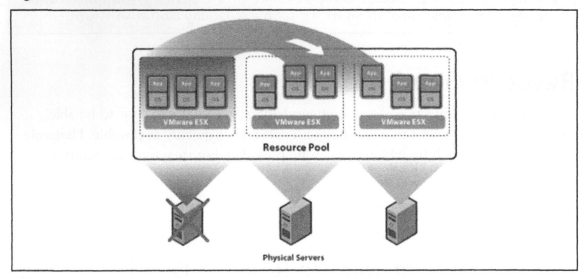

Citrix XenServer uses a similar methodology. With Citrix XenServer, the system monitors the health of the hosts in a pool, and if a host fails the virtual machines are moved to another host in the pool. Like VMware, this is only effective once a failure has occurred.

Utilizing Scripting or Other Mechanisms to Reset to Good

In addition to vendor tools, you can also use scripting or other mechanisms such as Microsoft Cluster Server (MSCS) to reset the environment to a good, functional state. For example, you can leverage powershell to monitor a virtual machine. If it detects that the virtual machine is not accessible or is not online, it will attempt to restart the virtual machine. In smaller or cost conscious environments this can be an easy way to provide for high availability without the cost of the vendor software that enables built in, automated high availability.

Another option is to utilize high availability cluster software such as MSCS on the virtual machines themselves. A benefit of this approach is that you may be able to provide zero downtime high availability in circumstances that otherwise would require a period of downtime during which the script or vendor tool could detect a failure and start the virtual machine again.

Degrading over Time

A common problem across virtually all software and operating systems is the periodic need to restart the system to get it functioning properly again. For example, memory leaks, orphaned sessions, and data caches may require that the system be rebooted in order to free up the corresponding resources and thus return the system to optimal performance. Utilizing high availability technologies (such as the migration of virtual machines to other hosts during the reboot process) can be done for underlying host servers with zero virtual machine downtime.

Configuring High Availability

Each virtualization vendor has its own unique details and steps in order to configure high availability, but virtually all of them have the same basic requirements and configurations to enable high availability in the environment. These include:

- Shared storage
- Network infrastructure that monitors for failure
- A pool or cluster of servers that participates in high availability

Configuring Shared Storage

A common element in most virtualization high availability configurations is the requirement for all of the virtualization hosts to use a common shared storage system that the virtual machine files reside on. The reason for this is simple: in order for a virtual machine to run on a host, the host has to be able to read the virtual machine files. If the virtual machine files are stored in local storage on HOSTA and HOSTA fails, it is not possible for HOSTB to read the virtual machine files. However, if the virtual machine files are stored on shared storage (such as Fibre Channel, iSCSI, and, in some cases, NAS or NFS) any host can potentially read the files, and, in the event of a failure the virtual machine can be powered up on any host.

Configuring the Network

In order to determine whether high availability mechanisms need to be activated, the virtualization systems need a means to determine whether a failure has occurred. The most common method of doing this utilizes heartbeats over the network infrastructure to determine whether a failure appears to be occurring. Consequently it is necessary to configure the network so that the systems that participate in the heartbeat activities are able to communicate with each other. In most cases you will want to use a common subnet for these communications, but some environments will use remote or WAN segments to provide for high availability between datacenters. This configuration is commonly referred to as stretch clustering. If any network devices such as firewalls reside between the systems, the firewall must be configured to permit the heartbeat traffic between the hosts. Finally, because the network infrastructure is used to determine whether a failure has occurred, it is important to utilize redundant network connections to reduce the likelihood of a false positive causing a failover to occur due to a minor or temporary network issue.

Damage & Defense...

Protecting against a Split Brain

Determining whether a failure has occurred is not a precise science. For example, if the network between two hosts has failed but the hosts themselves are still functioning, they may know a failure has occurred, but to each host it appears as though the other host is who has failed. This situation is known as split brain. Each host thinks that the other has failed, and thus attempts to bring the resources online locally. When the problem is remedied, you potentially wind up with the exact same virtual machines running at the exact same time but in different places. To protect against this you want to have network redundancy built into the design to prevent split brain from occurring due to a simple network issue. You also can configure most networks with policies to handle the situation when two hosts are isolated from each other, commonly referred to as isolation response.

Setting Up a Pool or Cluster of Servers

The final element of most high availability configurations is setting up the actual hosts that the virtual machines will reside on. Some vendors refer to setting up the hosts as configuring a cluster, while others refer to it as a resource pool or a pool of servers. Regardless of the taxonomy used, however, the underlying functionality is the same. The hosts are configured to operate as a logical grouping of servers allowing the virtual machines to be run on any of the hosts in the cluster or pool (for simplicity we will use the term cluster from here on).

Because the virtual machines can run on any host in the cluster it is important that the hardware in use be as close to the same as possible for all hosts. In fact, it's best to use physically identical systems. At a minimum most vendors require the following hardware to be the same within the high availability cluster:

- CPU from the same vendor (AMD or Intel)
- CPU the same model (except for stepping)
- CPU with the same features (for example, all CPUs support Intel Virtualization Technology)

Additionally, some vendors require that the exact same versions of hypervisor software be running on all hosts in the cluster. Although this is not required, it can greatly simplify troubleshooting by providing an easy means to compare systems in the event that there is a problem. Ideally the hosts will not only be running the same version of software, but they will be configured in the exact same manner.

Maintaining High Availability

Configuring high availability is only the first step in reducing downtime in a virtual environment. Once the initial configuration and implementation has occurred the task of maintaining the systems becomes the key to a successful high availability implementation. There are a number of issues, some unique to a high availability environment, to be aware of and to plan for accordingly.

Monitoring for Overcommitment of Resources

A primary motivator for virtualization is the ability to share the resources and capacity of the underlying virtualization hosts among multiple virtual machines. While over commitment of resources is not unique to a high availability implementation, in order for the high availability implementation to operate properly and provide the availability required effective capacity planning is critical.

In many cases for high availability to kick in something in the environment must be down, regardless of whether it is a planned or unplanned outage. By definition, for high availability functions to take effect, some portion of the normal production environment must be inaccessible. This can create a unique problem with high availability in that if you have allocated enough capacity to accommodate the failure of a host (or hosts), the high availability mechanism can have the exact opposite effect of what was intended. By oversubscribing the resources in the cluster, high availability can inadvertently take other resources down by making the performance of the remaining hosts so poor as to be unusable.

To mitigate this it is imperative that any high availability implementation be designed to accommodate N+1 capacity at a minimum. N+1 means that when you decide which resources are required to run the virtual machines in the cluster, you provide capacity for at least one additional host (though some environments might use N+2 or more in order to accommodate multiple failures) so that in the event that one host fails, all of the resources can still be brought online without adversely affecting performance. For example, if you have determined that in order to achieve the necessary performance for your environment you require five virtualization hosts, go ahead and implement capacity for six virtualization hosts. All six servers can typically be used for normal operations and capacity, and, in the event that a server fails, you still have the five servers required for optimal operations.

The catch with this is that there is always going to be a tendency to use "spare" capacity instead of buying "new" capacity. For example, if you need to add 10 more virtual machines and you effectively have 10 virtual machines worth of capacity in the high availability cluster, there may be a push to go ahead and just add the virtual machines without adding any additional recovery capacity. While this will probably work just fine for daily operations, in the event of a failure you will no longer have the capacity available to run all of the virtual machines in the environment. In fact, many vendors may even prevent a high availability recovery if there are not enough resources to effectively bring the virtual machines back online.

Security Implications

Another thing to consider are the security implications of high availability clusters. For technical or political reasons, it may be necessary for certain virtual machines to never run on the same host system. This could be due to security policies, for example, the HR resource must be isolated from other systems, or for technical reasons, such as not running all of your domain controllers on one host server since a failure could cause the entire domain to become inaccessible.

In the case of a failure, the high availability cluster could potentially bring virtual machines online on hosts they otherwise should not be running on. Some vendors can mitigate this by utilizing affinity and anti-affinity rules when making a high availability decision. Affinity rules define which virtual machines can be run together on the same virtualization host and in some cases may even require that the virtual machines be located together as a group. Anti-affinity rules are just the opposite; they define groups of virtual machines which should never run together on the same host. For example, you may be able to configure the domain controller virtual machines with an anti-affinity rule so that you never have the domain controllers running on the same virtualization host. While this may meet your security requirements, there is a delicate balancing act that must be performed. If you have an anti-affinity rule in place and the only place that a virtual machine can be recovered to run is on a virtualization host that the anti-affinity rule prevents from occurring, rather than bringing the virtual machine online it will stay offline in order to adhere to the anti-affinity rule.

The ultimate question that needs to be asked is whether it is more important for a virtual machine to remain isolated or to be brought online in less than ideal circumstances. If the answer is that security is the most important aspect, then your high availability implementation may not provide the protection you expect in certain circumstances. If it is more important that the virtual machine be running, then high availability can accomplish the goal, but you will want to make sure that the virtual machine is migrated to a host in order to provide the required separation at the earliest available time.

High availability is also frequently used to provide protection for virtual machines and resources by ensuring that the virtual machine remains operational as much as possible. While high availability can certainly help the overall security posture of an organization, it shouldn't be viewed as something to replace other defensive methods. If a virtual machine is compromised, all that high availability ensures is that the compromised virtual machine stays online and operational. You still need to implement traditional security and defensive mechanisms such as anti-virus and malware protection, intrusion detection/prevention, and firewalls.

Performing Maintenance on a High Availability System

One aspect of IT operations for which high availability can definitely reduce downtime is performing maintenance and patching of an environment, in particular, for virtualization hosts. While high availability can bring a failed virtual machine back online, many vendors have the ability if you can plan and schedule a server outage to move the virtual machines with zero downtime to other hosts in the cluster. Some good examples of this are VMware VMotion or XenServer XenMotion. By relocating all of the virtual machines on a particular host in a cluster to other hosts in the cluster, the freshly emptied host can be shutdown, patches can be applied, and maintenance can be performed with no downtime. When the maintenance is complete, you simply bring the host back online and reverse the process of relocating the virtual machines from the other hosts in the cluster back to the updated host.

When you do this you want to be mindful of something we discussed earlier, specifically the recommendation that as much as possible you should run all hosts in a cluster with the exact same software versions and configurations. Consequently you will want to test any patches or updates first, then roll them across the entire cluster in a structured fashion to minimize impact and downtime as well as to ensure that when maintenance is completed all of the virtualization hosts are as identical as possible.

Summary

One aspect of virtualization is its ability to leverage the technology to provide for high availability of virtual machine resources. Rather than requiring specialized hardware and software, as might be the case in a traditional environment, by leveraging the ability to build high availability clusters you can reduce or eliminate both planned and unplanned downtime.

There are a number of tools you can use to reset the environment to good, but they primarily fall into two categories: the first is vendor tools such as VMware HA or Citrix XenServer High Availability, and the second is scripted mechanisms that might include traditional HA tools such as Microsoft Cluster Server.

While the specific details of configuring high availability differ from vendor to vendor, most share three common elements. You must configure shared storage so that all of the hosts can read the virtual machine files. You must configure the network infrastructure to allow for heartbeats and failure detection mechanisms to operate. Finally, you need to define a cluster or pool of virtualization servers to provide high availability functionality for the environment.

Once the high availability implementation has been configured the task of maintaining the system takes precedence. You want to ensure that you guard against the over commitment of resources since this can not only prevent high availability operations from functioning but can also cause more problems to the entire environment than are solved by bringing the virtual machines online.

Another aspect of the high availability environment is the element of security. You need to be mindful of whether virtual machines can be run on the same virtualization host or not, and, if they cannot, the high availability solution must be configured accordingly. While high availability can help the general security posture of an organization by ensuring that resources are operational, it is not a substitute for other security mechanisms.

Finally maintenance of the systems should be planned and managed to ensure minimal impact and downtime for the virtual machines while at the same time ensuring that all of the hosts in the high availability cluster are running the same software and configuration for both stability and troubleshooting of the environment.

Solutions Fast Track

Understanding High Availability

☑ High availability is a mechanism to reduce or eliminate downtime.

☑ Planned downtime is scheduled in advance. High availability can frequently provide for zero downtime in these circumstances.

☑ Unplanned downtime is not scheduled in advance and is frequently the result of a system failure or compromise. High availability can frequently minimize this downtime by automatically identifying the failure and bringing impacted virtual machines back online.

Reset to Good

☑ Reset to good is the ability to reset an environment to a good, functional state as quickly as possible.

☑ Reset to good can be accomplished using vendor tools such as VMware HA or Citrix XenServer HA or via scripting or third-party technologies such as Microsoft Cluster Server.

Configuring High Availability

☑ Configure shared storage so that all hosts can read virtual machine files.

☑ Configure network connectivity for heartbeat and failure detection mechanisms.

☑ Set up a cluster or pool of servers for providing high availability functionality.

☑ All systems in a high availability cluster should use the exact same hardware, software versions, and configurations as much as possible.

Maintaining High Availability

☑ Proper capacity management must be performed to avoid over commitment of resources. Overcommitment can degrade the performance of the environment in the event of a failure or prevent the high availability from functioning altogether.

☑ If virtual machines require isolation from other virtual machines, you need to design your high availability solution to ensure adherence to affinity and anti-affinity rules.

☑ High availability is not a substitute for other security mechanisms.

☑ Virtual machine migrations can be used to patch host systems without impacting the virtual machines.

Frequently Asked Questions

Q: Does high availability prevent all downtime?

A: No. While high availability can prevent downtime in many circumstances, in some cases it doesn't prevent downtime rather it reduces recovery time by bringing impacted machines online faster.

Q: Do I have to use the same hardware for all hosts in a high availability cluster?

A: While you do not have to have the exact same hardware, it is highly recommended. In particular many vendors require the same processor type for effective high availability.

Q: Is resource over commitment a concern with high availability?

A: Yes. Because high availability functionality generally entails that some portion of the production capacity and resources have failed and are no longer accessible (in essence you are operating at reduced capacity to begin with), if you do not have spare capacity to allow for the high availability functionality to bring virtual machines online on alternate hosts, high availability operations may not be able to occur. You want to ensure that, at a minimum, you provide N+1 capacity to eliminate resource over commitment concerns.

Chapter 12

Best of Both Worlds: Dual Booting

Solutions in this chapter:

- **How to Set Up Linux to Run Both Natively and Virtually**

- **Issues with Running Windows Both Natively and Virtualized**

☑ **Summary**

☑ **Solutions Fast Track**

☑ **Frequently Asked Questions**

Introduction

Security professionals are often called upon to use a variety of tools to get their job done. Sometimes they need multiple operating systems while other times they need raw access to hardware for certain tools to work. I have seen many a consultant carrying multiple laptops so that they could have various tools at the ready. While carrying multiple laptops is a viable option, it can be a very tiring one, especially at the end of a long international trip. I have seen others juggling spare hard drives so they can switch between environments with only minor hardware adjustments (and a boot cycle). You can just imagine what they go through to transfer files between operating systems.

This chapter will explain one solution I've been using for the past few years that has met my needs in a variety of situations. It allows for both Windows and Linux to be run natively, as well as for Linux to be run in a virtual machine, giving me access to my Linux system while running under Windows.

The two biggest reasons I have for running Linux natively is for wireless tool access, and for using the open source security tool Nessus. Virtual machines are great for emulating hardware, but I have yet to be able to assign PCMCIA / miniPCI cards directly to a virtual machine. Because of this much of the low level driver operations required to perform wireless penetration testing must be done in native Linux. I really appreciate being able to be in both operating systems at once though when I am not performing low level network operations. The convenience of being able to write code and test tools while still connected to all of my corporate windows environments is very nice.

How to Set Up Linux
to Run Both Natively and Virtually

The easiest way to set this up is to install Linux in a virtual machine first. I prefer doing this for two reasons. The biggest current reason is that I have two hard drives in my laptop. The second hard drive is interchangeable with the DVD drive. I can either have the second hard drive or the DVD drive in but not both at the same time. This makes it a bit difficult to install Linux on the native machine first (although it can often be done by swapping the second physical drive with the primary drive for the duration of the installation).

By setting up a virtual environment first I am able to mount a DVD image file (also known as an ISO file) as though it were an actual disk. This allows me to leave both hard drives in at the same time. Migrating to a new laptop may require the purchase of a new drive bay, but this minor inconvenience is certainly worth the benefits of having both operating systems and the ability to use them concurrently.

Creating a Partition for Linux on an Existing Drive

If your machine is unable to support two hard drives (or you don't want to give up your DVD drive) it is possible to install Linux on a new partition. Partition Magic can be used to resize existing partitions to make room for the new installation.

The first step in this operation is to use the disk manager to defragment the drive. As a hard drive is used and files are allocated then deleted, a disk develops spaces between files. Modern file systems do a much better job of tracking and using these spaces, but spaces can develop none the less. By defragmenting the disk, the files on the disk are moved in such a way that these spaces are minimized. This ensures that the maximum amount of space is available for your alternate operating system.

After the disk is defragmented, the majority of its free space should be available in one large block. A new partition can then be created using a portion of this space. This operation requires a special tool such as Partition Magic shown in Figure 12.1.

Figure 12.1 Creating a New Partition with Partition Magic

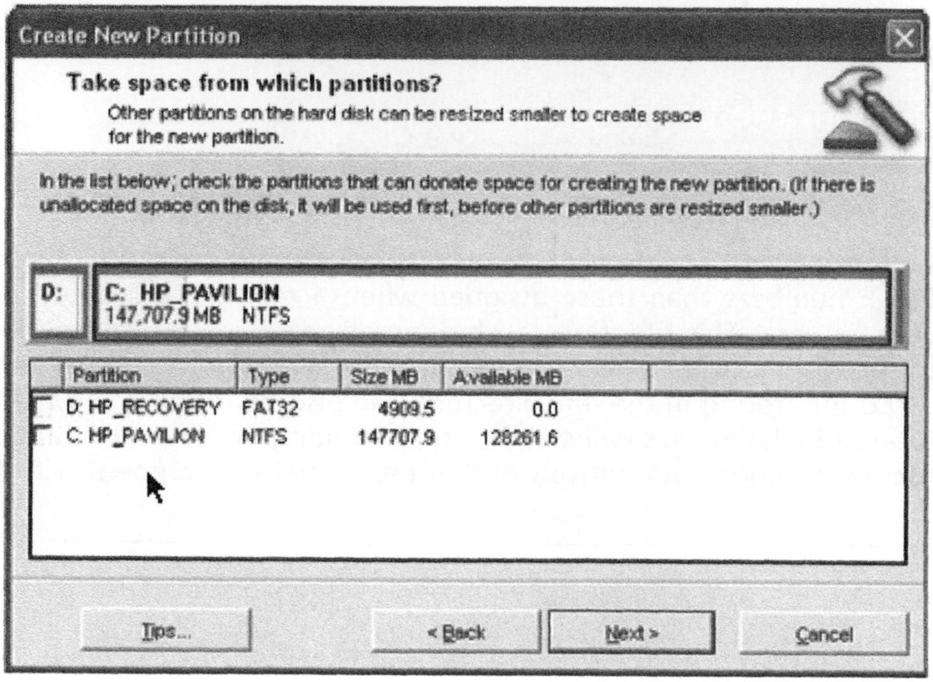

At this point the new operating system can be installed in one of two ways. Most operating systems are able to install on any partition, and normal installation procedures can be followed. Be sure to select the correct partition (installing on the wrong partition will almost certainly destroy your data). The other option at this point is to assign the new partition to a virtual machine. By selecting the partition and assigning it to a virtual machine, your alternate operating system can be installed without having to shutdown the primary operating system. In addition you also get the fringe benefit of not having to burn DVDs or CDs to do the installation. (You may also be able to use a DVD image on a system without a DVD drive.) It should be noted that the process of performing an installation using multiple CDs can be done without too much trouble. Whenever the installation process requires a new CD, the ISO images can be "virtually" ejected and the next image inserted by "mounting" it.

Continue with the installation process, although the master boot record should not be replaced. Here again, using a virtual machine can protect your primary operating system boot loader from being replaced. Unless you assign the primary operating system partition to the virtual machine deliberately, the virtual machine will not be able to read the primary partition at all.

Notes from the Underground...

Avoiding Problems with Changing Hard Disk Numbers

It should be noted that booting in a virtual environment can result in different hard disk numbers than those assigned when a machine is booted on the native hardware. This situation can be partially resolved by configuring the boot process to look for devices by disk label instead of by hard disk number. The fstab file (found in the /etc directory) can also be modified so that disks are located by label. This will stabilize the changing environments and allow your server to boot both natively and in the virtual environment with fewer issues.

At this point it's time to make it possible to boot to either operating system. This can be done in a couple different ways. First you may be able to use the bios to boot to an alternate hard drive. This is the method I used because it seems simplest. The other option is to use a boot loader to choose the operating system to boot.

The boot loader software is the first program loaded on your system. The two most common boot loaders are the Windows boot loader and the Linux boot loader known as Grub. Either of them can perform the function of booting both Windows and Linux. In order to boot Windows using Grub, you have to make the correct entries in the /boot/grub/menu.lst file. The following entries assume that Linux is installed on your primary disk and Windows is on a second hard drive.

```
title Windows XP
root (hd1,0)
rootnoverify (hd1,0)
map (hd0) (hd1)
map (hd1) (hd0)
chainloader +1
```

Booting Linux with the Windows boot loader is slightly more complicated. The Windows boot loader needs a copy of the boot sector (first sector) from the Linux box. This sector is enough to initiate the boot onto another partition. The easiest way to obtain the boot sector from the Linux partition is to boot it using a virtual machine. If this is not possible most Linux distributions allow you to boot using a Live CD configuration. It may also be possible to boot using a standalone Linux distribution such as Knoppix. Once you have booted into a Linux environment, the first sector of the disk should be copied to a file. The command DD accomplishes this task.

```
dd if = /dev/hda2 of = bootsector.sec bs = 512 count = 1
```

The preceding command copies the single 512-byte sector from the disk into a file called bootsector.sec. This file must then be copied over to the Windows partition. I usually put it in the root of the C drive. The boot.ini file must then be modified with an entry pointing to this boot sector. An example is shown in Figure 12.2.

Figure 12.2 Modifying the boot.ini file with the Linux Boot Sector

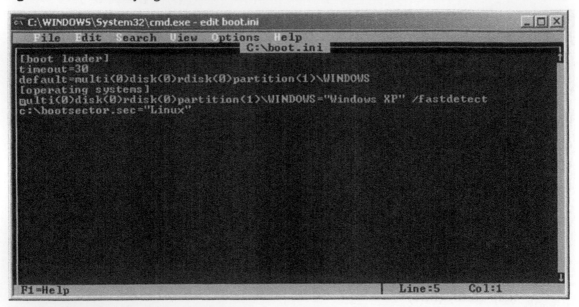

The first entry was already present in the boot.ini file. If you want to boot to the original partition by default then it should be left as the first entry in the file. If you want your new partition to be the default, then it should be first in the table. The timeout parameter determines how long the boot loader waits before the default entry is chosen. If you make this time too short you won't have time to pick the alternate operating system and may find yourself having to reboot often. If you extend the timeout you may end up taking too long to boot up without interaction (note that you can always hit Enter at the boot screen to pick the currently high-lighted choice). An example of the boot screen created by the boot.ini file in the preceding section is shown in Figure 12.3.

Figure 12.3 A Boot Menu with a Linux Option

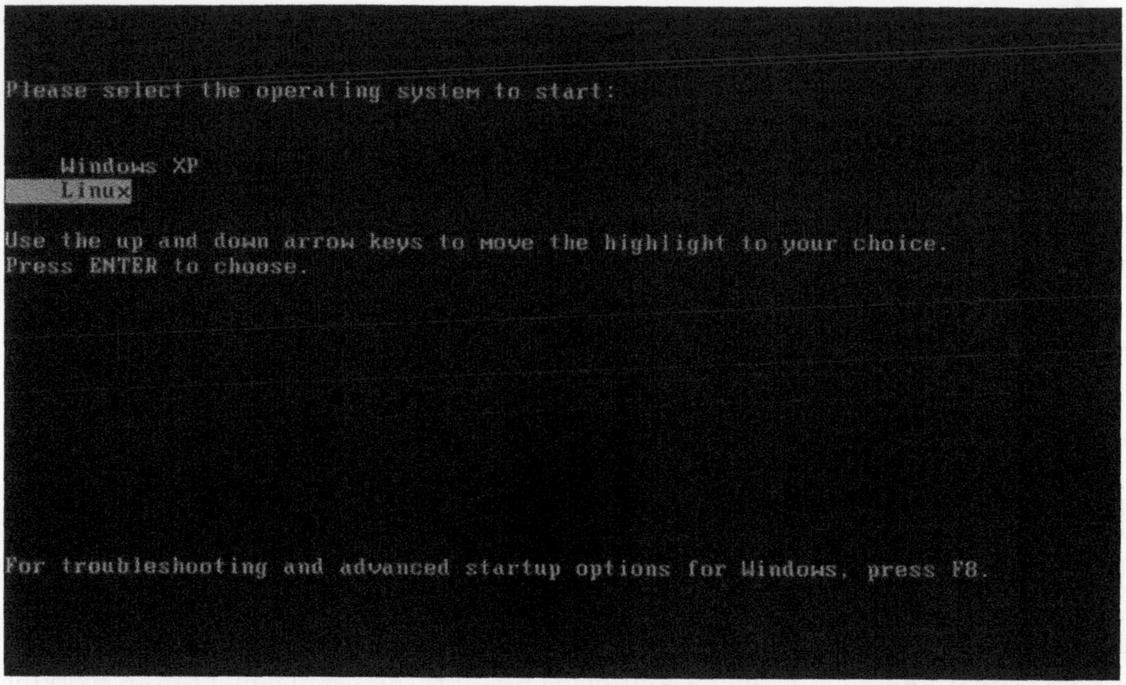

```
Please select the operating system to start:

     Windows XP
     Linux

Use the up and down arrow keys to move the highlight to your choice.
Press ENTER to choose.




For troubleshooting and advanced startup options for Windows, press F8.
```

At the completion of this procedure you will be able to boot either operating system on the machine natively.

At this point you need to configure a virtual machine hosted in one of the operating systems to boot the other physical partition. Chapter 4 discusses how to allow a virtual machine to access a physical drive. It is highly recommended that all of the other partitions be blocked from the virtual machine. Accessing an active partition can cause serious issues with your machine.

Setting Up Dual Hardware Profiles

The next step in making your alternate operating system function well is to configure dual hardware profiles. I will first discuss how to do this with Linux, and following that I will discuss doing it with Windows. When you boot an operating system both inside and outside of a virtual machine you are effectively booting the same operating system on two different sets of hardware. The operating system needs to be able to function on both sets of hardware. This effectively means it needs two different configurations, and the appropriate configuration needs to be activated at boot time.

Under Linux, VMware performs this switch using features installed when you add the VMware Tools package to the guest operating system. During boot time a process runs which determines if the operating system is running inside a virtual machine or not. If the system is a virtual machine, then the virtual machine's hardware profile is activated. This primarily consists of copying the appropriate display drivers and X server configuration into place. There are some other things activated depending on how you configured the virtual machine hardware (such as guest/host file systems and virtual memory monitors). Finally the clipboard linking functionality is activated.

If the system is booted on the native hardware, the original native configuration files are copied into the correct place. During upgrades this process can become a bit corrupted, and the update may have to be performed on both the native and virtual machines.

Issues with Running Windows Both Natively and Virtualized

At one time it was possible to run Windows in both environments. Unfortunately a new feature known as Genuine Advantage prevents this arrangement from working. Because the hardware appears significantly different inside than outside the virtual machine, the software believes it's been copied to another machine. At this point the Windows installation is deactivated, and key features no longer function correctly.

Precautions When Running an Operating System on Both Physical and Virtualized Platforms

In the section we'll discuss precautions to take when running an operating system on physical and virtualized platforms.

Booting a Suspended Partition

One of the benefits of having your operating system virtualized is the ability to suspend execution. I recommend you suspend any virtualized partitions using the virtualization software before you suspend or hibernate the native operating system. However, this can have complications for a dual booting machine. If you suspend a secondary partition and then boot it natively it recovers in much the same way it would if you shut the machine down by powering it off. Operating systems are normally set up so that they can recover from this situation without too much difficulty. The significant issue arises when you go to use the partition in a virtual environment again. When the virtualized environment is restored, it puts the memory back in place as though it had never been suspended. Unfortunately this memory state is not aware that the disks have been recovered. Any files that were open at the time the machine was suspended are still open, and even worse some file sectors may be cached or moved during file system maintenance processes. All of these actions can create unbelievable amounts of corruption on a machine. One of the worst incidents I have ever had to recover from on my Linux machine happened as a result of this unfortunate scenario. I highly recommend that the suspended files be removed and the system be rebooted cleanly.

In order to avoid this problem I make it a habit to shutdown the virtual machine unless I'm certain that I will be back in virtual mode next (such as a reboot to bring in new updates). If there's any chance I will boot Linux (my secondary partition) native then shutting down is the safest option.

Deleting the Suspended State

If for some reason you should discover that you're caught in the above scenario, you can delete the files that store the suspended state. The state is stored in files ending in vmss and vmem. VMware is then able to boot the machine cleanly, and you should not lose any data (beyond what you lost during the original recovery process).

Changing Hardware Configurations Can Affect Your Software

It should be noted that some software uses hardware parameters during execution. The most common package that I've observed doing this is Nessus. I had issues for months before I figured this problem out. We hope this description will save others the headache.

When Nessus is activated certain information is collected from the hardware to "fingerprint" the machine. This behavior is very similar to that of Windows Genuine Advantage as discussed previously in this chapter. When the machine is booted natively (as Nessus recommends), these hardware parameters change. This causes Nessus to behave as though you have copied it from one machine to another.

I was in the habit of updating Nessus in a virtual machine and then booting it natively for actual testing. Each time I did that I had to reregister then activate my installation again. This became a more serious issue when Tenable Security (the makers of Nessus) changed their licensing requirements, which now require commercial users to purchase licenses.

Any software that depends on hardware parameters for licensing requirements may behave very differently when run inside versus outside a virtual environment. Consideration and planning should be done before installing software to know in which environment the software is most likely to be run. The installation should be done in this environment.

Summary

The ability to boot an operating system both natively and within a virtual environment is a powerful tool that can greatly increase the convenience and productivity of a security professional. In addition hardware costs can be decreased significantly by reducing the number of "audit" machines that have to be deployed and maintained.

Solutions Fast Track

How to Set Up Linux to Run Both Natively and Virtually

☑ Add the Windows partition as an option to the Grub menu.lst configuration file

☑ Copy the Linux boot sector onto Windows using DD

☑ Change the boot.ini file to include the Linux boot sector as a bootable option

Issues with Running Windows Both Natively and Virtualized

☑ Create a new machine

☑ Assign the physical partition as the primary hard drive

☑ Ensure that no partitions are accessible by both the host and the guest operating systems at the same time

☑ Create a secondary hardware profile so that the virtualized operating system can be configured correctly

Frequently Asked Questions

Q: What advantages do you gain when booting a secondary operating system natively?

A: A secondary operating system has greater access to hardware devices. This is especially important when performing wireless assessments. It would be possible to perform similar work with USB wireless cards, but they are more expensive and do not always have the features required for wireless assessments (such as packet injection). There are also some tools (Nessus being a major standout) that do not function well in virtualized environments.

Q: What advantages do you achieve with the secondary operating system running in a virtualized environment?

A: The main advantage is that both the primary and secondary servers are running at the same time. You can use either one and transfer information between them with significantly less effort that would be required if only one were running and you had to reboot to switch between them.

Chapter 13

Protection in Untrusted Environments

Solutions in this chapter:

- ■ **Using Virtual Machines to Segregate Data**

- ■ **Using Virtual Machines to Run Software You Don't Trust**

- ■ **Using Virtual Machines for Users You Don't Trust**

☑ **Summary**

☑ **Solutions Fast Track**

☑ **Frequently Asked Questions**

Introduction

One great use of virtual machines is to provide the architecture to give someone access to a machine that can be used in an untrusted environment. Imagine one of your grandparents surfing the web. They enter a URL and make a typing mistake. They are confronted with a pop up message telling them that they have a virus and need to click on a link to fix it. How many of them would resist doing just that? There are obviously ways to prevent damaging the server and the underlying operating system, but these methods generally do not protect the user from hurting themselves. One method that has some merit is to use a virtual machine to perform everyday tasks such as browsing. The virtual machine is then reverted to the known good snapshot on a regular basis. This may be weekly, hourly, or even more often depending on the environment.

I have also seen technically savvy users utilize this method to browse sites they know are dangerous. They browse with the knowledge that their machine is almost certainly compromised, so no personal information should be used in it. They use these machines to read forums or run jokes sent to them by friends. Immediately after running the offending application, they revert the machine back to its pristine uninfected condition and continue with their day without worrying that the file they just executed may have damaged something.

Every day computer users face the choice of installing a new piece of software. Software is another consumer product neatly marketed, packaged, and made appealing by a host of pundits and influencers. Yet is that software good for your system or is it potentially malicious? Shades of gray are many, just like security postures practiced by consumers and enterprises. A healthy dose of caution when dealing with new and unknown software and documents is very much welcome.

For a curious user there's always a big question: do I take a plunge and install something I may not be able to easily remove later on, or do I simply give up. It can be a choice of biblical proportions. Virtual machines in most cases offer a simpler and safer playground than your primary machine.

Meaningful Uses of Virtualization in Untrusted Environments

As responsible computer users we need to be cognizant of modern computing realities. There is neither a warranty for software nor an international or government body that verifies software quality. In general we need to be skeptical or worried about alleged interoperability testing. Application separation for testing and pleasure is a good solution here, best implemented through virtual machines that unlike emulators implement the full richness of the original operating system.

But useful scenarios abound. For example, installing a VMware codec to record videos of virtual machines is not a big deal, but when it BSODs (Blue Screen of Death) my Vista machine, it is very much an inconvenience. As codecs and system drivers in general are potential deal killers on Vista, as a concerned user, I may have a valid and pressing need to find a solution for this problem. In my case my friendly QA department has recorded my failure scenario and demanded to review it. Instead of risking further trouble on Vista, I took a Vista VM image, installed the required VMware codec, and attempted to play the questionable clip there. The failure (with complete VM image) was then shipped to QA for further investigation. Obvious benefits were realized, the crash could be investigated, and my critical infrastructure was not affected.

This codec example was not security related, but it illustrates a straightforward benefit of a virtualization strategy. We can separate critical parts of our personal or business computing and isolate them to minimize application instability risk. Thus it can pay big for companies to distribute critical applications onto separate VM instances for operational as well as security benefits.

Consumers and enterprise users have discovered a wide variety of ways to use virtual machines as go-betweens for deferring security risks. It creates a new adage: what you can't do with a physical machine, you can do in a virtual machine. Some useful examples where complete functional segregation really does make sense are the following:

1. **Accessing your Internal CRM Implementation** CRMs and other line-of-business applications often bear the brunt of targeted malware attacks (which means that an AV signature is unlikely to be available). For example, Trend Micro Labs published that on September 12 of 2007 they saw 1,100 custom attacks in only 16 hours. As accurate data on custom attacks is hard to come by, we have to assume that our best security posture is the safest. So whether to discipline your call center staff or comply with various Sarbanes-Oxley or PCI requirements, keeping confidential application data (such as credit cards numbers or health records) separate from the polluted personal computing space is exceptionally prudent. This then allows enterprise administrators to define a so-called "application wall" and properly lock down virtual machine images providing assurance that only approved and

properly configured enterprise applications are used in a quarantined environment. Sometimes software applications distributed in this manner are called virtual appliances. But the term has a connotation that VM images are not for general users or average employees but rather something that belongs in a data center. Virtualization technology has significantly matured since the term was coined, and today we can virtualize VPN and a host of proprietary client applications fit for every type of user.

2. **Personal Playground** On the other side of the line separating line-of-business applications from personal computing is the employee's personal playground. Employees today expect to be allowed to do whatever they please with corporate PCs issued to them. Virtualization is then ideally used for segregating general Web browsing. Surfing the Web in a separate OS is a great way to limit your exposure to SQL Injection exploits and vulnerabilities directed against browsers and their add-on components. We will come back to this topic later in this chapter. Many enterprises could benefit by moving personal Web experiences onto a separate virtual "disk image" away from cumbersome and expensive compliance procedures that most companies need to implement. In a separate virtual machine a user can install all of their favorite IM, VOIP, and other tools, and quite literally, use it as a safer personal playground. In addition, enterprise administrators will be able to add to the mix a favorite anti-malware solution or could even opt for a controlled application whitelisting solution in order to maintain visibility and accountability. Once the first security products implementing the VMSafe program come to market that too can be transparently added to further protect these personal computing playgrounds. VMware's VMSafe program allows security vendors to scan and analyze virtual machines by not physically residing inside a virtual OS but rather being an application that is part of the virtualization server core. It is expected that other virtualization vendors will soon be making similar security announcements: a security product will run on the virtualization server or hypervisor level with full access to virtual disks and virtual memory (which is in effect on disk as well). Their efficiency will be improved as will be our security. Only let's not take it as a solution for zero-day or custom exploit attacks.

3. **System Rollback** Finally, reverting back to an initial image or to a last known trusted state can be done on a schedule that makes sense for users

and administrators. This in itself can help troubleshoot a host of other non-security related issues from sluggish performance due to large browser caches to instantly fixing disk defragmentation issues. It is often said that Windows and other operating systems suffer from memory loss over time as things get forgotten and operations take longer and longer. By effectively separating functional work spaces, for example, line-of-business applications and private computing, virtualization can help us regain control and rein in software application performance losses.

4. **Software Application Testing for Operating System Compliance** Most operating systems routinely release major new versions and with each such change risk breaking backward compatibility or various compliance policies. For example, it turns out that the best way to test new Vista compliant software applications is to actually run them in a Vista virtual machine (hopefully configured with your standard software and network settings) and see what happens before irreparably ruining your working system image. This seems like a silly recommendation, but given the level of incompatibility issues and serious consequences (hosed users and Blue Screens of Death), it is not surprising that major PC resellers like HP and Dell are offering XP downgrade paths for purchasers of their new hardware until at least June of 2009. Note that end-of-life for Windows XP has been announced with the availability of Vista.

5. **Quarantine of Suspicious Content** In the last year first serious attacks against Adobe Flash then media exploits of image files and videos were witnessed. It is no longer only unknown software, scripts, and documents with macro languages that are prone to malicious behavior. If you are investigating an exploit of an unannounced vulnerability, viewing images, video, or animations whose provenance cannot be proven is best done within a virtual machine. If you are doing this most likely you are on the forefront of malware research, whether working for one of the major security companies or a security analyst for Internet service providers (ISPs) or companies with known security exposures like banks and governmental institutions. Properly locked down virtual machines are best sandbox solutions for the job if you are working with a full OS and can install further tools to monitor behavior and actions of a questionable sample.

6. **Behavior Examination of Potential Malware** Unlike the use of sandbox tools, which usually give you a flavor for the capabilities of a potential piece

of code, building an environment for behavior forensics is another matter. For one you are implicitly more concerned about security and using gloves when necessary. On the other hand your role is more akin to that of a surgeon. You need better tools and more assistance. Debuggers like the free OllyDBG and disassemblers like IDA Pro are your tools; virtualization infrastructure is your assistant. At this stage, everything matters especially whether you are working with 16-bit mutex-es, 32-bit code or 64-bit code. For example, even the Beta version of OllyDBG 2.0 is not able to help you with 64-bit analysis. Anti-debugging libraries and exploits targeting vulnerabilities in virtualization software will also cause trouble. But as a safe first step virtual machines are a great choice for giving you a steady reading on what a piece of malware is up to.

Notes from the Underground...

Anti-debugging Libraries

The anti-malware industry has been using virtualization in malware research and product testing for some time now. Yet recent "commercial" anti-debugging libraries have made the industry re-examine this strategy as quite a few malicious samples change their behavior when run in a virtual machine. It has become increasingly difficult to detect dangerous samples, examine their behaviors, and build effective signatures. The Anti-Malware Testing Standards Organization (AMTSO) is attempting to address these issues by issuing guidance to both researchers and testers on how to observe malware in a virtualized environment. As today's security products rely primarily on "active protection" elements, they detect malware when it is actively executed. Such detection methods can be tested only in a controlled virtual environment that is as close to the real world scenario as possible. But to truly observe an application's behavior today, you need to be cognizant of modern anti-detection methods. If a piece of malware detects suspicious monitoring, it simply changes its behavior. In turn a researcher may realize thousands of instructions later that the code is running in a virtual loop or doing nothing significant.

Continued

E.G. Oreans's Themida protection mechanism used on many commercial games as well as malware adds to every dll as much as 2MB of bogus code to thwart any attempts at meaningful reverse engineering. In this way game software publishers as well as other legitimate companies that are worried about intellectual property theft are protecting themselves against software cracks and the most blatant of code thefts. Virtualization alone is not security's silver bullet. It can be exceptionally effective in reverting virtual images to their clean state. Starting from a known point is much faster than re-imaging your target system. But it is prone to modern detecting techniques. Hence for testing and research purposes not only one but rather two methods are critical: testing in a virtualized environment with all its efficiency benefits, and testing on a real system with all the volatility of an infected system. One effective method for doing this is combining a virtualized solution with a system re-imaging. For example, one can use Symantec Ghost. You would need to set up parallel installations that are blind to each other. Virtualization would be a preferred and optimal choice while oblivious to presence of a re-imaging solution. A re-imaging solution would then be able to replace a virtualization installation in cases where systems are deemed compromised or no virtual machine was able to yield malware detection on samples determined by other heuristic methods to be malicious in nature.

On the other side of the virtualization debate there are good arguments advocating caution when it comes to the exuberance that has recently marked public interest into virtualization technologies for malicious research. Recently, a surge in vulnerabilities with virtualization software has been reported. IBM's ISS X-Force team has spotlighted this trend in its 2008 Midyear Security Report (see note number one). As usual the more popular a software title is the more eyeballs it attracts from both users and researchers as well as attackers. The National Vulnerability Database (NVD) sets the tone. Of the total vulnerabilities assigned to VMware almost half were discovered in the last year, and a majority of them carry a "high severity" CVSS score (see note number two). Out of these a majority was discovered against products running on Windows and not enterprise products like ESX, which are not based on Windows. Yet the increase in vulnerabilities has been felt for all types of virtualization operating systems. Even more so up to now untouchable hypervisor micro–operating systems are increasingly coming under scrutiny. As a comparison, VMware had a one-fifth vulnerability ratio as compared to Microsoft products. The situation with Citrix was a bit different with 12 vulnerabilities out of 50 for all of the last year with only three marked with a "high severity" CVSS score.

One of the VMware Hypervisor architects boasted to me at the RSA Show in San Francisco in 2007 that VMware Hypervisor cannot be broken: A great promise, one of those that we always fear in software. Yet it appears to be holding water for now. Hypervisor technology is a great step forward as it locks down the micro-kernel to only the relevant set of components required to run the platform. To date most of the vulnerabilities found against VMware's Virtualization Server platform were related to packages not created by VMware, which has exposed the platform to standard vulnerabilities found against the Linux platform. This in itself has been a major driving factor for VMware and its customers moving to ESXi architecture, which promises to reduce ill effects of the underlying Linux platform. As the virtualization movement gains strength there will also be added scrutiny of virtualization server platforms. Similarly hypervisor installations (now few as the technology is rather new) will undergo further scrutiny, and any zero vulnerability boast will most likely not stand.

This is important because vulnerabilities in virtualization platforms invite security exploits that could potentially erase all the security benefits the virtualization platform provides. Hence the question: Is it okay to allow VM to be infected? After all it is a disposable VM instance that can be recycled at will regardless of the exploit vectors that it was exposed to. The truth is that you better be disconnected if you want to be sure. Vulnerabilities found against the core platform could lead to wholesale system compromise where the damage could be much worse than with standard setups. Proper management and network optimization of virtual switches and virtual machines will go a long way to limiting damage.

Looking back at the history of malware protection, we note that it didn't take very much for the blockbuster infections Sobig-F (see note number three) or MyDoom (see note number four) to circle the planet. And these are not the only ones. Sobig-F was the sixth variant in the Sobig virus series generating 300,000 infections per day. MyDoom extended this to 1.2 million infections per day. And this was still 2004. With today's broadband speeds you need to practice as much caution as possible. Hence I'd like to define levels of precaution, if not paranoia that are important when analyzing malicious samples. These precautions are increasingly costly and difficult to administer but nevertheless practiced widely in industry.

Levels of Malware Analysis Paranoia

Whether you are investigating suspicious software or an outright known and malicious piece of software, some core precautions are in order. Lessons from anti-malware and forensics industries are the best guidance. These are recommendations for the most paranoid and not necessary for all purposes. Trying out compatibility of new NVidia drivers on a Windows Vista image do not fall into this category.

1. **Set Up Proper VM Images** Create standard (based on Federal Desktop Core Configuration or FDCC) VM images with sandbox tools that trace registry, file, and network actions. Add ring 0 and ring 3 debuggers and install disassembles. Inventory registry and files so that you can do a baseline analysis at a later stage. Fingerprint all files. Stay away from MD5 hashes. Have fun: Execute new software or browse suspicious Web sites in a virtual machine.

2. **Set Up Virtual Network** Set up a separate Web network that is not connected to your corporate, private, or any other networks. You can at worst use conservative tools such as RSYNC or file drop points to exchange data and messages. IP KVMs help you seamlessly monitor disconnected networks and allow you to switch from one virtualized setup to another. A separate network allows malware to communicate with its command and control servers and behave as it would on a regular machine but will also limit the potential damage to your infrastructure if analysis gets out of hand.

3. **Set Up Disconnected Network** Create a surrogate Internet where all the outbound traffic is routed to your network sink. Log and evaluate traffic. Install IDS end point agents into your virtual machines. Monitor network traffic. Use Metasploit tools and HttpSinkholing to evaluate traffic.

One only needs to remember the "Hall of Fame" malicious attacks such as Blaster & Nachi Internet Worms whose rapid propagation had serious effects on many security labs. You may not have the ease of silently recycling every single instance of your Windows operating system. Even a few hours of downtime due to security restore could be deadly to companies who live and die by the 9 to 5 clock. You would theoretically have the ability to roll back many of your VM instances, but a failure to do so or the existence of a single unpatched endpoint could always trigger a re-infection one degree worse than the last.

CoreSecurity publicized in March of 2008 several VMware Player vulnerabilities (see note number five) that allowed an attacking malicious code or sample under investigation to get control not only over the Player application but also over the host system itself. Many malware analysts are using highly portable VMware Players to do a "back-of-the-envelope" first pass. That is a dangerous procedure as this vulnerability illustrates. This example involving shared folder traversals like the ones before them are serious but can be avoided by properly tuning the virtual machines and modifying the business process to limit obvious exposure points. When analyzing outright potentially malicious code one needs to exercise caution. Using fully blown virtualization products is a must as are cleanup and backup procedures in the unlikely scenario that the entire setup becomes corrupt.

Damage & Defense...

Shared Folders Vulnerabilities When Running Inside Windows

Several generations of vulnerabilities target VMware Shared Folder implementation when running inside Microsoft Windows. The ESX version of VMware is not affected. By not properly parsing the path, a very simple remote code execution attack can be performed. These vulnerabilities are well documented and tracked in CVE and NVD databases. Your best defense in this case is to implement your own shared folder functionality that does not run utilize VMware's flawed implementation. Even more so you should disable the feature in the VMware software that you are using.

One of the latest approaches to locking down VM images is to use application control or application whitelisting endpoint agents by companies such as Bit9. They employ positive security approaches to end point protection (see note number six). Currently, only a handful of companies are focusing on such an approach realizing that it is much easier to manage exceptions that diverge from a known and trusted software image. Any divergence—be it the existence of new files on the file system or suspicious registry entries and in-memory artifacts—could be a trigger for recycling a virtual machine or for performing in-depth forensics analysis. Allowing software to run and asking questions later is a sure recipe for disaster.

Having a measurable degree of a virtual machine lockdown cannot be emphasized more as proliferation of end point always implies the multiplication of your risk exposure even though your goal was to separate risky applications from business critical software. The reality is that your virtual machine instance is a fully fledged operating system carrying all the traditional exposure elements. For example, how often do you plan to update paused or running virtual machines to install the latest OS security updates? Are you planning to follow the same procedure for all other non-Microsoft produced code?

The simple answer is that there has to be a procedure for this especially if you are planning to expose your VM images to untrusted environments. Proper patching is no longer an exotic task. There are quite a few patch management vendors providing compelling solutions. Yet many of these solutions have only a limited grasp on existing security updates available. Take for example your typical Windows System Tray and you will see dozens of software applications that have automatic updaters available. That means that all those applications could automatically be updating your "trusted" image. They could also be new vectors for out-of-date security updates. In 2008 there were no less than 30 critical vulnerabilities in NVD attributed to software publishers not signing their software updates. These updates were distributed through their automatic update mechanisms. But the worst development of all is the increased focus on attacks against third party software, software that we have so far ignored when analyzing our security postures. That same software runs on your standard Windows image; whether it is running on iron or inside a virtual machine, it generates the same vulnerability exposure, which needs to be detected and dealt with.

Traditionally, Windows hardening initiatives were the only set of guidelines on how to de facto trickle down the performance and capacity of your operating system. Removing rights to one or the other operation, hiding or disabling icons, and preventing access to system or monitoring tools were all done as a proactive measure to keep intruders and malicious users from exploiting the system to its fullest. While credit has to be given to the richness of controls built into the GPO model—which addresses a multitude of levers from power consumption to identity management—in one specific area Microsoft GPO policies are a giant case study on how not to control software on an endpoint. This is not meant to bash the ecosystem of companies that provide valuable GPO tools such as NetIQ's Group Policy Administrator. GPOs are traditionally seen as a part of configuration change management where changes are controlled and audited by IT administrators.

Software application control is yet another matter. For example, it is highly unproductive to use GPOs to control and monitor how and when software applications execute. In such cases you have to dedicate at least one full sysadmin resource to manage fickle GPO rules that were not designed for software application control.

We say fickle because too many rules create a bizarre set of laws and regulations that can be explained only through historic intent and not through their functionality. For example, prevent execution based on filenames or extensions is not going to prevent people from doing what they want. Within the GPO object model software policies are not meant to be adaptive. They are either compliant or not. Yet with the proliferation of virtualized endpoints, GPO rules for software application management are bound to become more complex and as such utterly unmanageable. Clearly a better solution is necessary.

Tools & Traps...

Don't Let Your Processor Waste Cycles on Your Multiple Displays

It sounds obvious but the use of native graphic applications does help manage multiple displays. It is better to use your graphics card rather than abuse precious CPU time. Plus it's the best way to monitor actions on multiple virtual machines. For example, Matrox PowerSpace is a tool that has been specifically tuned for optimization of virtualized screens (see Figure 13.1). Of course, it runs on Matrox hardware, but this sort of tool is not exclusive to Matrox. Once you start running multiple virtual machines to examine and test software and malicious components, you will start to appreciate the convenience of having the graphics cards give back CPU cycles to virtual machines. Features you want to check out are: graceful log out of a virtual machine and application display management.

Figure 13.1 The Matrox PowerSpace Tool

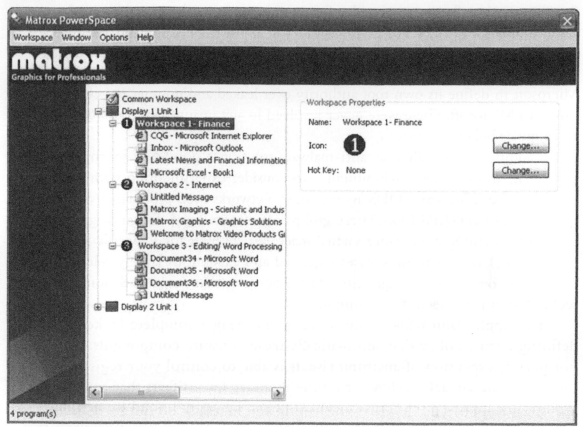

Source: Matrox.com

A better alternative is available from Tripwire when security servers and non–Windows operating systems. Faronics can help you with a simple single end point lockdown agent, while Bit9 can provide you with a complete enterprise application whitelisting suite built to manage access to all software applications whether malicious or benign. A typical tool that accomplishes a true end point lockdown does several things for you. For one it internally defines a software baseline. This internal cache can then be used to determine whether a new piece of software is automatically added to the approved set of components or is treated as a possible intruder. Automatism at this task is highly desired as any user interaction with automatic software installation procedures would only confuse. One does not need to be a home user to be confused over the existence of questionable reusable components claiming to be from Microsoft. Seamless automatism can be achieved by allowing flexibility in installation of trusted software components as long as they conform to some simple set of rules. For example, one can approve software from a known set of highly trusted software publishers who have never had an issue with their digital certificates. There was a longstanding dispute between Microsoft and VeriSign that led Microsoft to define its own root authority over leaked and now retired certificates issued to Microsoft. These were never involved in any unauthorized use contrary to the popular belief.

In addition to installing an anti-malware solution, a good way to improve your posture in an untrusted environment is to consider experimenting with stricter HIPS tools and host-based IDS agents. Altor Networks even produces a virtualization specific set of IDS/IPS tools. These groups of software were design to generally not trust executing code. Since virtual machines are built for a specific purpose, expected behavior is in most cases expected and exceptions largely relevant. Hence, the overwhelming quantity of false positives that come with some of these technologies is reduced to a minimum.

In an application whitelisting solution enforcing a complete lockdown means defining a trust policy that automatically trusts software components. It does not permit execution of anything else. It is able to control your registry and monitor your virtual machine's runtime memory for artifacts that are not specifically approved. The trust mechanism can be easily bound by defining a certain set of digital certificates, software sources, or administrative users that we inherently trust.

Another concept that could be leveraged is a so-called block-and-ask mode. In this mode a user is warned whenever a new executable software component is added to the virtual machine. This can be exceptionally powerful when working with browser appliances because downloading additional software or browser plug-ins is an action with expressed user intent. When warned, a user is able to affirmatively acknowledge their intent. If on the other hand a warning arrives when just browsing the Internet, it is a signal of an exploit being attempted against the virtual machine and the user is able to self-police by blocking such a request. In this way we expect the user to know what is appropriate and what is not. When browsing the Internet administrators could trust this general guidance as anti-malware tools and URL filtering devices are able to protect against outright violators.

A good starting point is always a healthy VM image. With Windows you can build your own golden image: your favorite configuration with your favorite tuning. Or you can leave this job to the government. Even though this may sound weird to the uninitiated, the National Institute of Standards and Technology (NIST) has done a tremendous amount of progress towards a common set of FDCC desktop operating system images (see Figure 13.2). The FDCC program stands for Federal Desktop Core Configuration and has received a fair amount of attention in the last few years as NIST, the National Security Agency with guidance from Microsoft, and other organizations have been looking at the best ways to certify software common desktop platforms and instill a level of configuration and platform control that we have required of automotive and pharmaceuticals industries but have not yet required from the software industry. As our power grid, waterways, and national defenses are controlled by systems that among others run Microsoft Windows, this seems reasonable. In 1.0 implementation FDCC offers images for Windows XP SP2 and Windows Vista that can be freely downloaded and used as an excellent baseline for all future virtualization and security projects. They include a standard OS installation with a series of hardening steps. Additional ones could be applied through a recommended set of GPO rules and IE7 and firewall hardening configurations. For example, it just makes sense to turn off autoplay for hardware devices and keep wireless devices off by default. RunOnce registry settings are disabled by default. A Vista-specific setting requires the use of signed device drivers, a policy that is usually left unenforced in today's Vista installations. As your purpose-built VM image is going to have as little contact with hardware devices, it makes sense that you go the extra mile and require signed device drivers, ones that are most likely going to come from a certified source. You may choose to alter or modify the hardened settings to fit your situation. Still many things are not addressed such as Vista audit policy settings, some tunneling protocols, and anonymous SID-name translations. Images can be found on http://fdcc.nist.gov. Of course, you will need to make sure that Windows licensing is your problem.

Figure 13.2 FDCC Downloads

Documentation	GPOs	SCAP Content
2008.06.20 FDCC Settings major version 1.0 - Final [xls, 456K] **SHA-1 Digest:** 06D8087A0CF572F 368B4DAB5CD15B4 69029A52DC **SHA-256 Digest:** 42AA5F3849D21E 54C8FF3187E46E 5D9EA7EC17E9D7 F2539F8F30D510 DE06E229	**2008.06.20** FDCC 2008 Q3 GPO Release -Final [zip, ~3 MB] **SHA-1 Digest:** 831F0755E3771 C4C47FC7B8847 D8AF2200DBB6AA **SHA-256 Digest:** B73D3A40CBEE922B77 3B038A8D00D839DC1A8 38A8D22109F35F80AB7 1D85FC09 Known Issues	**2008.06.20** Windows XP, Vista, firewall, and IE 7. - Final [zip, ~460K] **SHA-1 Digest:** 9E95E65D0623E8825A4 54EEF2FD01D9FD416 8266 **SHA-256 Digest:** 0511913B44E9522A693AF 0777FB37DB29C070B109EA 649D6A00B6B2423E6B87D Known Issues The preceding files are intended for use with "SCAP FDCC scanning capable" tools.
2008.06.20 FDCC Settings Changes major version 1.0 - [xls, 25K] **SHA-1 Digest:** 1B2C6FD06D78F31AA08E 29DFED887BE4E56D80F8 **SHA-256 Digest:** 2B8D404730A192E2B55D 44DC86773CE1D7E4B5433 FA4508AC87438F6A3FE997D		

VHD Files	SHA-1 Digest	SHA-256 Digest	Note
Windows XP FDCC VHD Release 1.0 - Part 1 of 7 - Final [zip, ~178MB]	C60D32A19D33785 7FCB72CCBC0246D E2AC107FBE	3227AD7C4BA5B0069B 5840DC840B03399C9B 9F57AD38A76D1B3EAA 886AC8B462	2008.06.20 2008 Q3 VHD released NOTE: Download the six files. Use WinZip to open the archive and extract the .VHD and .VMC files.
Windows XP FDCC VHD Release 1.0 - Part 2 of 7 - Final [zip, ~648MB]	6BAC158A308DBE2E 802A4CE46D28A06A B8D58286	D209D32EBEE50F9972 F3E2087BE1499C02B9 6E90F3B30FAD2C5F7D 448E94D147	

Source: http://fdcc.nist.gov

Using Virtual Machines to Segregate Data

The National Security Agency (NSA) has been spearheading the NetTop effort for the last six years. It is an effort that transposes many Virtual Desktop Infrastructure (VDI) ideas and complicates it by adding multiple parallel and disconnected networks. A fresh life was given to the effort in the large NSA booth at the RSA conference in San Francisco in April of 2008. NetTop provides guidance to security agencies that can truly harvest the power of virtualization. NSA's goal is to improve management and support for safe co-existence of confidential and non-confidential data and networks. Today a typical high security facility has a multiplicity of end point and networking equipment to address this unique security challenge faced by government and military facilities worldwide. But a similar principle applies for banking and pharmaceutical industries. Just for a second let's go back to a high security environment, and let's imagine a work desk with six different towers, all sporting different colored Ethernet wires leading into different hubs. At best you are looking at one monitor (using a KVM switch), but you could easily have multiple monitors in order to oversee status on several networks at the same time. It is obvious that this is costly and inefficient. Users are not happy, system administrators even less so, and the organizations that fund this mess hate it. Still it is the reality until NetTop gets widely implemented.

The NetTop project has produced several compliant prototype configurations that run on commonly available hardware (see note number seven). Many commercial companies such as HP and Juniper are seeing the future in the NetTop paradigm as well. Thin client vendors would like to reduce the desktop iron to a neat and light end point box that brings disparate networks together and only displays remotely powered applications on a single monitor. The real magic would happen on powerful virtualized switches and hardware serving perfectly separate and differently config-ured networks. If there is no way for a virtualized guest system to interact with the virtualization infrastructure, it is then assumed that it will not be able to break into guest system instances belonging to a different network with different security and confidentiality requirements.

This solution is also applicable to a host of other implementers. Government contractors for one will need to be able to integrate into this new paradigm. But more importantly financial institutions run parallel networks that need to clear and broker a wide variety of complex transactions. Pharmaceutical research and manufacturing floors are frequently segregated from the rest of the world with contact personnel using multiple systems and providing for failure points. Simple mistakes such as putting a USB key in the wrong socket or connecting a network cable to the wrong hub were "Doh!" moments that have in some instances brought down entire organizations for days at a time. In a national security scenario these exposures could be catastrophic.

Using Virtual Machines to Run Software You Don't Trust

Developing your ultimate set of VM images for the analysis and running of software that you generally do not trust should not be an impossible task. But as anyone who has tried to diligently install a major OS upgrade such as Windows Vista from scratch, this process can take a long time. I am not picking on Vista here, but OS installations in general are always time consuming efforts. The steps given here are not mandatory but are rather presented in an order describing an ascending level of depth and control that you may want to exercise over your ultimate disposable testing environment.

The first step is to create or obtain a baseline OS image with relevant corporate and security software installed. FDCC's Windows XP and Windows Vista images (see note number eight) are a great start, but many organizations have already pre-configured and pre-installed "golden" images. FDCC images can be easily downloaded from the NIST Web site.

An operating system baseline is at some points an artistic decision. Different people for different purposes might include networking or corporate applications that they do not trust into a baseline for testing software. Whether unknown software is trying to kill pop-ups generated by your Oracle CRM application, installing a filter into your corporate VPN application, or hooking into your legacy terminal application is best determined when a potentially vulnerable target is part of the baseline OS. Targeted attacks do not happen if the configuration does not correspond to reality.

Keeping a running tally of VM template images is a good procedure for maintaining configuration consistency across a multitude of different virtual instances. For example, OS install should be followed by network and VPN setup if you are building browser or internal application appliances. Critical applications should follow not in order of their importance but rather in the software stack order: device drivers first, followed by middleware, and ending with end client applications such as Web browsers and Oracle and SAP end user agents.

The next step following the application stack metaphor is system hardening. It can be built as a separate and isolated step that can be managed separately. Security postures could evolve by including less or more strict policies. These should naturally build on top of a well configured VM template and before target applications are installed. Windows Vista has introduced a host of new GPO policies and lockdown functionality. On the one hand you should not expect to truly lock down a Windows Vista system. This means that there would be no native way in Vista to prevent the installation of unauthorized software, be it through temporary browser cache or elsewhere in the VM image. On the other hand tweaking GPO policies is a very worthwhile step. The FDCC recommended GPO policy settings are a great start.

After installing software applications that are part of your purpose-built virtual appliance, you could optimize user experience by launching and pausing VM instances. VM image in paused states can then be used for reverting back to a known good state or performing a differential analysis in order to identify what has changed in the file system or the Windows registry since the last known point.

Some effort should be taken at hardening the environment outside of the VM instance. Tools are available on the market, for example, Configuresoft's Compliance Checker, that will assess the health of a virtualization server looking for basic security exposures such as vulnerable password policies, root login restrictions, Mac address spoofing, misconfiguration among console firewall, and syslog services.

An extremely useful step to consider is building your own HTTP Sinkhole which intercepts and terminates all HTTP network traffic. ShadowServer Foundation has expressed intention to build what many people have accomplished through multiple scripts into a stand-alone offering (see note number six). Another open source project is underway with leadership coming out of AOL Time Warner but is without an official Web page. This project plans to aggregate tools required to offer easy installation and configuration of HTTP Sinkholes whose importance resides in being able to intercept botnets outgoing traffic, analyze it properly, and potentially reverse the command and control protocol to allow security professionals to assume control over infected systems and instantly shut down their malicious behavior.

Inside the virtual machine instance a proper set of tools can bring exceptional visibility over software execution of unknown components. Logging all file system and registry access is a great first step. There are a number of tools available from HijackThis, Metasploit, and Mandiant that can help monitor application activity.

If you are interested in an in-depth malware or binary analysis or a true form forensics, a next step down is mandatory use of debuggers and disassemblers. OllyDBG provides a good solution for 32-bit environments, though we still do not have appropriate 64-bit ring 3 or user mode debuggers (see Figure 13.3). This could lead to some serious trouble if the penetration of 64-bit Windows systems was any more common. On the ring 0 kernel level Norman provides the best tool for reversing and monitoring the execution of unknown code in a Windows kernel. As the popularity of various packing or compression and software protection techniques is on the rise especially among the writers of malicious code, debugging and analysis is not complete without a proper disassembly tool such as IDA Pro. Disassembly can help identify binary protection artifacts or bogus code designed not to look suspicious or to frustrate researchers. Some modern software protection techniques add a sufficient amount of redundant or indirect code through parallel threads, countless assertions and code re-interpretation that it requires reverse engineers of the highest caliber to be able to extract the potentially malicious payload.

To make matters worse anti-debugging and anti-VM tricks have made it to the commercial market place and are now available as software libraries. They detect whether your software is running in a virtual environment; it then alters its behavior. There are numerous methods to perform this check. In one scenario all a malicious code needs to do is to look for the presence of rdtsc hooking. Rdtsc is present on newer processors such as Pentium Pros and AMDs and has been available for the last several years. It controls the processor clock and is very important to the function of the VMware server unlike a traditional OS, which needs to coordinate execution of multiple kernels and as such needs to have complete control over the system clock.

If all of these steps are followed, you will end up with an operating system image loaded with all the software that is the key to the success of your enterprise, and it will have all the required monitoring and forensics tools needed to properly assess the trustworthiness of any given piece of executable code.

Figure 13.3 OllyDBG Binary Level Analysis

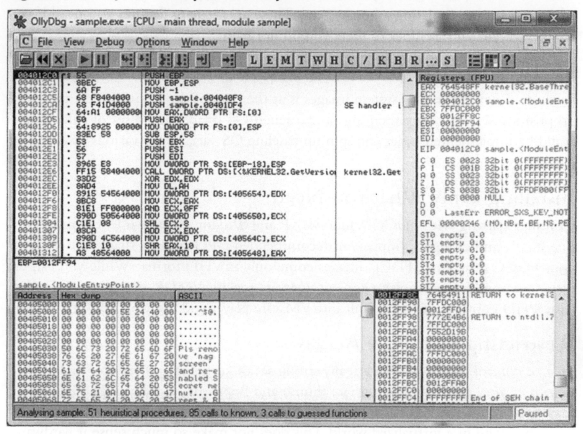

Using Virtual Machines for Users You Don't Trust

VMware's ACE product line is exceptionally useful for generation of disposable images for public use including users you do not trust. There are other vendors in this market as well; so if more control over VM is desired one should certainly do well in evaluating competing solutions.

What is attractive about the ACE model is an additional level of management that you can apply to virtual machine instances that you issue. ACE allows you to encrypt your virtual image. This can then be used by a single user or given to a designated group of users all sharing similar settings. Furthermore these images can be run directly from a USB drive for ultimate portability. You should not expect lightning fast performance though. ACE also allows you to control VM image with rules-based

network access (locking out systems by port or traffic type) and to better implement
a host quarantine (isolating a host system). These are security features you need if you
are to give virtual machines to users you do not trust.

Setting up the Client Machine

Setting up new operating system images is at the core of the virtualization value
proposition. Here we are focusing on hardened OS images and a set of rules that
could be implemented to let you spin up baseline OS variants for various investigative
purposes.

Installing Only What You Need

Consider starting with FDCC Windows XP and Windows Vista hardened images
(see note number eight). Implement recommended GPO policies that come with
your FDCC download. FDCC images come only in VHD format. While you can use
http://vmtoolkit.com tools to convert VMware specific VMDK images to VHD files,
basic VHD converter VHD is built into VMware player and the workstation.

Restricting Hardware Access

Device control solutions offer a really strong set of kernel ring 0 features that allow
you to custom tailor the appropriate thumb and floppy drive policies. The best bet
may be to simply disable them for good because access to hardware devices may not
be appropriate in a virtualized world. This does not make so much sense if hardware
is locked up in a data center unless of course an organization has hundreds of IT
administrators. It does make a lot of sense for thin computing stations where host
hardware still has some functionality.

Restricting Software Access

Application control solutions from vendors like Bit9 allow you to drastically reduce
the attack surface of the operating systems residing in your virtual machine by
expressly defining what is and is not approved (see Figure 13.4). In this way any
divergence is reported and can be instantly acted upon. You may want to be notified
in a Vista Universal Access Control (UAC) manner or you may want to block from
execution anything that does not belong to the software image of the type of software
that you want to allow to execute. For example, you may want to allow all Microsoft
security updates to automatically install, and you do not want the arduous task
of continually updating your baseline images.

Figure 13.4 Software Lockdown

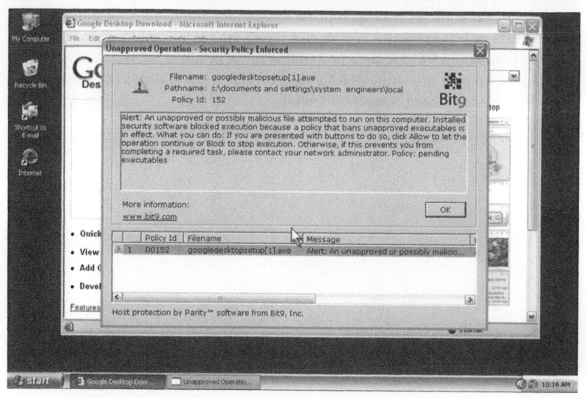

Scripting the Restore

Basic approaches to virtual machine restore depend on the number of personalized data settings that need to be recovered. The most basic approach is to stop and destroy the corrupted virtual machine image. But if more flexibility is necessary a backup procedure can be implemented with the backup agent of your choice. Most of this can be easily scripted and put on a schedule. Another option is to use specific backup features available with products such as VMware VCB (VMware Consolidated Backup) where you do not need to have an individual backup agent inside of each VM Image. This option can be scripted as well. The basic difference between these two approaches is in the way the backup is performed. If you do it from within each image you can do a file by file backup optimization, but you will lose efficiency if all your VM instances decide to start performing backup at the same time. VMware VCB on the other hand will perform better but will not give you visibility inside each VM image for a more optimal backup experience. Still, backing up entire images is an appropriate solution for protecting your purpose-built VM appliances. It is important to note that there's yet a third option geared toward big iron installations. VCB is quite powerful as it was designed for large VMware installations running primarily on SAN devices. This solution also is not a breeze to implement so one should consider it carefully.

Summary

Security has high hopes for virtualization as it gives researchers an unprecedented view into the behavior of unknown software applications. Virtual machines have been used for quite some time among top anti-malware companies. A recent surge of reported vulnerabilities and the emergence of commercial anti-VM libraries have pushed for these companies to change their posture and begin adapting to a world where virtualization is a highly valuable tool but is also an untrusted environment.

In the enterprise virtualization is improving security procedures by allowing purpose-built appliances to be built and deployed in untrusted environments. It redefines how enterprises think about their software risk exposure and how to best manage their business critical software assets. Separation between critical and risky has been long a conundrum of personal computing. The disposable nature of virtual machine images is about to change where and how we use software applications.

Solutions Fast Track

Using Virtual Machines to Segregate Data

☑ Business critical software applications are best run in isolation

☑ Purpose-built appliances need to implement prudent system hardening methods

☑ Application whitelisting and application control solutions give the best lockdown

Using Virtual Machines to Run Software You Don't Trust

☑ Unknown applications are best tested in virtualized network and end point settings

☑ Be cognizant that virtualization vulnerabilities and anti-VM libraries exist

☑ Implement network and end point system segregation

☑ Monitor all aspects of file system and network activity with all relevant debugging and reversing tools at your disposal

Using Virtual Machines
for Users You Don't Trust

☑ Virtual machines are perfect for segregating untrusted users from themselves

☑ Be cognizant that virtualization vulnerabilities and anti-VM libraries exist

☑ Harden each virtual machine security posture and validate virtualization server security settings

☑ Manage untrusted users by permitting approved and denying all other software execution

Frequently Asked Questions

Q: What should I consider when using VM images for testing suspicious Web sites or potential malware?

A: You should be cognizant of the fact that there are commercial anti-debugging and anti-VM toolkits out there. Based on their information some advanced malware alters its execution, aborts, or launches virtual machine specific exploits. Consider building a specialized lab that is as separate from your mission critical infrastructure as possible. Consider building a HTTP sinkhole so that you can easily analyze, spoof, and redirect HTTP traffic. Most recent botnet traffic has migrated to the HTTP protocol as it affords a larger surface attack area.

Q: What tools could help me in analyzing the behavior of VM images?

A: HijackThis is a freeware application that offers a really good summary of behavior of unknown software. Today additional information is available on the Trend Micro Web site. Metasploit offers tools to understand their behavior. Going deeper, OllyDBG and IDA Pro are good ring 3 debugger and disassemblers for in-depth forensic analysis of unknown applications. Norman's Sandbox is the best tool for going deeper into ring 0 and examining kernel level interactions.

Notes

1. *IBM Internet Security Systems X-Force 2008 Mid-Year Trend Statistics* (Somers, NY: IBM Global Services, 2008), www-935.ibm.com/services/us/iss/xforce/midyearreport/xforce-midyear-report-2008.pdf.

2. "National Vulnerability Database Version 2.2" (Gaithersburg, MD: National Institute of Standards and Technology, Computer Security Resource Center), http://nvd.nist.gov/.

3. John Leyden, "Sobig-F is fastest growing virus ever — official outlook grim," *The Register*, August 2003, www.theregister.co.uk/2003/08/21/sobigf_is_fastest_growing_virus/.

4. "Mydoom Surpasses Sobig.F to Become Fastest Spreading Virus Ever, with 1 in 12 Emails Now Infected," *BNET* (from Business Wire, January 2004), http://findarticles.com/p/articles/mi_m0EIN/is_/ai_112589554.

5. "PATH TRAVERSAL VULNERABILITY IN VMWARE'S SHARED FOLDERS IMPLEMENTATION," Core Security Technologies, 2008, http://www.coresecurity.com/content/advisory-vmware.

6. "OWASP NYC AppSec 2008 Conference," the Open Web Application Security Project, 2008, www.owasp.org/index.php/OWASP_NYC_AppSec_2008_Conference.

7. "Technology Profile Fact Sheet: NetTop," from *Technology Profile Fact Sheets* (Fort George G. Meade, MD: National Security Agency, Central Security Service), www.nsa.gov/techtrans/techt00011.cfm.

8. "Federal Desktop Core Configuration," National Institute of Standards and Technology, July 2007, http://nvd.nist.gov/fdcc/download_fdcc.cfm.

Chapter 14

Training

Solutions in this chapter:

- Setting Up Scanning Servers
- Setting Up Target Servers
- Creating the Capture-the-Flag Scenario
- Out Brief
- Cleaning Up Afterward
- Saving Your Back

☑ Summary

☑ Solutions Fast Track

☑ Frequently Asked Questions

Introduction

During my early years as a security professional I had a role in training other members of my team in penetration testing. Because of the nature of penetration testing, we had to go through special precautions to ensure that surrounding network environment would not be damaged by the students. In addition, because we were using it as a training environment we wanted to keep the systems that the students were using fairly standard. We didn't want them to have to install new operating systems, and we didn't have hardware to pass out to everyone for the class.

Initially, we tried to do things using multiple physical servers, Knoppix CDs and lots of rebooting. Setting up for class each day meant coming in one to two hours early to wire everything up, and make sure the environment was ready to go. The end of day brought a similar level of effort to shut everything down. We had to find a good place to store five servers, along with the switches and cabling needed to make it work.

Virtualization significantly reduced complexity of the environment. As you will see in the chapter our requirements went from dragging around five physical servers and nightmare administration down to a single server and eventually to a remotely accessible server which stayed in our lab. As an added advantage, resetting the environment for the next class was a matter of reverting to snapshots created before the class started. No more server rebuilds were required. We could also revert during the class when the students crashed too many services for the box to be considered operable. Restarting the services/rebooting the box would have been possible, but it was no longer necessary thanks to the benefits we gained from using virtual servers.

Our users were able to move to an environment that they could alter when they wanted, but could be restored in a simple manner. They could install tools which would be there the next day. No reboots were required to use Linux tools on their Windows laptops.

Setting Up Scanning Servers

One of the first tools used during a penetration test is the scanner. During our class the goal was to give each student the opportunity to configure and run a scan from an operational server. We did not want the students installing software for two reasons. First of all installing software can be tedious, and certainly wouldn't have been a valuable use of time. The other reason is that our students were often new to Linux, and may not have been able to install the required software in a "clean" Linux distribution.

Advantages of Using a Virtual Machine instead of a Live-CD Distribution

Our first solution involved using a Linux distribution designed for security testing. The environment was distributed in the form of a Live-CD. A Live-CD is a bootable CD that boots into a preconfigured environment. One can think of them as a computer image on a disk. Normally, a Live-CD boots a kernel, and creates a virtual disk in memory. The kernel then creates a file system on this memory disk, containing all of the files that the environment will need to function. This usually includes commands and utilities to accomplish a specific task, but can be as complex as an entire application environment.

The Live-CD distribution we chose booted to a fully functioning Linux workstation designed for security testing. It had a large number of tools installed, and would have been a great base to learn from. There were however two drawbacks that made this environment slightly less than ideal.

Persistence

The first drawback of a Live-CD environment is persistence. Each time a Live-CD environment is rebooted, all changes are lost, and the environment is restored to a clean directory. They are great for a short-term demonstration, but for the purposes of our class we wanted somewhere to store information for the duration of the class. The students were using their laptops, and permanent alterations would have been frowned upon.

Another option would have been to have students put their customizations on a USB storage device. At one point we encouraged students to use these with their Live-CD environments and it seemed to work, but at that time USB storage devices weren't terribly popular.

Customization

Each class we would run into something we wanted to improve. During one class we might have noticed that the version of Nessus was way out of date. During another class we would wish that we had a tool to look at WebDav shares. We always had to weigh the educational value of a change against the inconvenience of having every student try and install tools. Inevitably someone would miss an instruction, and we would have to troubleshoot their installations. We spent significant amounts of class time teaching students how to install and configure software which they might never use again.

We did have a goal for students to learn to install simple software, however. Life as a penetration tester involves a willingness to go out and find tools appropriate for the job at hand. There is a vast knowledge base which has been developed which is available for public use (for which we all owe a debt of gratitude). Students needed the ability to install and configure tools to their liking.

Disadvantages of Using a Virtual Machine instead of a Live-CD

There were some disadvantages of using a Virtual Machine instead of a Live–CD distribution. The biggest issue in our minds was that students couldn't take their virtual machine home with them after the class was complete. Although some of our students were very new to Linux and security in general, others were quite capable of handling their own machines. Nowadays we could have arranged for it by copying their virtual machine to their local box, and using VMware Player. This would have worked ideally, but at the time all of the VMware products required additional licensing fees. Assuming the student's hardware was capable of the additional workload, the student would have been able to boot the image and run the tools in the same manner as they had on our server.

Another drawback to using virtual machines instead of CDs is that we lost the ability for the students to do wireless assessments. As we've discussed in other portions of the book, wireless assessments can require significant hardware control right down to the firmware level. Virtualization software does not allow virtual machines to access the hardware in a direct manner. In order to demo wireless software, tools must either be installed on the native operating system, or they can be loaded from a CD.

Default Platforms As Well to Use a Variety of Tools

There was also call for semistable environments for students to install software into (I wouldn't recommend installing individual clients for single tests onto "master" scanning servers, but onto an image dedicated to a single test shouldn't be a problem). Examples of such software might be a Lotus Notes client. Lotus Notes uses a proprietary protocol which is most conveniently tested using the actual Lotus

Notes Client. The client is able to talk to the server and discover information about default databases and configuration options which, while remotely accessible, are not easily obtained using any other tools.

The testing of exploits also often requires a default platform to be ready at a moment's notice. Exploits obtained from the internet can be unpredictable. In some cases they are very reliable, and perform their action with minimal impact to the server in question. In other cases they crash the server multiple times trying to brute force parameters before they are able to perform their intended action. In still other cases the author of the exploit has deliberately coded the exploit to perform malicious actions. A professional network penetration tester should know the exact effect that an exploit might have, and have permission from the client to perform such a test. Ideally the tester has the ability to read through the code and determine at some level what the exploit is doing, but in many cases that may be difficult or impossible. At a minimum the exploit should be run against a test server to verify that the exploit works as advertised.

Scanning Servers in a Virtual Environment

For all of the reasons above, we decided that preconfigured virtual servers for each student would be the way to go. That way we could give each student a "root" password to log in, and manage their own server. Students were encouraged to customize things to their own liking and become familiar with the server throughout the weeklong course.

The base configuration looked very similar to our favorite Live-CD distribution with regards to tools chosen to be installed. From there we added some additional tools that we wanted to use to demonstrate various concepts from the class. Students were given copies of the master scanning server, and each was then encouraged to customize as they saw fit. The first recommended action was to change the root password. For one class in particular this was an important instruction. For some reason they spent much more time trying to attack each other than they did training against the official target servers. This behavior also caused the instructors to curtail the amount of "dangerous" techniques we taught. If they couldn't refrain from attacking each other, we didn't feel teaching them advanced techniques would be a wise course of action.

We did not elect to create servers to test exploits against (although we did recommend this for testing in the "wild"). The students were encouraged to test exploits that they obtained from the web against their scanning server (and to read through the code to get an idea of how it worked). We deliberately structured the class so that commercial clients/test servers would not be required (for licensing issues as much as anything else).

One obstacle that we did have to overcome was that each machine had to be able to exist on the same network at the same time. This meant that their MAC/IP addresses needed to be changed. We ended up scripting the MAC address change, and using DHCP to handle the IP address modifications. This proved to be fairly effective.

Students were able to access their boxes using the VMware console software. Thankfully this was readily available from the VMware server management web portal. Students could download the flavor of their choosing (Linux or Windows), install it, and be presented with the console of their scanning machine. This gave them some exposure to managing virtual machines in addition to learning the basics of security testing. The teachers could also use the consoles to observe the students and check that they were keeping up with the progressive nature of the scenarios. If any student required assistance, the teacher could either use the console to demonstrate the technique or go directly to the student's desk to provide personal attention.

The virtual machines could also be accessed and managed in the same manner as any other remote server. Because the scanning servers we were using were Linux based, the preferred remote management tool was SSH. In some cases they used GUI type tools tunneled through SSH as well. SSH was also used for transferring files to and from the scanning servers. The steps in setting up these tunnels were used as teaching opportunities. Students were taught how to work in the presence of firewalls.

The testing environments were set up with firewalls governing traffic in both directions. Because the target servers were "weakened" live servers, we did not want them on the primary corporate network. One can imagine the scandal if the security group were to be infected by a worm because of an un-patched training server. In addition, we wanted all testing to be done from the scanning servers inside of the test environment. This was done to ensure that tests performed during the class would not accidentally be directed at targets outside of our environment. As mentioned above, the only two ports open to incoming connections were SSH and the VMware console port. Outbound connections were blocked entirely from both the scanning servers and the target servers.

Setting Up Target Servers

Because the class was supposed to be about penetration testing and exploitation, we needed to have servers to scan and attack. Virtualization made it easy to create additional servers and start/stop them one at a time as our demonstrations required.

We were even able to keep them in a suspended state so that the demonstrations took very little time to initialize and execute. The first set of machines was used during the first three days of the class. A second set of boxes was used for the final day where the class was able to practice the techniques they had learned.

Very "Open" Boxes
for Demonstrating during Class

The target servers for the first half of the week were set up using un-patched operating systems plus a number of services with known vulnerabilities. In addition, we deliberately installed some additional "vulnerable" third-party packages with exploitable issues. The intent was to give the students experience in exploiting a wide variety of vulnerabilities. While an in-depth discussion of developing their own exploits was beyond the scope of the class, it was well within their abilities to do research on publicly available sites, and to determine if the exploits they found would apply to the environment we provided. We deployed the servers with no firewall rules restricting traffic from the scanning servers. We set up both Linux and Windows environments using "older" generation platforms to ensure there were enough issues to work with.

Suggested Vulnerabilities for Windows

The first type of vulnerability we wanted to demonstrate were default configuration issues and poorly chosen passwords. We created a number of users on the test server. Some users had no passwords, and others had simple or predictable passwords. The class was taught how to look up default passwords for various software installations, as well as how to enumerate users on servers which allow it. They were also taught how to look at the password policy to determine if it would be safe to attempt to brute force passwords. Of course on our test server brute forcing was configured to be safe so that we could demonstrate tools to perform such attacks. We also installed MS SQL server, and had the password set to blank as was the default a number of years ago. This allowed the students to both learn how to connect to such a server, as well as how to exploit a database server using SQL commands.

We also made sure that significant information was available using publicly available tools. SNMP community strings were set to public. I believe this server even displayed configuration information using the built in IIS web server with some custom ASP scripts (which had vulnerabilities in them as well).

In addition, we installed some open source software with known exploits. The goal in installing this software was to simulate a real environment which was performing useful functions. The software we chose had a buffer overflow in the portion of the application which collected data from the network. We also chose software that had "non-overflow" vulnerabilities. If a tester issued a properly formatted request, then the tester could retrieve any file on the system.

Finally, the operating system was left unpatched. We had to be careful to keep the firewall rules in place, as putting such a server on the corporate network would have been a violation of the usage guidelines, and likely would have been a victim of the occasional worm outbreaks.

Suggested Vulnerabilities for Linux

We also deployed a highly vulnerable Linux box so the students would have experience attempting to exploit a UNIX-like server. Again we installed a number of vulnerable software packages. From there we modified the server configuration so that even more vulnerabilities existed.

Again the configuration of the installed software was changed so that there would be even more vulnerable to exploitation. One example of this was modifying the FTP server so that when one logged into the server using anonymous, you were given read and write access to a user's home directory. The students were then taught how to exploit a server if you had access to that directory.

Finally, a number of packages were installed which had known buffer overflow issues. Again these were packages with known buffer management issues. The goal was to allow students to perform their own research and collect vulnerabilities to be used during the test.

Suggested Vulnerabilities for Application Vulnerability Testing

We also installed a handful of applications that would be exploited using web servers, as these types of servers would be the ones most commonly encountered during penetration tests. Again the class did not have enough time to teach a significant amount of application exploitation, but the students were given some exposure to it. At the time the most significant type of vulnerability being exploited in the wild was SQL injection. SQL injection vulnerabilities arise when an application creates an application query using input from the user without ensuring that it is in the proper format. Students were taught to extract data from tables, as well as how to gain shell access to a database server which was accessed by a vulnerable application as shown in Figure 14.1.

Figure 14.1 An Example of a Successful Exploit Returning a Shell from a Windows Machine

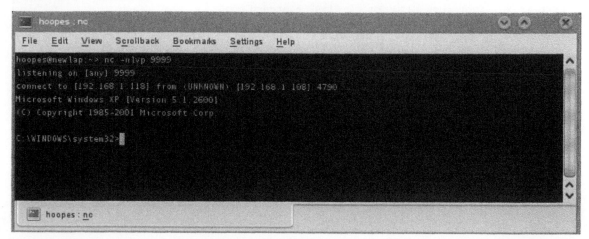

Students were also taught how to test and exploit some forms of vulnerable CGI-BIN scripts. My first successful exploit was actually a vulnerable CGI script which I had installed on a test server. I had read about how one performed an exploit against a particular CGI script, and wanted to know if it worked. It appeared too simple to actually be effective. I installed the package by following the instructions which came with the package. I then attempted the exploit that I had read about. Much to my surprise the exploit worked, and I was presented with a shell prompt originating from my victim server. I was absolutely shocked, and hooked at the same time. I wanted to give my students that same thrill. Figure 14.2 shows how the exploit of a vulnerable cgi script might look.

Figure 14.2 A Successful Exploit against a Linux Server

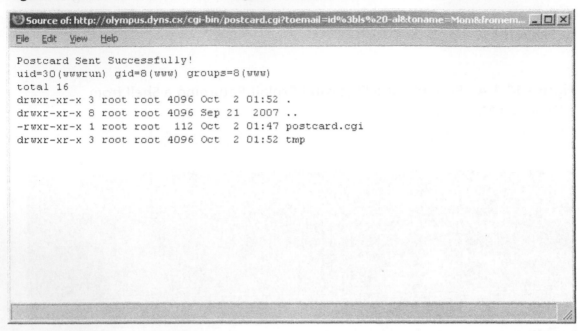

Although cross site scripting attacks were not terribly popular at the time I was teaching my class, talk about the exploitation of cross-site scripting attacks. The students were presented with a vulnerable application and taught how to spot issues in the applications. They were also taught some minor exploitation techniques.

During each of the application vulnerability scenarios we spent a limited amount of time looking at the vulnerable source code. Our students were not all capable of understanding the raw source code, but because the examples we were using were so blatant I believe the majority of them could understand how the issues arose. Figure 14.3 shows how the XSS demonstration appeared.

Figure 14.3 An Example of a Successful XSS Demonstration

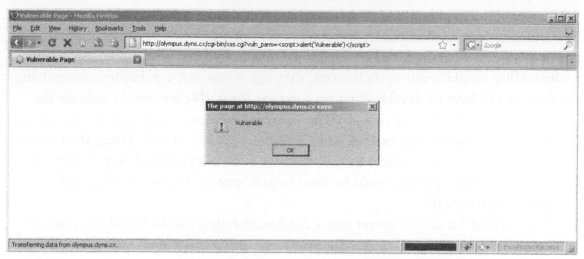

Creating the Capture-the-Flag Scenario

The final day's activities were devoted to a capture-the-flag scenario. Students were divided into teams of two and were told to conduct a penetration test. We provided the teams with a sample "Statement of Work" indicating the boxes that were considered in scope to be tested, along with some information regarding the purpose of each server. The team with the best report would be declared the winners. The measurement of "best" report was a subjective analysis done by the class using an approach of each team presenting vulnerabilities, and then we discussed the results. Finally, teams were given the opportunity to choose whose report best captured the state of the environment.

Each team used their own virtual machines to conduct scans and perform testing against the targets.

Harder Targets

Each server had some vulnerabilities deliberately installed, as well as some false positives that appeared vulnerable on a scan but which would ultimately prove vulnerable. On each server there were multiple vulnerabilities to exploit.

The first server (and only server the students could reach directly from the scanning server) was a web server. It had an older version of apache, as well as an exploitable version of openssl. The versions installed were both vulnerable to buffer overflow exploits which allowed arbitrary code execution. This would result in shell access on the server if you used exploits that were published in a number of places (which we had covered during class). The web server also had a CGI vulnerability on it which was vulnerable to shell character insertion (a type of attack where a user-submitted input is used as a parameter to an application run from a command line). Again this vulnerability would result in shell access, although it was not a published vulnerability so they would have to develop their own exploit for it. (Nessus would indicate the exact format of the exploit, though). The operating system on the web server was also a bit old, and a number of exploits were available against it as well. Using the remote vulnerabilities the servers could gain shell access as an unprivileged user. Following this the local vulnerabilities could be used to gain root on the server, and crack the shadowed password file.

The second "in scope" server was a database running on the Windows platform. The web server had access to the database server using credentials stored in a file in the web environment. In addition, the database server had one account that would have been easily guessed from the username. By using the database credentials, the students could gain access to the database server as SYSTEM, or using the guessed password they could obtain administrator access.

Finally, another "internal" server was in scope which had simulated payroll data on it. This server was exploitable by using the same usernames and passwords found in the shadowed password file on the Linux server. It could also be exploited using an old FTP vulnerability. Either of those would get the attacker onto the server with the flag.txt file.

While it sounds pretty simple, exploiting the three boxes usually took the majority of the day and allowed the students to use a significant portion of what we had taught them.

Snapshots Saved Us

There were a large number of times that the ability to restore to a snapshot helped us restore the environment. During the initial days of the class, a reboot of one or more servers was required to fix various problems that arose. It was especially annoying when the first class managed to lock everyone (including the instructors) out of the server. We had to boot that server into single user mode to recover. Obviously, the members of the class were anxiously awaiting this repair to continue their work. Happily, the virtualized environment alleviated many of these types of problems. A hung server could be recovered in about 30 seconds by restoring to a snapshot created before the class even started. Unfortunately, this would delete the tools of the students who had already gained access to the box, but that couldn't always be helped. This experience can also happen in the real world.

Require Research to Accomplish the Task

A key portion of the class consisted of the students detecting the vulnerability using the scan, and then going out on the internet to research the vulnerability. We encouraged them to read about who discovered the vulnerability, what the problem actually was, how it was repaired, and how the exploit worked. Wherever possible we encouraged them to test the vulnerability against a test server, with sniffers in place so that they would see each step of the exploit in action.

Introduce Firewalls

During the capture-the-flag scenario we also brought firewalls into the environment. Up to this point the students hadn't had to contend with a firewall's effects on their testing. Firewalls blocked access to ports that they were accustomed to using such as FTP, Telnet, and SSH. In addition, they had to understand the effects that egress filtering would have on their attempts to create connections back to their "attack" servers. The primary web server was only reachable on ports 80, and 443. We also left a range of ports open from 1100–1200 open in the firewall but with no services running on them. These ports were intended to be used by students to forward ports of internal services, and to transfer tools onto the web server. Egress filtering was not in place (a possible finding for the teams). The firewall also allowed the students to make connections back to their scanning server without issue.

Multiple Servers Requiring Chained Attacks

Another technique that was introduced during the capture-the-flag scenario was the idea of chaining attacks together. While the statement of work indicated the presence of a number of servers, only one was actually accessible from the students' scanning servers. They were required to exploit this server in one of a number of ways. From there they were able to (but not required to) escalate privileges to root on the server. From this point they were to exploit boxes on the "inside" of the network. Again there were a number of methods to go from the front web server to the other servers inside the environment. Students were required to get any tools they wanted to use onto this server in order to exploit the remaining servers. These tools often include scanners and remote administration tools. It was interesting to see to what length each group would go to in order to gain graphical access to the server they had just exploited. Although it was not necessary for the testing, some groups would work on it for extended periods of time.

This exercise of having to chain their attacks together taught them both to really think about what they were doing, as well as practice using the tools. Each time they messed up and accidentally closed their tunnels, they would have to start them over. By the end of the day they were getting pretty adept at it, and in some cases would script major portions of it.

Adding Some Realism

As mentioned earlier, we made every effort to keep the scenarios realistic. This included a statement of work that was very close to statements which we had used on previous real-world engagements. In some cases the customer would "reboot" a box without letting the testers know. This was normally done to recover the environment from a "misbehaved" exploit that someone had run. In addition, if service was somehow interrupted, the customer would "call" and let the testing team know that they were not pleased. Each of these devices was used to prepare the students for situations they might encounter as they moved out of the classroom environments.

Loose Points for Damaging the Environment

We had to create some rules to get the students to realize that they had to be better behaved than the bad guys. Exploits couldn't be run unless you could describe what their effect would be. At one point we also deployed some servers in the environment which were not mentioned in the statement of work. Any attacks against these servers were penalized. I guess in some ways we had deployed honey pots hoping to catch the careless students in our groups.

For some reason, during each and every class at least one of the students tried to shutdown the firewall on the primary web server. I assume this was their way of getting some more "room to work with". They didn't know how to operate with the firewalls in place, so they tried to drop the firewall rules. Every class we tried to increase the amount of instruction on working with limited network access, but apparently it wasn't enough. Obviously shutting down a firewall would not be an appropriate action to perform on a customer server, but never the less someone always managed to attempt it. And every class they did it in a way that locked everyone out of the server, instead of opening it to the world. This was normally the cause of our "customer" calling to say that they were severely displeased with the service interruption that had been caused by the testing. Instead of changing the final rule on the firewall to accept all packets, they flushed all of the rules except the default rule which was set to deny all traffic.

Demonstrate What the Attack Looks Like on IDS

One aspect that I would have liked to add to the class would have been an IDS server. It would have been interesting for the instructors to observe the progress of the class. It also could have been an educational experience for the students to see how their attacks were registering on the console. It might also have been yet another "deterrent" for any students who might have wanted to take their newly learned skills out on the road. If I were to set up the class again, I would take advantage of one of the virtual appliance programs to install a preconfigured IDS system. Using an appliance would give me all of the benefits of an IDS system without me having to expend significant effort. Expending less effort has always been a goal of mine, and I've spent considerable effort trying to achieve it.

Out Brief

At the conclusion of the day we had a short out brief meeting. We used this time to discuss the major vulnerabilities that were found. Teams were given the opportunity to present how they discovered a particular vulnerability, the information they discovered while researching the vulnerability, as well as how well their exploits worked. We also attempted to commend teams for finding additional vulnerabilities. During each stage of the scenario we attempted to have more than one path, to remind the students that even though the situation was called "capture the flag", their goal was to find all vulnerabilities in the environment, not just a valid path to the end goal.

Cleaning up Afterward

The best part of our new virtualized classroom environment was the ability to get ready for the next class. We didn't have to help anyone fix their laptops. Each of the student's scan boxes could be deleted, and the configurations removed from the virtual server manager.

The target boxes for both the weeklong instruction, as well as the capture-the-flag scenarios, could be reverted to the snapshots taken at the beginning of the week. Finally, the scenarios could be updated with new vulnerabilities, or more likely with hints to cause the students to move in a more productive direction. These changes were then incorporated into a snapshot to be used during the next time we taught the class.

Saving Your Back

The last improvement that we made was the use of a VPN to be able to access the virtual server host. Servers with enough horsepower to run a decent sized class were not terribly portable. By using a VPN into our lab environment, we were able to reduce the needs of the class down to my laptop (which was also used for the class presentation materials). The solution we chose was Openvpn. This would allow me to connect to the environment, and then students could route their management connections through my workstation, into the VPN tunnel, and finally the lab environment. Openvpn was fairly simple to set up, and seemed to allow us to perform any actions we might need. I was amazed to see tools such as Nessus, and Nmap be able to perform with near real-time speed through the tunnel.

To simplify even further, a hardware device could have been used to give instant access to the environment (without me needing to be in the correct configuration). Devices such as the Linksys WRT54G router can be configured to connect to Openvpn gateways. Anyone connecting to either the wired or wireless interfaces can be directed into the tunnel, and given access to the lab network. Note that some caution should be used when deploying a wireless network on a corporate infrastructure. It is highly likely that you may be breaking corporate policies. It is certainly recommended to use appropriate encryption precautions to prevent unauthorized users from accessing the lab, or the corporate network using your hardware.

Another advantage of deploying your own hardware is to test out a number of attacks which are not advisable for use on a corporate network. Tools which perform ARP packet spoofing in an attempt to become the gateway for a segment can cause significant damage. By using our own hardware, the students could be shown both the techniques and the effects without causing interference or damage to production systems.

Summary

Virtualization made my class significantly more productive. I was much happier to teach the class when I didn't have to cart around five different servers and spend significant amounts of time trying to get each student's environment set up appropriately. It also made the time much more effective for the students. They were able to concentrate on learning what they had come to learn instead of learning how to configure an operating system they may or may not ever use again.

Solutions Fast Track

Setting Up Scanning Servers

- ☑ We wanted something for students to use that was easily reproducible.
- ☑ We needed something that had a variety of tools installed.
- ☑ We wanted each student to have access to their own server.

Setting Up Target Servers

- ☑ We used older versions of software.
- ☑ We created additional holes to illustrate key concepts during demonstrations.
- ☑ Virtualization was used to run multiple servers on less hardware. In this case we only used servers for short periods of time (often minutes), and then suspended it, freeing up resources to be used for other machines.

Creating the Capture-the-Flag Scenario

- ☑ This environment was more complicated; it included multiple networks, firewalls, and interconnected applications.
- ☑ Virtualization allowed us to monitor students' progress.
- ☑ Virtualization allowed us to quickly restore the environment in the event that a student damaged something.

Out Brief

☑ Students reported their findings on the environment.

☑ Emphasis was placed on listing all of the vulnerabilities, and not just the ones that led to further exploitation.

Cleaning Up Afterward

☑ Virtualization allowed us to restore all of the environments used in class to a known functional state for the next session.

☑ We often reverted, updated, and took another snapshot as we encountered issues we wanted to change.

Saving Your Back

☑ VPN technology was used to access the virtual hosting server remotely.

☑ VPN technology allowed us to have even more processing power without having to transport bulky equipment.

☑ The effect of the VPN on the students was minimal. We didn't have to chance the class at all to make it work.

Frequently Asked Questions

Q: Was it safe to teach ethical hacking?

A: We were confident that the students were attending the class with the intent of learning more about security and the attacker's mind-set. The students were professionals and understood the issues involved with performing tests against systems owned by others.

Index

Printed and bound by CPI Group (UK) Ltd, Croydon, CR0 4YY

03/10/2024

01040341-0009